Matters of Style

MATTERS OF STYLE

J. MITCHELL MORSE
Temple University

THE BOBBS-MERRILL COMPANY, INC.

*A Subsidiary of
Howard W. Sams & Co., Inc.
Indianapolis and New York*

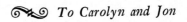 *To Carolyn and Jon*

THIS IS A TEXTBOOK FOR GOOD STUDENTS: for students who don't need drill in writing correctly and who therefore can profit by guided practice in writing well. It has been worked out, tested, revised and developed in the classroom.

The method is to have students analyze a variety of literary styles and then write in those styles—not in order to wind up writing like Lyly or Dr. Johnson or Herman Melville or William Faulkner, but in order to discover some of the possibilities of English prose: to develop a consciousness of form and some skill in devising form, two things without which no individual style is possible. This is the method all good writers have used, instinctively or deliberately, in learning their common craft and developing their personal art.

The models include familiar and unfamiliar writers from a variety of periods; each has been chosen because his style has certain clearly visible characteristics. The headnotes to the selections give brief analyses of their styles, pointing out such things as the use of chiasmus (in Saint Augustine, James Joyce and Samuel Beckett), of rhythmic repetition (in the King James Bible and Oscar Wilde), of visual imagery (in Lafcadio Hearn and John Dos Passos), of dead-pan solemnity with big words (in Thorstein Veblen), etc. Since the passages are chosen for their style rather than their subject matter or point of view, some of them are very short; this makes it possible to provide more illustrations.

I have found that it pays to have the students concentrate

their work rather than extend it. In the process of learning to write with some style, it is better to design each sentence carefully than to write a lot of sentences that have no good qualities beyond the basic requirement of grammatical correctness; it is better to write a short piece that catches the essence of a style than a long one that doesn't. Better a small diamond than a big slag pile. I have therefore suggested that each exercise be limited to two pages or less.

In addition to models, I have given my students a number of brief collateral readings. I include here as appendices the three that have proved most stimulating. The translations of Sartre and Spire are my own.

Dr. James R. Kreuzer, Acting Dean of the Faculties at Hunter College of the City University of New York, read the manuscript and made many valuable suggestions, which have greatly enhanced the book's usefulness. To him I am warmly grateful. And I am indebted beyond estimation to my wife, for her remarkably sensitive judgment of language, her wise restraining hand, and her deep sustaining enthusiasm.

J. M. M.

ACKNOWLEDGMENTS

Thanks are due to the following individuals and publishers for their permission to reprint copyrighted material:

Appleton-Century-Crofts: St. Augustine, ON THE IMMORTALITY OF THE SOUL, *translated by George B. Leckie, 1938.*

The Atlantic Monthly Company: Gertrude Stein, THE WINNER LOSES: A PICTURE OF OCCUPIED FRANCE, *1940.* Copyright © *1940, by The Atlantic Monthly Company, Boston, Mass., 02116. Reprinted by permission.*

Doubleday & Company, Inc.: Vladimir Nabokov, NABOKOV'S DOZEN, *1958. Excerpt from "Mademoiselle O," copyright 1942 by The Atlantic Monthly Company; and from "First Love," copyright 1948 by Vladimir Nabokov, both from* NABOKOV'S DOZEN *by Vladimir Nabokov. Reprinted by permission of Doubleday & Company, Inc.*

Editions Gallimard: Valéry Larbaud, BEAUTÉ, MON BEAU SOUCI, *1921.* © *Editions Gallimard.*
Jean-Paul Sartre, SITUATIONS III, *1949.* © *Editions Gallimard.*

Grove Press, Inc.: Samuel Beckett, MURPHY, *1936.*
Samuel Beckett, WATT, *1953.*
———, MOLLOY, *1951, translated from the French by Patrick Bowles in collaboration with the author, 1955.*
———, MALONE DIES, *1956, translated from the French by the author, copyright* © *1956 by Grove Press, Inc.*
———, HOW IT IS, *1961, translated from the French by the author, copyright* © *1964 by Grove Press, Inc.*

[ix]

CONTENTS

Matters of Style

GOOD TEA, GOOD MAYONNAISE, GOOD PROSE

MR. LEOPOLD BLOOM, the hero of Joyce's *Ulysses*, a naively ignorant man who likes to think that he has what he calls "the scientific temperament," makes tea according to the formula "one spoonful per cup and one for the pot." But his wife, Molly, an aggressively ignorant woman who has no use for science, for art or for Leopold, scorns his "measuring and mincing." Her way is to "throw in a handful of tea."

Let us not waste any time considering Molly's way; it hopes for a miracle, but has every chance of producing a disaster. As for Bloom's way, I have drunk some very excellent tea and some very bad tea made with equal care according to the same formula and with the same brand. The secret of good tea is elusive. For many years I had to struggle against a temptation to believe that it depended less on the formula than on the person. But I knew that any such undemonstrable whimsy would be unscientific, and my twentieth-century conscience required that I make at least some effort to analyze what takes place in the making of tea. So, after years of close observation, careful comparison and conscientious notekeeping, suppressing all prejudices, taking all variables into account, and reducing all my equations to graphs, I have concluded that the secret of good tea lies in the grace with which the teamaker handles the pot, the kettle and the spoon.

That is to say, it is a matter of judgment. Bear with me; for the scientific temperament, with which I like to think I am endowed at least as generously as Leopold Bloom, often connects one phenomenon with another by a graceful intuitive leap. The ability to make such leaps, I need hardly add, is a special talent. As Enrico Fermi once remarked, the lucky accidents always happen in the same laboratories. In this case, I connected tea-making with mayonnaise-making. A French friend of ours, a successful business man who in his earlier years had been a blue-ribbon chef, invited us to a magnificent dinner for which he made everything himself, including a large dish of really superb mayonnaise. My wife asked him how he made it, and he gladly told her—but didn't mention any quantities. "How much oil do you use?" she asked. "I don't measure," he said simply, "I judge." My heart sang. For what is judgment? We had arrived while he was preparing the steaks, and had gone into the kitchen and watched; he had worked with the grace and sure touch of an artist; and now I concluded that judgment was grace, grace judgment; that is all we know on earth, and all we need to know.

This truth is especially true of the art of writing. Literary genius is, or at least begins with, an unteachable gift; but short of genius a high degree of literary competence can be cultivated. Our merely normal intelligence does not condemn us to write poorly; within its rather generous limits we can learn to write well and even brilliantly. This is not a matter of learning formulas; like the making of excellent tea or superb mayonnaise, it is a matter of cultivating grace and exercising judgment—which, as I have suggested, are not two but one.

We can cultivate grace and strengthen judgment only by practice: not the worse than futile practice that consists in repeating our mistakes over and over again, but guided practice in finding better ways to express ourselves.

This implies that some ways really are better than others: that true judgment in literary matters is possible: that the difference between good writing and bad is not a matter of opinion but a matter of fact: that we can demonstrate just how and why and in what ways one piece of writing is better than another.

I am not talking about correctness alone. Not all correct writing is good, and not all incorrect writing is bad. I doubt that any editor has ever accepted a manuscript merely because it was free of grammatical errors, or that any reader has ever enjoyed a book, article, story, play or poem for that reason; on the other hand, the letters of Sacco and Vanzetti are often adduced as examples of good writing that is not correct. But English was a foreign language for Sacco and Vanzetti, and the very incorrectness with which they wrote it expressed their naive honesty and goodness and the poignancy of their situation. That was too special a case to afford us a general conclusion. Most incorrect writing is bad. It is either unintentionally funny or merely dull. Even when it isn't really bad, it would be better if it were correct: I say this after having just read some half-dozen volumes of letters and diaries by privates in the Civil War, looking for examples of good incorrect writing. The most striking thing about these writers is the inadequacy of their prose to the experiences they report. These honest men write about the most hideous battles in the same tone that they write about setting up a new camp or being reviewed by the President or getting a package from home. Their grammatical incorrectness is not in itself what makes their writing bad, except when it prevents our discovering what they are trying to say; more often it is a symptom of a general incompetence with language: other symptoms being a limited vocabulary, a deaf ear, and a blank unawareness that there is such a thing as design. Either their insipid idiom doesn't express what they felt, or it does. If it doesn't, it is plainly inadequate; if it does—and I suspect that in some cases it does—then it puts rather narrow limits not only on what a man can say but also on what he can think, and even on what he can feel. That is why the quality of our prose is so vitally important. It constitutes the quality of our thought, and to some extent the quality of our feeling.

A musician, as musician, thinks and feels in terms of sounds and the notes that represent them; a painter, as painter, thinks and feels in terms of color, drawing, composition, light, shadow, texture—the organization of the space at his disposal; a writer, as writer, thinks and feels in words. A person who says, "I know what I mean, but I just can't say it," is wrong. He can't say it because he doesn't know what he means, and he doesn't know what he means because he can't say it. He hasn't worked out his thought. When he works it out—when he composes it as a sentence—then he will know what he means, for it will be clear. Thoughts are not born clear, they are made clear. The thought *is* the sentence that constitutes it. No clear sentence, no clear thought. We can't have deep or subtle or clear thoughts if we lack language to construct them.

But correctness is not everything. Beyond correctness, we want a certain brilliance, grace, color, flavor, personality: *style*. To do anything brilliantly, with the brilliance that is called style, we must intensify the grace of nature with the grace of art. Only thus can we emphasize the individuality of our performance. When we walk we all make the same motions, but no two people walk exactly alike: we can recognize our friends and acquaintances by the way they walk, even when we can't see their faces; and when we are upstairs we can tell who is coming up by the sound of the footsteps. The process of recognition gives us a certain pleasure, which is partly a matter of self-satisfaction at making the identification and partly a matter of the release of tension that comes of ending our incertitude. But writing is not a natural activity like walking, in which we reveal some of our natural differences; it is a highly artificial activity, a matter of rules, formulas and conventions; and few of us master the rules, formulas and conventions well enough to use them in an individual way that expresses our individuality. In Vladimir Nabokov's novel *Despair*, the villain receives a letter from his intended victim and observes, "As often happens with uneducated people, the tone of his letter was in complete disagreement with that of his usual conversation."

In most of the things we say, whether in speech or in writing, there is no need to express our individuality. For purposes of simple communication, standard formulas are best. When somebody knocks at the door, we say "Come in"; when we want the butter, we say "Pass the butter, please." Rather than make a speech or burst into poetry, we use an accepted formula to convey an accepted meaning. Good technical writing is of this kind. The owner's manual that comes with a new car, or the instruction booklet that comes with an adding machine, tells us nothing about the author. Its prose doesn't express his personality—it isn't supposed to. That would be irrelevant, distracting, and annoying. The prose of technical instruction, if it is well made, is impersonal and anonymous. It has no personal timbre, no voice. The sign "STOP" is mute; a red light would do just as well or even better. In the international traffic code, the sign ⃠ means "No Parking." Writing that gives impersonal infor- mation of this kind is and should be mute writing.

But expository writing that deals with human beings in action should not be mute. Nothing is more boring than mute history, for example, or mute psychology, or mute education. There are hack historians who can make the Italian Renaissance seem dull, the French Revolution trivial, Periclean Athens dreary, Elizabethan London empty, and the discovery of America unimportant; there are hack psychologists who can make the operations of the mind seem boring, and hack educationists who can make teaching and learning seem as mindless as scratching. A hack is a writer who reduces everything to formulas, for whom language is a set of stencils or cookie cutters, and whose thought is accordingly mechanical, automatic, predictable, unoriginal, stale, dead.

To write about human life in the same way that we write about mechanical processes is to be false to our subject. No two human beings are alike, no two human encounters are identical, no two human situations are more than vaguely analogous. To see the encounter or the situation as it is, in its irreducible uniqueness and freshness, to sense its essential incommunicability, and to try to convey to as many readers as possible its vital individuality, that precious essence which certain medieval philosophers called its *haecceitas*—its "thisness"—to see and convey the situation as nearly as possible as it is, we need to think of it in language as concrete and precise as possible.

This is partly a matter of accuracy of vocabulary. We should be aware, for example, that the difference between "pretty" and "beautiful" expresses more than a difference of degree—that a storm in the mountains may be beautiful but is not pretty, whereas the prose of *Euphues* is pretty but not beautiful. To understand the difference we must not only look up the words in a dictionary and observe how good writers use them; we must also think of them in terms of our own experience. The meanings of words are derived from the life we live. And of course the dictionary is a part of our life. We should know the different uses of such words as "pensive" and "thoughtful," "verbose" and "wordy," "tautological," "pleonastic," "redundant" and "circumlocutory," "rational" and "reasonable," "baby" and "infant," "lunch" and "luncheon," "attempt" and "effort," "predominate" (verb) and "predominant" (adjective), "incomplete," "uncompleted" and "unfinished," and "perhaps" and "maybe." The whole tone of a sentence differs as we use one word or another. The dictionary will help us with "tautological" and "redundant," but only living can teach us the difference between "lunch" and "luncheon" or "perhaps" and "maybe."

Language, however, is more than words. We can give simple information and simple directions by pointing or by single words: "There." "Right." "Left." "Up." "Down." "Exit." "Slow." "Curve." "Danger." "Slides." But the development of more complex ideas involves putting words together in sentences: in certain sequences or arrangements or patterns that are generally agreed upon as the forms of ideas. For example, it is generally agreed (though there are many exceptions and special cases) that in English the subject precedes the active verb and the object follows it: we have no difficulty in distinguishing the meanings of the sentences "The matador killed the bull" and "The bull killed the matador." The same words are used in both sentences; by arranging them differently we indicate different facts or construct different ideas; and in the passive voice we reverse the order and change the tone. This is a matter of using conventions.

A skillful user of the conventions of language can manipulate them and play with them to construct and set forth his own most personal ideas and feelings: to express himself. And here we have a paradox: freedom comes through discipline. Freedom is the ability to do what we want to do. A skillful swimmer, who has perfect control of his body, can make it do whatever he wants —assuming that he is sane. Of course our knees bend in only one direction, our elbows bend in only one direction, our head will turn only so far and no farther; to distress ourselves about these limits, to waste time and psychic energy wishing there were no limits, to mope and refuse to go into the water under such restrictive conditions as nature imposes on us, is to be insane. A skillful swimmer, accepting the limits of the human body, learns to express himself within them. He becomes free to the extent that he masters the body's possibilities. If he makes a series of ridiculously awkward moves, it is by choice, not by accident. Likewise a skillful guitarist, who has mastered all the possibilities of the instrument, can express himself within its range with perfect freedom. If he plays a passage out of tune, it is by choice, not by accident. An unskillful performer, in the water or on the guitar, cannot express himself. He can't make his body, or his instrument, execute his wishes. His performance is a series of accidents and disasters. He is not free, he has no choice, because he has no discipline. He doesn't take liberties with the technique, the technique takes liberties with him. It makes him do things he doesn't want to do. There are, to be sure, situations in which a grunt may be more eloquent than the most cogently designed and clearly articulated speech; but cogency and clarity also have their occasions, and we should be able to choose. We should not utter a series of grunts in the belief that we are uttering a syllogism—or a poem.

One more analogy. In chess, a bold, risky, dangerous but successful and absolutely deadly maneuver—such as sacrificing a knight in order to get into position to take your opponent's queen ten moves later—is technically called a "brilliancy." Players who execute brilliancies do so within the rules of the game. They don't frustrate themselves childishly wishing that a knight could move like a castle, or a bishop like a knight. One such move would destroy the game. No rules, no game. No discipline, no skill. No skill, no freedom. No freedom, no self-expression. Look at Appendix I, "The Prankquean." This is an episode from Joyce's great experimental novel *Finnegans Wake*. Read it aloud. Observe the sentences. Their syntactic patterns are quite orthodox. Only the words are strange; and even they are rooted in orthodoxy, for they are not mere sounds but real words which Joyce has made by blending words from at least nineteen different languages, in order to make one word carry several different meanings simultaneously. The word "handworded," for example, suggests the German *antwortet* (answered) and also the primitive language of gesture; and "panuncular cumbottes" suggests "peninsular gunboats" (from the Peninsular War of 1808-1814), the Duke of Wellington's famous gumboots, and Uncle Sam's "avuncular gumboots," as well as "combat boots" and French "thrusts" or "lunges"–*bottes*. A great many things remain to be identified in *Finnegans Wake*; but enough have already been identified to indicate that what we have here is not nonsense, not meaningless sounds carelessly strung together, but a multiplicity of meanings awaiting our ingenuity.

Everyone who has spent any time on *Finnegans Wake* agrees that it is full of brilliancies.

In writing as in everything else, we gain skill by mastering the possibilities of the medium. A writer's medium is language: words, phrases, sentences, paragraphs, and larger structures: articles, essays, short stories, novellas, novels, plays, poems of one kind and another. Within the limits of the English language a great many structural forms are possible. The purpose of this book is to introduce you to certain forms and point out the principles of their design so that you can practice constructing them. Since it concentrates on style, it is devoted entirely to the construction of sentences. Its aim is to help you achieve the freedom of an expert in constructing English sentences. You will then have a very considerable advantage when you undertake to develop larger structures.

The method is simple, but not easy. There is no easy method of learning to do anything well: as Aristotle is said to have said to the young Alexander, there is no royal road to geometry. In the course from which this book grew, I have had my students analyze and then write in a variety of styles whose basic pattern is symmetry, trying to match the prettiness of Lyly, the finical dancing of Florio, the vigorous eloquence of Burke and Paine, the ponderous dignity of Dr. Johnson, the magisterial sweep of Gibbon, the absurd bombast of P. T. Barnum; I have also had them write several different kinds of poetic prose, and try their hands at writing like Rabelais, and like James, Hemingway, Faulkner, Dos Passos, Beckett, the Joyce of *Ulysses*, the Gertrude Stein of *The Autobiography of Alice B. Toklas*, and other good twentieth-century writers. Some of these writers write in extremely eccentric ways; but their eccentricity is deliberate, as firmly controlled and at least as artful as the regularity of the eighteenth-century neo-classicists. Every writer in this book has a clear and unmistakable pattern of his own. I have avoided artless writers, such as John Mandeville, and clumsy writers, such as Theodore Dreiser. There is no point in imitating them. But there is much to be gained from imitating writers who know what they are doing. If you consciously write according to certain patterns, as a swimmer consciously practices certain patterns of movement, you will learn how to do a variety of things with language. The more ways in which you learn to use it, the better it will serve you; the more fully you master and control it, the more freedom you will have; and to the extent that you achieve freedom, you will be able to develop a style of your own: a style that suggests your personal voice.

BALANCED STYLES

So bold, yet so judiciously you dare,
That your least Praise, is to be regular.

DRYDEN TO CONGREVE

Symmetry, Balance, Antithesis, Parallelism

FOR OBVIOUS REASONS, many of the examples of style in this book will come from the twentieth century. For reasons that I hope will be equally obvious, the first examples you will be asked to analyze and follow come from ancient Greece and Rome. I take from my shelves, not quite at random but without much deliberation, eight books: an eighteenth-century history, a bit of nineteenth-century natural history, a nineteenth-century novel, a twentieth-century autobiography, and four twentieth-century novels. In the first book, as we might expect, we find the beautiful symmetry and parallelism of the classic style as it was practiced in the eighteenth century, noun balancing noun, verb verb, phrase phrase, clause clause, thought thought. We don't customarily expect balance and symmetry in the prose of the romantic nineteenth century or the seething twentieth, but they are there, though in less obvious ways; for the classic style has been for centuries and to a large extent remains the basic form of European thought and hence of American thought. Since this is a book about English style, I have taken only one of these preliminary examples from a continental writer; you can find plenty of others, however, in any decent library; and later in this chapter I will give you a number of examples from the Greek and Latin writers who founded the style. But let us read a few lines from each of those eight volumes chosen not quite at random.

Chapter 26 of Voltaire's *The Age of Louis XIV* (1751) begins thus:

> To the glory, to the pleasures, to the gallantry that filled the first years of this reign, Louis XIV wished to add the sweetness of friendship: but it is difficult for a king to make happy choices. Of

two men in whom he placed the highest confidence, one meanly betrayed him, the other abused his favor.

Though we might very well not expect it, the influence of this style is clear even in Thoreau. It is an artful, poised, intellectual style; its sentences are well-designed, well-constructed and well-managed, and its influence on the patterns of Thoreau's thought gives his prose a firmness, a tone, that is lacking in most writers about the great innocuous outdoors. This is the opening paragraph of a book review entitled "A Natural History of Massachusetts" (1842):

> Books of natural history make the most cheerful winter reading. I read in Audubon with a thrill of delight, when the snow covers the ground, of the magnolia, and the Florida keys, and their warm sea-breezes; of the fence-rail, and the cotton-tree, and the migrations of the rice-bird; of the breaking up of winter in Labrador, and the melting of snow on the forks of the Missouri; and owe an access of health to these reminiscences of luxuriant nature.

Here too we have balance and symmetry, though not so obviously as in Voltaire: three nouns before the first semicolon are balanced by three nouns after it; and though the third noun of the second triad is the simple "migrations," it is supplemented by the compound noun "rice-bird," paralleling the compound "fence-rail" and "cotton-tree." After the second semicolon, "the breaking up of winter" is balanced by "the melting of snow," and "in Labrador" by "on the forks of the Missouri." This is no accident, this is art.

What can we say of Herman Melville? A writer of genius does not lend himself easily to our academic definitions and classifications: he overspills all categories. What is the style of Melville's *Moby Dick* (1851)? The midnight dance in Chapter 40 has counterparts no better in *Faust, The Temptation of Saint Anthony,* and *Ulysses;* the legal discussion in Chapter 90 is as good as any in Rabelais; the irony in many a chapter would do proud by Sterne.

But the style of the opening paragraphs, romantic as it is, unique and unmistakably Melville's as it is, shows the classic influence as surely as Voltaire's—or Goethe's, or Flaubert's, or Joyce's, or Rabelais', or Sterne's. Observe, for example, the parallelism of "Whenever . . . whenever . . . whenever . . . and especially whenever," "deliberately stepping . . . and methodically knocking," and "tied to counters, nailed to benches, clinched to desks"; and the quiet antithesis of "With a philosophical flourish Cato . . . ; I quietly."

> Call me Ishmael. Some years ago—never mind how long precisely—having little or no money in my purse, and nothing particular to interest me on shore, I thought I would sail about a little and see the watery part of the world. It is a way I have of driving off the spleen, and regulating the circulation. Whenever I find myself growing grim about the mouth; whenever it is a damp, drizzly November in my soul; whenever I find myself involuntarily pausing before coffin warehouses, and bringing up the rear of every funeral I meet; and especially whenever my hypos get such an upper hand of me, that it requires a strong moral principle to prevent me from deliberately stepping into the street, and methodically knocking people's hats off—then, I account it high time to get to sea as soon as I can. This is my substitute for pistol and ball. With a philosophical flourish Cato throws himself upon his sword; I quietly take to the ship. There is nothing surprising in this. If they but knew it, almost all men in their degree, some time or other, cherish very nearly the same feelings towards the ocean with me.
>
> There now is your insular city of the Manhattoes, belted round by wharves as Indian isles by coral reefs—commerce surrounds it with her surf. Right and left, the streets take you waterward. Its extreme down-town is the battery, where that noble mole is washed by waves, and cooled by breezes, which a few hours previous were out of sight of land. Look at the crowds of water-gazers there.

Circumambulate the city of a dreamy Sabbath afternoon. Go from Corlears Hook to Coenties Slip, and from thence, by Whitehall, northward. What do you see?—Posted like silent sentinels all around the town, stand thousands upon thousands of mortal men fixed in ocean reveries. Some leaning against the spiles; some seated upon the pier-heads; some looking over the bulwarks of ships from China; some high aloft in the rigging, as if striving to get a still better seaward peep. But these are all landsmen; of week days pent up in lath and plaster—tied to counters, nailed to benches, clinched to desks. How then is this? Are the green fields gone? What do they here?

In the twentieth century the classic influence is still clear. These are the first three sentences of Samuel Beckett's *Murphy* (1938):

> The sun shone, having no alternative, on the nothing new. Murphy sat out of it, as though he were free, in a mew in West Brompton. Here for what might have been six months he had eaten, drunk, slept, and put his clothes on and off, in a medium-sized cage of north-western aspect commanding an unbroken view of medium-sized cages of south-eastern aspect.

The antithesis of north-west and south-east in the last sentence is obvious; perhaps less obvious is the antithesis, in the first two, of the sun and Murphy, "shone" and "sat out of it," and "having no alternative" and "as though he were free."

The next book shows how Beckett, the best and boldest master of English since Joyce, uses classic balance and antithesis in the most advanced avant-garde writing. In his most recent novel, *How It Is* (1964, translated by himself from his own French original, *Comment c'est*, 1961), Beckett's nameless hero hears a voice:

> . . . a voice which if I had a voice I might have taken for mine which at the instant I hear it I quote on is also heard by him whom

Bom left to come towards me and by him to go towards whom Pim left me [.]

Here we have not only antithesis but chiasmus as well. The term chiasmus, from the Greek letter *chi* (X), indicates a crossing over, a change of direction:

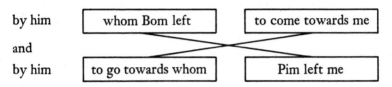

Here the reversal may indicate the different directions of the two hearers, though on the other hand, as Beckett would say, it may not, for they may be crawling in the same direction. However that may be, chiasmus is another figure in the verbal dance of good classic stylists. Here is an example by Joyce, in *Ulysses* (1922):

> On Newcomen bridge the very reverend John Conmee S. J. of saint Francis Xavier's church, upper Gardiner street, stepped on to an outward bound tram.
> Off an inward bound tram stepped the reverend Nicholas Dudley C. C. of saint Aagatha's church, north William street, on to Newcomen bridge.

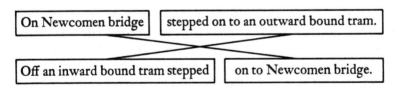

You will find another and more complex example of chiasmus in the first quotation from St. Augustine later in this section.

Here is the opening paragraph of *World Within World: The Autobiography of Stephen Spender* (1951):

I grew up in an atmosphere of belief in progress curiously mingled with apprehension. Through books we read at school, through the Liberal views of my family, it seemed that I had been born on to a fortunate promontory of time towards which all other times led.

Here too we have classic balance and antithesis, though in a much less obvious way: "belief in progress" is balanced by "apprehension," "Through books" by "through the . . . views," and "a . . . promontory of time" by "all other times."

And here is the opening paragraph of Iris Murdoch's *The Bell* (1958):

Dora Greenfield left her husband because she was afraid of him. She decided six months later to return to him for the same reason. The absent Paul, haunting her with letters and telephone bells and imagined footsteps on the stairs, had begun to be the greater torment. Dora suffered from guilt, and with guilt came fear. She decided at last that the persecution of his presence was to be preferred to the persecution of his absence.

These last two sentences take us back to the eighteenth century with Voltaire. The first two sentences also balance each other; and in the third—"The absent Paul . . . had begun to be the greater torment"—the present Paul is unmistakably implied. Miss Murdoch might have written, "The absent Paul . . . had begun to be a greater torment than the present Paul." That, however, would have been awkward, since "the present Paul" suggests "the past Paul" more strongly than it does "the absent Paul." Miss Murdoch has avoided an evident awkwardness but left us with an implicit awkwardness; we do not read the sentence easily; it gives us pause; it is not a very good sentence. I point this out for two reasons: (1) to indicate—as I said in the Introduction—that no style should be regarded as a magic formula that will save us from bad writing, and (2) to illustrate another point I made in the

Introduction, that the quality of a piece of writing can be objectively demonstrated.

Ancient, Medieval, and Early English-Renaissance Classicists

ꙮ THE FOOLISH POLONIUS' wise advice to his son (*Hamlet* I.iii.59–80) was not a reflection of any wisdom in him. It was quoted almost verbatim from a book of maxims widely used in Elizabethan grammar schools—maxims only too familiar to every literate male in Shakespeare's audience. Beyond that schoolbook they go back through various windy writers to the ancient windbag Isocrates (436–338 B.C.): a professional speech writer, who wrote several speeches to be read silently as models of elegant writing, who worked on one speech for fifteen years, and whom the ironical Socrates, arguing against all bad writers and all readers of ready-made speeches, commended to the dim-witted Phaedrus as a bubbling fount of freshness and spontaneity. I mention him by way of allegory: he represents a danger inherent in the classic style, the danger of sententiousness. This style, with its neatly balanced pairs and parallels, encourages a facile tendency to think in terms of opposites and hence of abstractions: Virtue and Vice, Reason and Passion, Wisdom and Folly, Nobility and Baseness. It tends to obscure our view of particular persons and actual situations: Polonius broke up an affectionate leave-taking with his grammar-school commonplaces.

In the following selections from Isocrates I have spared you most of the maxims Polonius owed to him. In practicing his style, emulate his virtues, not his vices; his wisdom, not his folly; his nobility, not his baseness; and use the same wariness with regard to the variations of that style in other writers.

❧

ISOCRATES [436–338 B.C.]

Excerpts from "To Demonicus"

[I have used George Norlin's translation with a few minor modifications to indicate Isocrates' lust for symmetry. For example, the sentence that Norlin translates, "If you love knowledge, you will be a master of knowledge," reads literally, "If you are a philomath, you will be a polymath." But that is hardly English; certainly it is not the idiomatic twentieth-century English we find most readily intelligible. Therefore, having considered and rejected such fancy alternatives as "If you love knowledge intensely you will possess it abundantly" and "If you are a lover of all knowledge you will be a possessor of much knowledge," I have stayed close to Norlin's version: I have rendered it "If you are a lover of knowledge, you will be a master of knowledge." I mention all this in order to emphasize the value of revision and the difficulty of weighing the often conflicting claims of euphony, precision, and intelligibility. I have made similar modifications in the other translations from ancient writers.]

In many respects, Demonicus, we shall find that much disparity exists between the principles of good men and the notions of base men; but by far the greatest difference is in their relations with others. The base honor their friends only when they are present; the good cherish theirs even when they are absent; and whereas a little time can dissolve the intimacy of the base, not all eternity can disrupt the friendship of the good. Therefore, since I deem it fitting that those who strive for distinction and are ambitious for education should emulate the good and not the base, I have dispatched this discourse to you as a gift, in proof of my good will toward you and in token of my friendship for Hipponicus; for it is fitting that a son should inherit his father's friendships even as he inherits his estate. I see, moreover, that fortune is on our side and circumstances are in league with us; for you are eager for education and I profess to educate; you are ripe for philosophy and I direct students of philosophy. . . .

Observe here the antithesis of "principles" and "notions," "good men" and "base men," "only when they are present" and "even when they are absent," "a little time" and "not all eternity," etc. You will also find a symmetrical pairing of things that are not opposites, such as "my good will toward you" and "my friendship for Hipponicus."

Virtue . . . is better than riches and more serviceable than high birth; it makes possible for us what is impossible for others; it bears with courage things that the multitude shrinks from in terror; and it considers sloth a disgrace and toil an honor. . . . But it is not possible for the mind to be so disposed unless it is equipped with many noble maxims; for, as it is the nature of the body to be developed by appropriate exercises, it is the nature of the soul to be developed by moral precepts. . . .

If you are a lover of knowledge, you will be a master of knowledge. What you have come to know, preserve by exercise; what you do not yet know, seek to add to your knowledge; for it is as reprehensible to hear a profitable saying and not grasp it as to be offered a good gift by one's friends and not accept it. Spend your leisure time in cultivating an ear attentive to discourse; for in this way you will find that you can learn with ease what others have worked out with difficulty. Believe that many precepts are better than much wealth; for wealth quickly fails us, but precepts abide through all time; for wisdom alone of all possessions is imperishable. Do not hesitate to travel a long road to those who profess to offer some useful instruction; for it were a shame, when merchants cross vast seas to increase their wealth, that the young should not endure even journeys by land to improve their under-standing.

Be courteous in your manner, and cordial in your address. It is the part of courtesy to greet those whom you meet, and of cordiality to enter into friendly talk with them. Be pleasant to all, but cultivate the best; thus you will avoid the dislike of the former and have the friendship of the latter. Avoid frequent conversations with the same persons, and long conversations on the same sub-jects; for there is satiety in all things.

This goes on and on; it is the source of Polonius' advice to his son. No wonder the son was reckless, impatient and impulsive!

CICERO [106–43 B.C.]

Excerpt from "Against Quintus Caecilius," VERRINE ORATIONS

There are other qualities, Caecilius, which you may think of small account, but without which no man can manage any case, and especially not one of this magnitude. He must have some little capacity as a pleader; some little experience as a speaker; some little training either in the principles or in the practice of the Forum, the law-courts, and the law. I am aware that I am here treading on dangerous and difficult ground. Vanity of every kind is disagreeable; but vanity concerning intellectual and oratorical gifts is far more detestable than any other kind. I shall therefore say nothing of my own intellectual capacity. There is nothing I can say, nor, if there were, would I say it. For either the powers, be they more or less, with which I am credited, are sufficient for my purpose; or, if they are not, I can make them no greater than they are by talking about them. But as for you, Caecilius—and I would assure you that I am now going to speak to you as one friend to another, without reference to the present competition between us—I earnestly advise you to examine your own mind. Recollect yourself. Think of what you are, and of what you are fit for. This is a formidable and very disagreeable case, which involves the cause of our allies and the welfare of our province, the rights of our own nation, and the authority of our law and our courts of law. These are not light or simple matters to take upon you: have you the powers of voice and memory, have you the intelligence and the ability to sustain such a burden? Think of the crimes that Verres has committed as quaestor, as legate, and as praetor, at Rome, in Italy, in Achaia and Asia and Pamphylia: do you think yourself able to charge him with all these, arranging and distinguishing them properly, according to the times and places at which they respectively occurred? Do you think you can do what is especially necessary in prosecuting a man on such charges as these —make all his acts of lust and impiety and cruelty excite as much pain, and as much indignation, in those who are told of them here, as they excited in those who underwent them there? I assure you, these things of which I tell you are no trifles, and you must not think of them lightly. You have to mention everything, establish every fact, expound everything in full. You have not merely to state your case: you have to develop it with impressive wealth of detail. If you wish to achieve any sort of success, you must not only make people listen to you: you must make them listen with pleasure, with eagerness. Even had you the advantage of great natural gifts; had you from boyhood received the best teaching and enjoyed an elaborate and thorough education; had you studied Greek literature at Athens instead of at Lilybaeum, and Latin at Rome instead of in Sicily: even so, with a case of such magnitude, a case that has aroused such wide public interest, it would be hard to find the industry to master it, the eloquence to set it forth, and the strength of voice and body to carry it through.

Observe the hard-hitting force of the reiterated sarcastic "some little . . . , some little . . . , some little. . . ." The devices of parallelism, symmetry, antithesis, etc., which less serious writers used merely for smoothness and elegance, Cicero used in order to get practical results. He used them unobtrusively, not in order to call attention to them but in order to produce certain desired effects on his audiences. "There is nothing I can say, nor, if there were, would I say it." That is an example. The beautiful economy of the sentence seems the most natural thing in the world, an expression of the modesty it boasts of, a product of moral sincerity, not of rhetorical art. An almost equally fine example is "the cause of our allies and the welfare of our province, the rights of our own nation, and the authority of our law and our courts of law." Cicero repeatedly hits his opponent with parallelisms: "have you the . . . , have you the . . . and the. . .?" "You have to. . . . You have not merely to . . . , you have to. . . ." "Even had you . . . ; had you . . . ; had you. . . ."

SALLUST [86–34 B.C.]

Excerpt from the speech of Philippus in the "Histories"

I pray you consider how the order of things is inverted; formerly public mischief was planned secretly, public defence openly; and hence the good easily forestalled the wicked. Nowadays peace and harmony are disturbed openly, defended secretly; those who desire disorder are in arms; you are in fear. What are you waiting for, unless perchance you are ashamed or weary of well-doing? Are you influenced by the demands of Lepidus? He says that he wishes to render unto each his own, and keeps the property of others; to annul laws established in time of war, and uses armed compulsion; to establish the citizenship of those from whom he

denies that it has been taken, and in the interests of peace to re-
store the power of the tribunes, by whom all our discords were
kindled.

Note: I record this last met-
aphor, without condoning it. A discord can be perpetrated, caused,
or brought about; it cannot be kindled. One might as well speak
of untuning a fire.

☙

SENECA [4 B.C.?–A.D. 65]

Excerpt from "On Anger," MORAL ESSAYS

Whether it is in accord with nature will become clear if we turn
our eyes to man. What is more gentle than he while he is in a
right state of mind? But what is more cruel than anger? What is
more loving to others than man? What more hostile than anger?
Man is born for mutual help; anger for mutual destruction. The
one desires union, the other disunion; the one to help, the other
to harm; one would succor even strangers, the other attack its
best-beloved; the one is ready to devote himself to the good of
others, the other to plunge into peril if it can imperil others.

Here anger is personified;
observe the same device in the passage from Gibbon, pp. 63–66.

☙

TACITUS [A.D. 55?–117?]

Excerpt from "Dialogus," in DIALOGUS, AGRICOLA, GERMANIA

Likewise at Rome, so long as the constitution was unsettled, so
long as the country kept wearing itself out with factions and dis-

sensions and disagreements, so long as there was no peace in the
Forum, no harmony in the Senate, no restraint in the law courts,
no respect for authority, no decorum in the magistrates, the
growth of eloquence was doubtless sturdier, just as untilled soil
produces certain vegetation in greater luxuriance. But the benefit
derived from the eloquence of the Gracchi did not make up for
what the country suffered from their laws, and too dearly did
Cicero pay by the death he died for the orator's renown he
enjoyed.

ST. AMBROSE [340–397]

Excerpt from ON THE DUTIES OF THE CLERGY

We then must strive for that wherein is perfection and wherein is
truth. Here is the shadow, here the image; there the truth. The
shadow is in the law, the image in the Gospel, the truth in heaven.
. . . Here, then, we walk in an image, we see in an image; there face
to face where is full perfection. For all perfection rests in the
truth. Whilst, then, we are here let us preserve the likeness, that
there we may attain to the truth.

ST. AUGUSTINE [354–430]

Excerpts from the CONFESSIONS

In Thee abide, fixed for ever, the first causes of all things unabiding; and of all things changeable, the springs abide in Thee unchangeable; and in Thee live the eternal reasons of all things unreasoning and temporal. . . .

Here we have a beautiful double chiasmus, in which the design of the whole is repeated in each of its parts:

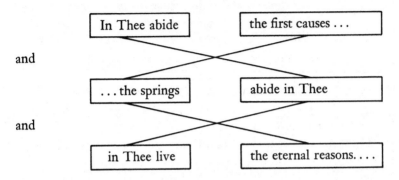

Observe the antithesis of "abide, fixed" and "unabiding," "changeable" and "unchangeable," and "reasons" and "unreasoning." Observe also the double chiasmus of "the first causes of all things," "of all things . . . the springs," and "the eternal reasons of all things."

Excerpts from the CONFESSIONS

In those years I taught rhetoric, and, overcome by cupidity, made sale of a loquacity to overcome by. Yet I preferred (Lord, Thou knowest) honest scholars (as they are accounted), and these I, without artifice, taught artifices, not to be practised against the life of the guiltless, though sometimes for the life of the guilty. . . .

Blessed whoso loveth Thee, and his friend in Thee, and his enemy for Thee. For he alone loses none dear to him, to whom all are dear in Him Who cannot be lost. And who is this but our God, the God that made heaven and earth, and filleth them, because by filling them He created them? Thee none loseth, but who leaveth. And who leaveth Thee, whither goeth or whither fleeth he, but from Thee well-pleased, to Thee displeased? . . .

And it was manifested unto me, that those things be good, which yet are corrupted; which neither were they sovereignly good, nor unless they were good, could be corrupted; for if sovereignly good, they were incorruptible; if not good at all, there were nothing in them to be corrupted. For corruption injures, but unless it diminished goodness, it could not injure. Either then corruption injures not, which cannot be; or, which is most certain, all which is corrupted is deprived of good. But if they be deprived of all good, they shall cease to be. For if they shall be, and can now no longer be corrupted, they shall be better than before, because they shall abide incorruptibly. And what more monstrous, than to affirm things to become better by losing all their good? Therefore, if they shall be deprived of all good, they shall no longer be. So long therefore as they are, they are good: therefore whatsoever is, is good. . . .

Excerpt from ON THE IMMORTALITY OF THE SOUL

And even if there be no destruction without change, and no change without motion, yet not all change is engaged in destruction, nor is all motion engaged in change.

Excerpt from ON THE FREE CHOICE OF THE WILL

Wherever thou turnest, He speaketh to thee by traces, which He has impressed upon His works, and by the very forms of outward things recalls thee, when sinking down to things outward.

ॐॐ

ST. ANSELM OF CANTERBURY [1033–1109]

Excerpt from PROSLOGIUM

O supreme and unapproachable light! O whole and blessed truth, how far art Thou from me, who am so near to Thee! How far removed art Thou from my vision, although I am so near to Thine! Everywhere Thou art wholly present, and I see Thee not. In Thee I move, and in Thee I have my being; and I cannot come to Thee. Thou art within me, and about me, and I feel Thee not.

Excerpts from St. Anselm's THIRD MEDITATION

Ah! from what height hast thou fallen, to what depth hast thou plunged! Woe! what blessedness hast thou contemned, what cursedness hast thou embraced! What hast thou done, O conscious madness, mad foulness, foul wickedness, what hast thou done? . . .

Prodigious horror, what a perverse will! Horrible prodigy, what willful perversity! How, God, can such depravity in me be corrected? How, God, can such wickedness to Thee be redeemed? . . .

Horrible terror, terrible grief, grievous sorrow, overwhelm me, crush me, bury me, shake me, engulf me, possess me! It is just, it is just. . . . If indeed I am not worthy to lift my eyes to Heaven in prayer, surely I am not unworthy to blind them with weeping. . . .

This meditation has to do with Anselm's remorse for what he calls the loss of his virginity in youth—under circumstances that made it necessary for him to leave town in a hurry. The expression of his grief is full of formal elegance, but is not on that account unmoving. In the original, it even rhymes:

Heu! de quam sublimi cecidisti, in quam profundum corruisti! vae! quam benignum contempsisti, quam maligno te junxisti! Quid fecisti, o mentis amentia, amens spurcitia, spurca nequitia, quid fecisti? . . .

Horror mirabilis, quam perversa voluntas! Miraculum horribile, quam voluntaria perversitas! Unde mihi, Deus, tantae pravitatis correctio? unde tibi, Deus, tanti sceleris satisfactio? . . .

Terror horribilis, dolor terribilis, moeror inconsolabilis, aggregate vos super me, irruite, obruite, perturbate, obvolvite, possidete. Justum est, justum est. . . . Si enim non sum dignus oculos ad coelum orando levare, certe non sum indignus eos vel plorando caecare. . . .

Observe the rhymes: "cecidisti . . . corruisti . . . contempsisti . . . te junxisti . . . quid fecisti . . . quid fecisti," etc. Observe that each has four syllables. Observe also, in the last sentence of the first paragraph, the linking of "amentia" with "amens," and of "spurcitia" with "spurca." Literally, the sentence reads, "What hast thou done, O mindlessness of mind, mindless foulness, foul wickedness, what has thou done?" But since "mindlessness of mind" is not idiomatic English, and since the combination of "mindlessness" with "mindless foulness" is clumsy and cacophonous, I have sacrificed literality to readability. Likewise, at the end of the second paragraph, a literal translation would read, "Whence to me, God, the correction of so much depravity? Whence to Thee, God, the satisfaction of so much wickedness?" But that just isn't English; and to write bad English is to be profoundly unfaithful to a good original. Hence the changes. Most translations involve such changes. The difficulty

lies in judging how far to go. See, for example, J.-P. Vinay and
J. Darbelnet, *Stylistique Comparée du Français et de l'Anglais*
(Paris, 1964), which deals with problems of translation from
English to French and from French to English.

BISHOP HUGH LATIMER [1491–1555]

Excerpts from SERMON ON THE PLOUGHERS, *1549*

And thus if the ploughmen of the country were as negligent in
their office [their duty] as prelates be, we should not long live for
lack of sustenance. And as it is necessary for to have this plough-
ing for the sustentation of the body, so must we have also the
other for the satisfaction of the soul, or else we cannot live long
ghostly [spiritually]. For as the body wasteth and consumeth
away for lack of bodily meat [food], so doth the soul pine away
for default of ghostly meat. . . .

But now for the default of unpreaching prelates, methinks
I could guess what might be said for excusing of them: they are
so troubled [occupied] with lordly living, they be so placed in
palaces, couched in courts, ruffling in their rents [making a display
of their wealth], dancing in their dominions, pampering their
paunches like a monk that maketh his jubilee [a monk on an offi-
cially permitted vacation], munching in their mangers, and moiling
[busying themselves] in their gay manors and mansions, and so
troubled with loitering in their lordships, that they cannot attend
[to] it.

                              In the second paragraph we
have not only parallelism but also alliteration. This is a rather
cheap affectation, which becomes obnoxiously noticeable in
Euphuism. See the next section of this chapter.

൦ᘻᓀ

THOMAS LEVER [15??–1577]

Excerpts from A SERMON PREACHED AT PAUL'S CROSS, *1550*

Some peradventure will be offended not because I speak against
the buying of benefices [church jobs], which be spiritual charges,
but for that [because] I also include the buying and selling of
[government] offices, which, as they say, be temporal promotions.
As for benefices, ye know so well, that I need not to stand [to waste
time] about the declaration or proof in them [as far as they are
concerned].

No, I am sure that ye perceive how that through the
abuse of one benefice, the Devil ofttimes is sure to have many
souls:

First the patron [the one who has control of the job and
sells it] for his presentation, then the Bishop for admission [for
permitting the buyer to take the job], the parson for his unworthiness, and a great many of the parish that be lost for lack of a good
parson's duty. [Lever seems to be objecting not only to the selling of such jobs, but to making presents of them to unworthy
friends, relatives, political allies, etc.]

But now as concerning the buying of [government] offices:
to come thereby into the room [the place] of an auditor, surveyor
[supervisor], chancellor, or any such like, surely no man will
attempt it but he which is so covetous and ambitious that he doth
neither dread God nor love man. . . . If we say that the offices be
not meet for God's servants, then we confess that the officers
which be in them be God's enemies. If we say that they be ordained for the faithful servants of God, how can we think that
they may be bought unto the bribing servants of wicked
Mammon?

🙰

ROGER ASCHAM [1515–1568]

Excerpts from THE SCHOOLMASTER, *1570*

Yet some will say that children of nature [by nature] love pastime and mislike learning: because, in their kind [by their nature], the one is easy and pleasant, the other hard and wearisome: which is an opinion not so true as some men ween: for the matter lieth not so much in the disposition of them that be young as in the order and manner of bringing up by them that be old, nor yet in the difference of [the difference between] learning and pastime. For, beat a child if he dance not well, and cherish him though he learn not well, ye shall have him unwilling to go to dance, and glad to go to his book. . . .

But now the ripest [most facile] of tongue be readiest to write: and many daily in setting out books and ballads make great show of blossoms and buds, in whom is neither root of learning nor fruit of wisdom at all. . . .

Sallust is a wise and worthy writer: but he requireth a learned reader and a right considerer of him. My dearest friend, and best master [teacher] that ever I had or heard [of] in learning, Sir J. Cheke—such a man as, if I should live to see England breed the like again, I fear I should live over long—did once give me a lesson for Sallust, which, as I shall never forget myself, so is it worthy to be remembered of all those that would come to perfect judgment of the Latin tongue. He said that Sallust was not very fit [suitable] for young men to learn out of him the purity of the Latin tongue, because he was not the purest in propriety of words, nor choicest in aptness of phrases, nor the best in framing of sentences: and therefore is his writing, said he, neither plain for the matter, nor sensible [perspicuous] for men's understand-

ing. "And what is the cause thereof, Sir?" quoth I. "Verily," said
he, "because in Sallust writing is more art than nature, and more
labor than art."

In Latimer, Lever and As-
cham we see men who were masters of Latin struggling with
English. To the extent that they follow the old Latin patterns
they write clearly; but the many clumsy sentences in the three
foregoing passages indicate how hard it was to write clear English
prose in the Renaissance period of transition between old forms
and new. These pioneers helped to work out the basic forms of
modern English.

Exercises

As I write, racism at home and the war in Vietnam are our most serious
public concerns. For many of us they have become deeply personal
concerns, as important as love and more important than anything else.
They are obviously better subjects to write about than "How I Went
Home Over the Weekend," or "The Difference Between High School
and College," or "My Ideal Girl/Man," or "Greek Week," or "Fresh-
man Customs." Nevertheless, I suggest that in this course it will be
useful to suppress for the time being your deepest moral and emotional
preoccupations and concentrate on learning to handle our native
language skillfully. I am of course not suggesting that you write on
any such paltry subjects as those I have just listed: all themes on such
subjects are alike: there is neither thought nor passion in them, but
only a kind of reflex twitching: has there ever been an Ideal Girl/Man
who didn't Have a Sense of Humor? What I am suggesting is that in
this course you concentrate all your thought and passion on mastering
ways of constructing thought and expressing passion. Plato, Aristotle,
St. Augustine, St. Thomas Aquinas, Wordsworth, Flaubert, Oscar
Wilde, Joyce, Proust, Kafka, Mann and Nabokov, among others, agree
that there is no necessary connection between moral rectitude and

literary skill, or between the intensity with which a writer feels emotion
and the effectiveness with which he expresses it. A good writer concentrates on his sentences, not on the beating of his heart. It will therefore be wise, at the beginning, to avoid subjects on which your emotion
may distract you from the choice and marshaling of words.

I suggest also that you resist the temptation to write on subjects
that you have recently begun to think about for the first time, or that
you have often thought about but never read about. The worst sin a
writer as writer can commit is to be unconsciously naive. There are
dozens or hundreds or thousands of books on any intellectual question
you can mention, and if you haven't read at least two or three you can
only utter naivetés. At least for our immediate purposes it is better to
write one well-made paragraph about three mirrors, each of which
reflects the reflections in the other two, than ten pages of formless
generalities about Fate And Free Will or The Individual And Society.
The first is an intellectually demanding exercise; the other two are
not. In any intellectual effort, form, content and significance are one;
in any such intellectual effort as that of describing those mirrors accurately, content and significance are aspects or by-products of form.
In the beginning, we have it on the very best authority, was the Word.
The following topics are by way of suggestion and illustration.

1. Six waiters are setting tables in a large restaurant, three of whose
walls consist of alternate full-length windows and full-length mirrors.
Describe the comings and goings of the waiters, and of the passersby
who can be seen through the windows, and of their various reflections.
Remember that in a mirror your right hand is your left hand. Think
of the whole as a kind of walking ballet; try to contain your choreog-
raphy in two pages. You will find the classic sentence patterns very
useful. Use them. Use parallelism and antithesis. Use chiasmus. Use the
chains of St. Anselm. They will help you to free yourself.

2. On the campus of your college or university, three meetings are
going on simultaneously: of the trustees in their board room, the
Liberal Arts faculty in a dingy auditorium, and the student council in
a dorm necking parlor. All three meetings are devoted to the same
question: Should controversial public figures be invited to speak on

campus? The trustees are concerned with public relations and the reactions of legislators or rich alumni—i.e., with money, as they must
be; the faculty is concerned with such questions as freedom and responsibility, the search for truth and the propagation of propaganda,
the difference between discussion and proclamation, the desirability of
hearing all sides of a question, the undesirability of encouraging crack-
pots, clowns and charlatans by inviting them to perform under serious
auspices,[1] and the problem of how to determine objectively whether a
man is worth taking seriously or not; they are haunted on the one hand
by those doctors of the church who refused to dignify Galileo's demon-
stration of the law of falling bodies by attending it, and on the other
hand by notorious demagogues and dope pushers who profit by our
imbecile relativistic reluctance to reject anything at all. The students
are concerned with various things: freedom of speech, intellectual
curiosity, morbid curiosity, curious curiosity, fun and games, moral
outrage, social concern, sexual frustration, etc. I am not sneering, I am
stating facts. Recount the simultaneity of the three meetings, the
parallels, the antitheses, the convergences, the divergences, etc., by
means of classic devices.

See the postscript on page 317.

Euphuism

EUPHUISM WAS an affected
manner of writing and speaking affected by many members of polite
society in Elizabethan England. Shakespeare made fun of it: see,
for example, the speeches of Polonius in *Hamlet* II.ii, of Falstaff
in *I Henry IV* I.ii, and of Armado, Biron and Holofernes throughout *Love's Labour's Lost*. The term is derived from the title of
a didactic novel by John Lyly, *Euphues* (1579), which means
"The Gentleman." This mincing, finicking, posing, posturing,

---

[1] Some of the faculty may be silently wondering, "*Is* this a serious institution?"

dancing, prancing novel had a mad vogue for about a dozen years; its direct influence on other writers continued for perhaps a dozen more; and in the long run and on the whole, its own impossible cheapness notwithstanding, the exercises it encouraged seem to have contributed to the grace and firmness of English prose. It was a fictional supplement or companion to the many "courtesy books" that professed to teach courtly manners to the rising middle class; the irony is that it taught high-born courtiers themselves to speak like bourgeois gentlemen trying too hard. As Dr. Johnson was to say of Lord Chesterfield's book of letters, it inculcated the manners of a dancing-master.

Euphuism involves the dressing up of harmless commonplace ideas in ridiculously fancy language, decorated all over with aphorisms, alliterations, assonances, consonances, rhymes, ratios, examples from history and mythology, and analogues from nature and imaginary nature. It is a perverse exaggeration of the classic style; it is a fake style, in which gaudy language fails to dissemble poverty of thought. To cultivate it seriously would be absurd, but it is well worth practicing for the sake of exercise.

JOHN LYLY [1553–1606]

Excerpts from EUPHUES, *1579, and* EUPHUES AND HIS ENGLAND, *1580*

This old gentleman having finished his discourse, Euphues began to shape him an answer in this sort.

Father and friend (your age showeth the one, your honesty the other), I am neither so suspicious [as] to mistrust your good will, nor so sottish [as] to mislike your good counsel; as I am therefore to thank you for the first, so it stands me upon [is incumbent upon me] to think better on the latter: I mean not to cavil with you, as one loving sophistry, neither to control you, as one having superiority: the one would bring me into the suspicion of fraud, the other convince me [convict me] of folly.

Whereas you argue (I know not upon what probabilities, but sure I am upon no proof) that my bringing up should be [is] a blemish to my birth, I answer, and swear to, that you were not therein a little overshot: either you gave too much credit [credence] to the report of others, or too much liberty to your own judgment: you convince my parents of peevishness [convict them of senselessness] in making me a wanton, and me of lewdness [stupid wickedness] in rejecting correction. But so many men so many minds: that may seem in your eye odious which in another's eye may be gracious. Aristippus a philosopher, yet who more courtly? Diogenes a philosopher, yet who more carterly? Who more popular than Plato, retaining always good company? Who more envious than Timon, renouncing all human society? Who more severe than the Stoics, which like stocks [blocks of wood] were moved with no melody? Who so secure [carefree] as the Epicures, which wallowed in all kinds of licentiousness? Though all men be made of one metal, yet they be not cast all in one mold; there is framed of the selfsame clay as well the tile to keep out water as the pot to contain liquor; the sun doth harden the dirt and melt the wax; fire maketh the gold to shine and the straw to smother [to give off smoke]; perfumes doth refresh the dove and kill the beetle, and the nature of the man disposeth the consent of the manners [his manners tend to follow his nature]. Now whereas you seem to love my nature and loath my nurture, you betray your own weakness in thinking the nature may any ways be altered by education; and as you have examples to confirm your pretense [the view you set forth], so I have most evident and infallible arguments to serve for my purpose. It is natural for the vine to spread; the more you seek by art to alter it, the more in the end you shall augment it. It is proper for the palm tree to mount; the heavier you load it, the higher it sprouteth. Though iron be made soft with fire, it returneth to his [its] hardness; though the falcon be reclaimed to the fist, she retireth to her haggardness [returneth to her wildness]; the whelp of the mastiff will never be taught to retrieve the partridge; education can have no show [effect] where the excellency of nature doth bear sway. The silly [innocent] mouse will by no manner of means be tamed; the subtle fox may well be beaten, but never broken from stealing his prey; if you pound spices, they smell the sweeter; season the wood never so well, the wine will taste of the cask; plant and translate [move, transplant] the crab tree where and whensoever it please you, and it will never bear sweet apple unless you graft it by art, which nothing toucheth [has nothing to do with] nature. . . .EUPHUES.

Observe here Lyly's soporific sententiousness—his long chains of proverbs and clichés; his tireless balancing of words and phrases—"your age . . . your honesty," "so suspicious . . . so sottish," "to mistrust . . . to mislike," "your good will . . . your good counsel," etc., etc., etc.; his many alliterations—"cavil . . . control," "sophistry . . . superiority," "probabilities . . . proof," "bringing up . . . blemish . . . birth," "parents . . . peevishness," "many men . . . many minds," "courtly . . . carterly," "severe . . . Stoics . . . stocks," "moved . . . melody," "men . . . made . . . metal . . . mold," "love . . . loath," "nature . . . nurture," "hardness . . . haggardness," "returneth . . . retireth," etc., etc., etc.; and his many illustrations from nature and from popular superstitions about nature, such as the notion that perfumes refresh doves but kill beetles, and the notion that the heavier you load a palm tree the higher it will grow. Watch for the same features in the passages that follow.

Lucilla, either so bewitched that she could not relent or so wicked that she would not yield to her father's request, answered him in this manner.

Dear Father, as you would have me to show the duty of a child, so ought you to show the care of a parent; for as the one standeth [consisteth] in obedience, so the other is grounded upon reason. You would have me (as I owe duty to you) to leave Curio; and I desire you (as you owe me any love) that you suffer me to enjoy him. If you accuse me of unnaturalness in that I yield not to your request, I am also to condemn you of unkindness in that you grant not my petition.

You object I know not what to Curio; but it is the eye of the master that fatteth the horse, and the love of the woman that maketh the man. To give reason for fancy were to weigh the fire and measure the wind. If therefore my delight be the cause of your death, I think my sorrow would be an occasion of your solace. And if you be angry because I am pleased, certes I deem you would be content if I were deceased: which if it be so, that my pleasure breed your pain, and mine annoy your joy, I may well say that you are an unkind father and I [am] an unfortunate child. But, good Father, either content yourself with my choice or let me stand to the main chance; otherwise the grief will be mine and the fault yours, and both untolerable.   EUPHUES

If travelers in this age were as wary of their conditions as they be venturous of their bodies, or as willing to reap profit by their pains as they are to endure peril for their pleasure, they would either prefer their own soil before a strange land, or good counsel before their own conceit [conception, opinion]. But as the young scholar in Athens went to hear Demosthenes' eloquence at Corinth and was entangled in Lais' beauty, so most of our travelers, which pretend [undertake] to get a smack [a taste, a little bit] of strange language to sharpen their wits, are infected with vanity by following their wills. Danger and delight grow both upon one stalk, the rose and the canker in one bud; white and black are commonly in one border [of a garden]. Seeing then, my good Philautus, that we are not to conquer wild beasts by fight, but to confer with wise men by policy: we ought to take greater heed that we be not entrapped in folly, than fear to be subdued by force.

EUPHUES AND HIS ENGLAND

When I was young as thou now art, I never thought to be old as now I am: which caused lusty blood to attempt those things in youth which aching bones have repented in age. I had one only brother, which also bore my name, [we] being both born at one time as twins. . . .

As we grew old[er] in years, so began we to be more opposite in opinions: he grave, I gamesome; he studious, I careless; he without mirth, and I without modesty.

And verily, had we resembled each other as little in favor [in looks] as we did in fancy, or disagreed as much in shape as we did in sense, I know not what Daedalus would have made a Labyrinth for such monsters, or what Appelles could have colored such misshapes.

EUPHUES AND HIS ENGLAND

To love and to live well is wished of many but incident to few. To live and to love well is incident to few but indifferent to [equally wished by] all. To love without reason is an argument [a sign] of lust, to live without love a token of folly. The measure of love is to have no mean, the end [the purpose] to be everlasting.

EUPHUES AND HIS ENGLAND

ROBERT GREENE [1558–1592]

Excerpt from PANDOSTO: THE TRIUMPH OF TIME, *1588*

Dorastus, thy youth warneth me to prevent the worst, and mine age to provide the best. Opportunities neglected are signs of folly;

actions measured by time are seldom bitten with repentance; thou art young, and I old; age hath taught me that which thy youth cannot yet conceive.

I therefore will counsel thee as a father, hoping thou wilt obey as a child. Thou seest my white hairs are blossoms for the grave, and thy fresh colors fruit for time and fortune; so it behooveth me to think how to die, and for thee to care how to live. My crown I must leave by death, and thou enjoy my kingdom by succession. Wherein I hope thy virtue and prowess will be such as, though my subjects want [lack] my person, yet they shall see in thee my perfection. That nothing either may fail to satisfy thy mind or increase thy dignities, the only care I have is to see thee well married before I die and thou become old.

Dorastus (who, from his fancy, delighted rather to die with Mars in the field than to dally with Venus in the chamber), fearing to displease his father, and yet not willing to be wed, made him this reverent answer.

Sir, there is no greater bond than duty, nor no stricter law than nature: disobedience in youth is often galled with despite in age. The command of the father ought to be a constraint to the child; so, parents' wills are laws, so they pass not all laws. [Thus, parents' wills are laws, provided that they don't overstep all limits of law.] May it please your Grace, therefore, to appoint whom I shall love: rather than by denial I should be appeached of disobedience, I rest content to love, though it be the only thing I hate.

Egistus, hearing his son to fly far from the mark, began to be somewhat choleric, and therefore made him this hasty answer.

What, Dorastus, canst thou not love? Cometh this cynical passion of prone desires, or peevish forwardness? What, dost thou think thyself too good for all, or none good enough for thee? I tell thee, Dorastus, there is nothing sweeter than youth: nor swifter decreasing, while it is increasing. Time passed with folly may be repented, but not recalled. If thou marry in age, thy wife's fresh colors will breed in thee dead thoughts and suspicion, and thy white hairs her loathsomeness [unwillingness] and sorrow. For Venus' affections are not fed with kingdoms or treasures, but with youthful conceits [thoughts] and sweet amours. Vulcan was allotted to shake the tree, but Mars allowed to reap the fruit. Yield, Dorastus, to thy father's persuasions, which may prevent thy perils. I have chosen thee a wife, fair by nature, royal by birth, by virtues famous, learned by education, and rich by possessions: so that it is hard to judge whether her bounty or fortune, her beauty or virtue, be of greater force: I mean, Dorastus, Euphania, daughter and heir to the King of Denmark.

THOMAS LODGE [1557?–1625]

Excerpt from ROSALYND: EUPHUES' GOLDEN LEGACY, *1590*

Aliena, having read over his sonnet, began thus pleasantly to descant upon it. I see, Saladin (quoth she), that as the sun is no sun without his brightness, nor the diamond accounted for precious unless it be hard, so men are not men unless they be in love; and their honors [their reputations] are measured by their amours, not their labors, counting it more commendable for a gentleman to be full of fancy than full of virtue. I had thought

> *Otia si tollas periere Cupidinis arcus,*
> *Contemptaeq iacent, et fine luce faces:*
>
> [*Take away leisure and Cupid's bow is broken,*
> *And his torch lies extinguished and despised:*]

But I see Ovid's axiom is not authentical, for even labor hath her loves, and extremity is no pumice stone to race out [to erase] fancy. Yourself exiled from your wealth, friends and country by Torismond (sorrows enough to suppress affections), yet amidst the depth of these extremities Love will be lord and show his power to be more predominant than Fortune. But I pray you, Sir (if without offense I may crave it), are they some new thoughts, or some old desires? Saladin (that now saw opportunity pleasant) thought to strike while the iron was hot, and therefore taking Aliena by the hand sate down by her; and Ganymede, to give them leave to their loves, found herself busy about the folds, whilst Saladin fell into this prattle with Aliena.

Fair Mistress, if I be blunt in discovering [revealing] my affections, and use little eloquence in leveling out my loves, I appeal for pardon to your own principles, that say, Shepherds use few ceremonies, for that they acquaint themselves with few subtleties; to frame myself therefore to your country fashion with much faith and little flattery, know, beautiful Shepherdess, that whilst I lived in the court I knew not love's cumber, but I held affection as a toy [a trifle], not as a malady; using fancy as the Hyperboreans do their flowers, which they wear in their bosom all day, and cast them in the fire for fuel all night. I liked all because I loved none, and who was most fair, on her I fed mine eye: but as charily as the bee, that as soon as she hath sucked honey from the rose, flies straight to the next [nearest] marigold. Living thus at mine own list, I wondered at such as were in love, and when I read their passions [love songs] I took them only for poems that flowed from the quickness of the wit, not the sorrows of the heart. But now, fair Nymph, since I became a forester, Love hath taught me such a lesson that I must confess his deity and dignity, and say, as there is nothing so precious as beauty, so there is nothing more piercing than fancy. For since I first arrived in this place, and mine eye took a curious survey of your excellence, I have been so fettered with your beauty and virtue, as, sweet Aliena, Saladin without further circumstance loves Aliena. I could paint out my desires with long ambages [circumlocutions], but seeing [that] in many words lies a mistrust, and that truth is ever naked, let this suffice for a country wooing: Saladin loves Aliena, and none but Aliena.

Although these words were most heavenly harmony in the ears of the shepherdess, yet to seem coy at the first courting, and [to seem] to disdain love howsoever she desired love, she made this reply.

Ah, Saladin, though I seem simple, yet I am more subtle than to swallow the hook because it hath a painted bait: as men are wily, so women are wary, especially if they have that wit by others' harms to beware. Do we not know, Saladin, that men's tongues are like Mercury's pipe, that can enchant Argus with an hundred eyes; and their words as prejudicial [harmful] as the charms of Circe, that transform men into monsters? If such sirens sing, we poor women had need stop our ears, lest in hearing we prove so foolish hardy [foolishly bold, foolhardy] as to believe them, and so perish in trusting much and suspecting little. Saladin, *Piscator ictus sapit* [The fisherman knows when he has a bite]; he that hath been once poisoned, and afterwards fears not to bowse [drink] of every potion, is worthy to suffer a double penance. Give me leave then to mistrust, though I do not condemn. Saladin is now in love with Aliena?—he a gentleman of great parentage, she a shepherdess of mean parents?—he honorable, and she poor? Can love consist of contrarieties? Will the falcon perch with the kestrel, the lion harbor with the wolf? [The kestrel, or windhover, is a small hawk that is useless for purposes of falconry.] Will Venus join robes and rags together? Or can there be a sympathy between a King and a beggar? Then, Saladin, how can I believe thee, that Love should unite our thoughts when Fortune hath set such a difference between our degrees [social ranks]? But suppose thou likest of Aliena's beauty; men in their fancy resemble the wasp, which scorns that flower from which she hath fetched her wax; playing like the inhabitants of the island Tenerifa, who when they have gathered the sweet spices use the trees for fuel: so men when they have glutted themselves with the fair[ness] of women's faces hold them for necessary evils; and wearied with that which they seemed so much to love, cast away fancy as children do their rattles; and loathing that which so deeply before they liked, and having their eyes attractive like jet apt to entertain any object, are as ready to let it slip back again. [Jet, a hard black mineral, when electrified by rubbing attracts paper, cloth, etc.; the word "attractive" here means magnetic.] Saladin, hearing how Aliena harped still [always] upon one string, which was the doubt of men's constancy, broke off her sharp invective thus. [Etc.]

༄

HENRY CHETTLE [15??–1607?]

Three brief and unconnected excerpts from PIERS PLAINNESS: SEVEN YEARS' APPRENTICESHIP, *1595*

The sun no sooner entered Gemini, but Nature's plenty and Earth's pride gave the husbandman hope of gainful harvest, and the shepherd assurance of happy increase; the first [was] cherished [made easy in mind, cheered] with the lively spring [springing forth] of his dead-sown seed; the second cheered by the living presence of his late yeaned [born] lambs. . . .

Aeliana, what new fires are these kindled in thy bosom? what sudden changes, what unwonted passions? Hast thou thus long offered olive boughs to Pallas, and wilt thou now present Venus with myrtle branches? Hast thou followed Diana over the lawns [fields] with exercise, and wilt thou prove the follower of her adversary by idleness? No, Aeliana, extinguish these fond [foolish] loves with mind's labor, and nip thy affections in the bloom, that they may never be of power to bud. . . .

Aeliana, center of all my joy, divinest beauty's essence, light of my soul, my life's lode-star, how miserable am I to see thee placed in so high a sphere, myself dejected in so low a clime; thou most happy [fortunate], I most hapless; I a slave, thou a sovereign.

In the sixteenth century, spelling and punctuation were irregular, erratic and often confusing; I have therefore modernized the spelling and punctuation of the foregoing passages, in order to make the shapes and structures clearer. I have left in its original glory, however, one particularly fine piece of fancy prose, which follows. For a just and sensitive appreciation of John Florio's qualities, see Douglas Bush, *English Literature in the Earlier Seventeenth Century*, Oxford, 1945.

JOHN FLORIO [1553?–1625]

First two paragraphs of "The Epistle Dedicatorie" to his translation of Montaigne's ESSAYS, *1580*

To the Right Honorable my best-best Benefactors, and most-most honored Ladies, *Lucie, Countesse of Bedford*; and hir best-most loved-loving Mother, *Ladie Anne Harrington*.

Strange it may seeme to some, whose seeming is mis-seeming, in one worthlesse patronage to joyne two so severallie all-worthy Ladies. But to any in the right, it would be judged wrong, to disjoyne them in ought, who never were neerer in kinde, then ever in kindnesse. None dearer (dearest Ladies) I have seene, and all may say, to your Honorable husbands then you, to you then your Honorable husbands; and then to other, then eyther is to th'other. So as were I to name but the one, I should surely intend the other: but intending this Dedication to two, I could not but name both.

Exercise

A man asks a woman to marry him, and she refuses. He demands to know why, and she tactfully tells him she likes him fine but has always thought of him as an uncle rather than as a husband, and she hopes they will always be good friends. He then tells her all the advantages she would enjoy as his wife: unlimited money, mansions in all the glamour cities and resorts, breakfast in bed, his private jet plane, his private ocean liner, his private archipelago in the Pacific, and his large collection of green stamps. Realizing then that her tact was lost on him, she tells him frankly that she finds him physically uninteresting, intellectually insipid, and morally boring.

Put this conversation in the style of *Euphues*. Remember Lyly's addiction to proverbs and analogies, animal, vegetable, mineral, meteorological, mythological and historical. Above all, be sententious.

Neo-Classicism

THE EXCESSES of euphuism gave way in time to the restraints of neo-classicism; the exuberance of the seventeenth century to the decorum of the eighteenth; the Renaissance delight in fancy to the Augustan delight in reason. All such antitheses are of course misleading: restraint, decorum and reason were not lacking in the Renaissance, nor excess, exuberance, fancy, enthusiasm, vitality, gusto, grossness and madness in the misnamed Age of Reason. Were Swift and Sterne cool? And was that prince of Burma-Shave poets, the Elizabethan Sir Henry Wotton, passionate? Who can look at the drawings of Hogarth and Rowlandson and then with a straight face call their age the Age of Reason? It was indeed the Age of Reason; but it was also the age of Rousseau, Casanova, Blake, the Marquis de Sade, the Wesley brothers, the revival of Anglo-Saxon, and the invention of gin. Renaissance England had let Chaucer die; Tyrwhitt, an eighteenth-century scholar, resurrected him. The romantic Macpherson, Chatterton and Bishop Percy were all eighteenth-century men; the egregiously sentimental Werther came weeping into the world in 1774, the same year that Lord Chesterfield published his egregiously cold letters. In literary history each period seems to begin about the middle of the previous period and end about the middle of the succeeding period. From the first Scholium in Newton's *Mathematical Principles of Natural Philosophy*—the first specimen of neo-classic prose in this chapter—it is evident that the eighteenth century was already under way in 1686; Dryden had written *MacFlecknoe*, whose tone is thoroughly Augustan, in 1678; and Marvell's "Fleckno," published posthumously in 1681, had undoubtedly been written before 1678.

So, with all these cautions, reservations and provisos, let us call the eighteenth century the Age of Reason. In England the gay clothes of Elizabethan fops and Restoration bucks had given way to the sober suits—if you'll pardon the pun, we can say the sober habits—of Georgian business men; in English ballrooms the running coranto and the gay five-stepping cinquepas or gaillard had given way to the decorous pacing of the minuet and the somewhat faster but still quite decorous gavotte; in literature, on the whole and generally speaking (and let us remember that the leaping saltarello was also an eighteenth-century dance), the tone was one of decorum, dignity, correctness, propriety, restraint, rationality and—which is not quite the same thing—reasonableness. The civil and religious wars having ended, the form and general principles of government having been settled, and the conquest of empire having got well under way, the growing number of well-to-do Englishmen liked to compare their condition to that of Roman citizens of the Augustan age. (See the passage from Gibbon in this chapter.) They called King George I Augustus with much more

conviction than their fathers had called King Charles II Augustus
or Queen Anne Augusta. Handel's august and gloriously pleasing
"Water Music," played by an orchestra on a barge that accompanied George's royal outings on the Thames, expressed a serenely
energetic joy that many felt.

Many didn't, of course. Not everybody was a prosperous
business man or his comfortable wife; Justice often peeped through
her gauzy blindfold, and her scales were not always true. Many
pathetic scenes in *Joseph Andrews* and *Tom Jones* must have been
drawn from Fielding's experience as magistrate and police com-
missioner; Pope, though not a rebel against the god of things like
they are, was hardly one of his worshipers; nor was Defoe; nor
was Dr. Johnson; and what shall we say of Swift? But even the
critics of Augustan society often took its tone, if only in mockery.
What could be more magisterial—mockery or no mockery?—than
Dryden's

> All human things are subject to decay;
> And, when Fate summons, monarchs must obey.

What could be more magisterial in tone, or more commonplace in
substance? I have said that the language is the thought. Do I con-
tradict myself? No. The magisterial is often commonplace; in any
case, these words and this arrangement of them were carefully
chosen to give just that effect and make their readers smile; and we
do smile, not only at their pomposity but also at Dryden's wit in
writing about MacFlecknoe in the style of MacFlecknoe. In the
same way, Swift's account of the Lilliputian Emperor's terms for
Gulliver's freedom has the Augustan tone, and Gulliver's review
of English life for the King of Brobdingnag is delightfully earnest,
complacent, bombastic and fatuous. But Defoe's moralizing in
Robinson Crusoe, though equally earnest, is not altogether fatuous; for, as Joyce observed some time later, it was men like Defoe
who made the British Empire, and it was their self-confident moral

earnestness, humorlessness and doggedness that made their conquests possible.[1]

But the Augustan or neo-classic prose style reached its best development not in fiction but in exposition and argument. How it continued to flourish in the nineteenth century is indicated by the last two specimens in this chapter, the eloquent Macaulay and the bombastic Barnum.

Perhaps it will be helpful here to point out some things in the passages that follow.

Newton, explaining a difficult subject to specialists, his fellow mathematicians, writes plainly and clearly. We who are not mathematicians find his work difficult or impossible to follow, because we don't know the vocabulary or the grammar of mathematics; but the passage quoted here, which doesn't require such knowledge, is written so clearly that even I, who can't understand the simplest mathematical problems, can follow it without much difficulty. Newton was not concerned with literary form or rhetorical effect; the tournure of his phrases never occupied his mind. His prose is not expressive; it is the nearest thing in this book to what I have called in the Introduction mute writing; nevertheless, its design is clearly that of the Age of Reason, balanced and symmetrical. Observe the antitheses "absolute and relative, true and apparent, mathematical and common"; observe the next stage of their development in "Absolute, true, and mathematical time, . . . relative, apparent, and common time"; and their full elaboration in separate paragraphs beginning "Absolute space," "Absolute motion," and "Absolute time." Within this larger design the individual sentences, though contrived merely to give complex information and without any thought for their own beauty, are often pleasing —as in the account of the relative and absolute motion of the sailor on the ship, the ship on the earth, and the earth in space.

[1] See James Joyce, *Daniel Defoe*, edited from Italian manuscripts and translated by Joseph Prescott, Buffalo Studies, Vol. I, No. 1, Buffalo, N.Y., 1964.

(I have included Newton because a former colleague said, "Why don't you put in some scientific writing, for the engineers and the technical writers?" He suggested something from Francis Bacon's *The Advancement of Learning.* But I'm tired of Francis Bacon. I began to be tired of him the first time I opened his *Essays.* His notion that reading maketh a full man, conference a ready man, and writing an exact man, flies in the face of all observation and experience; anybody who believes *that* will believe anything he tells himself. It's a fine example of a cliché that isn't true. William Harvey, a real scientist, said Bacon wrote about science like a Lord Chancellor. You can find this remark under "Harvey" in John Aubrey's *Brief Lives;* for an explanation of its meaning, see Charles Sanders Peirce's essay "The Fixation of Belief," in his *Collected Papers,* Vol. V, paragraphs 358–387.)

For those of us who are not accustomed to the ways of mathematical thought Dr. Johnson's style is much clearer, and, since he consciously aimed at beauty, much more beautiful. Observe, for example, the elegant parallelism of "till I am indifferent," "till I am solitary," "till I am known," "and cannot enjoy it," "and cannot impart it" [his wife had died], "and do not want it." In the letter to Macpherson, observe the parallelism of "a cheat" and "a ruffian," "an imposture from the beginning" and "an imposture still," "I despise you" and "I reverence truth," "your rage," "your abilities" and "your morals," "what you shall say" and "what you can prove." In the letter to Mrs. Thrale, observe the forceful reiteration of "without." Each of these devices has its full intended effect. A less artful writer might have written to Macpherson, carefully avoiding any repetition of words, "From the very beginning, I thought your book was an imposture; and now that I have cogitated about it some more, I still believe it to be a fraud." This is almost as bad as the phony cleverness of those bush-league sports writers who say, "In the first inning, . . ." "In the second stanza,

. . ." "In the third encounter, . . ." "In the fourth set-to, . . ." etc. (See "Elegant variation" in H. W. Fowler's *A Dictionary of Modern English Usage.*)

In the last sentence of the passage from Johnson's preface to Shakespeare's works, envy and time are personified. In Gibbon, such abstractions are used not quite as personifications but rather as faculties of the mind or soul, and sometimes as independent entities. In the first paragraph of the passage quoted here, observe "the policy of the senate," "the active emulation of the consuls," and "the martial enthusiasm of the people." (In this context, it is evident that "policy" means something like "skill" or "wisdom.") In the second paragraph, observe "the wisdom of Augustus" and "the fears and vices of his immediate successors." In the third paragraph, observe "their avarice," "the fortitude of Caractacus," "the despair of Boadicea," and "the fanaticism of the Druids." In each case, the quality is represented as acting or being acted upon. This is perhaps the most salient identifying characteristic of Gibbon's style.

The passages from Burke, Paine, Macaulay and Barnum offer additional illustrations of the classic manner. You will easily observe in them the same features I have pointed out in Newton and Johnson.

ISAAC NEWTON [1642–1727]

> *Excerpt from first scholium in* THE MATHEMATICAL PRINCIPLES OF NATURAL PHILOSOPHY, *1686, translated from Newton's Latin by Andrew Motte, 1729*

[The Oxford English Dictionary defines a scholium, in mathematics, as "A note added by the author illustrating or further developing some point treated in the text." What Newton called "natural philosophy" we now call "science."]

Hitherto I have laid down the definitions of such words as are less known, and explained the sense in which I would have them to be understood in the following discourse. I do not define time, space, place and motion, as being well known to all. Only I must observe, that the vulgar conceive those quantities under no other notions but from the relation they bear to sensible objects. And thence arise certain prejudices, for the removing of which, it will be convenient to distinguish them into absolute and relative, true and apparent, mathematical and common.

I.   Absolute, true, and mathematical time, of itself, and from its own nature, flows equably with regard to anything external, and by another name is called duration: relative, apparent, and common time, is some sensible and external (whether accurate or unequable) measure of duration by the means of motion, which is commonly used instead of true time; such as an hour, a day, a month, a year.

II.   Absolute space, in its own nature, without regard to anything external, remains always similar and immovable. Relative space is some movable dimension or measure of the absolute spaces; which our senses determine by its position to bodies; and which is vulgarly taken for immovable space; such is the dimension of a subterraneous, an aereal, or celestial space, determined by its position in respect of the earth. Absolute and relative space, are the same in figure and magnitude; but they do not remain always numerically the same. For if the earth, for instance, moves, a space of our air, which relatively and in respect of the earth remains always the same, will at one time be one part of the absolute space into which the air passes; at another time it will be another part of the same, and so, absolutely understood, it will be perpetually mutable.

III.   Place is a part of space which a body takes up, and is according to the space, either absolute or relative. I say, a part of space; not the situation, nor the external surface of the body. For the places of equal solids are always equal; but their superfices, by reason of their dissimilar figures, are often unequal. Positions properly have no quantity, nor are they so much the places themselves, as the properties of places. The motion of the whole is the same thing with the sum of the motions of the parts; that is, the translation of the whole, out of its place, is the same thing with the sum of the translations of the parts out of their places; and therefore the place of the whole is the same thing with the sum of the places of the parts, and for that reason, it is internal, and in the whole body.

IV.   Absolute motion is the translation of a body from one absolute place into another; and relative motion, the translation from one relative place into another. Thus in a ship under sail, the relative place of a body is that part of the ship which the body possesses; or that part of its cavity which the body fills, and which therefore moves together with the ship: and relative rest is the continuance of the body in the same part of the ship, or of its cavity. But real, absolute rest, is the continuance of the body in the same part of that immovable space, in which the ship itself, its cavity, and all that it contains, is moved. Wherefore, if the earth is really at rest, the body, which relatively rests in the ship, will really and absolutely move with the same velocity which the ship has on the earth. But if the earth also moves, the true and absolute motion of the body will arise, partly from the true motion of the earth, in immovable space; partly from the relative motion of the ship on the earth; and if the body moves also relatively in the ship, its true motion will arise, partly from the true motion of the earth, in immovable space, and partly from the relative motions, as well of the ship on the earth, as of the body in the ship; and from these relative motions will arise the relative motion of the body on the earth. As if that part of the earth, where the ship is, was truly moved toward the east, with a velocity of 10010 parts; while the ship itself, with a fresh gale, and full sails, is carried towards the west, with a velocity expressed by 10 of those parts; but a sailor walks in the ship towards the east, with 1 part of the said velocity; then the sailor will be moved truly in immovable space towards the east, with a velocity of 10001 parts, and relatively on the earth towards the west, with a velocity of 9 of those parts.

Absolute time, in astronomy, is distinguished from relative, by the equation or correction of the vulgar time. For the natural days are truly unequal, though they are commonly considered as equal, and used for a measure of time; astronomers correct this in-equality for their more accurate deducing of the celestial motions. It may be, that there is no such thing, as an equable motion, whereby time may be accurately measured. All motions may be accelerated and retarded, but the true, or equable, progress of absolute time is liable to no change. The duration or perseverance of things remains the same, whether the motions are swift or slow, or none at all: and therefore it ought to be distinguished from what are only sensible measures thereof; and out of which we collect it, by means of the astronomical equation. The necessity of which equation, for determining the times of a phaenomenon, is evinced as well from the experiments of the pendulum clock, as by eclipses of the satellites of *Jupiter*.

As the order of the parts of time is immutable, so also is the order of the parts of space. Suppose those parts to be moved out of their places, and they will be moved (if the expression may be allowed) out of themselves. For times and spaces are, as it were, the places as well of themselves as of all other things. All things are placed in time as to order of succession; and in space as to order of situation. It is from their essence or nature that they are places; and that the primary places of things should be movable, is absurd. These are therefore the absolute places; and translations out of those places, are the only absolute motions.

❧

SAMUEL JOHNSON [1709–1784]
Letters

To the Right Honorable the Earl of Chesterfield

February 7, 1755

My Lord:

I have been lately informed, by the proprietor of the *World*,
that two papers, in which my Dictionary is recommended to the
public, were written by your lordship. To be so distinguished is
an honor which, being very little accustomed to favors from the
great, I know not well how to receive, or in what terms to
acknowledge.

When, upon some slight encouragement, I first visited your
lordship, I was overpowered, like the rest of mankind, by the
enchantment of your address; and could not forbear to wish that
I might boast myself *le vainqueur du vainqueur de la terre* ["the
conqueror of the conqueror of the earth"—from Georges de
Scudéry's fatuous epic *Alaric*, 1664];—that I might obtain that
regard for which I saw the world contending; but I found my
attendance so little encouraged, that neither pride nor modesty
would suffer me to continue it. When I had once addressed your
lordship in public, I had exhausted all the art of pleasing which a
retired and uncourtly scholar can possess. ["The art of pleasing is a
very necessary one to possess, but a very difficult one to acquire,"
Lord Chesterfield wrote to his son on Oct. 16, 1747; Chesterfield's
letters were not published, however, until 1774; so that Johnson
was quite aware of Chesterfield's one and only concern in life, and
was able to mock it, without having read its most explicit expressions.] I had done all that I could; and no man is well pleased
to have his all neglected, be it ever so little.

Seven years, my Lord, have now passed, since I waited in
your outward rooms, or was repulsed from your door, during

which time I have been pushing on my work through difficulties of which it is useless to complain, and have brought it, at last, to the verge of publication, without one act of assistance, one word of encouragement, or one smile of favor. Such treatment I did not expect, for I never had a patron before.

The shepherd in Virgil grew at last acquainted with love, and found him a native of the rocks. [*Eclogues*, I.43 ff.]

Is not a patron, my Lord, one who looks with unconcern on a man struggling for life in the water, and, when he has reached ground, encumbers him with help? The notice which you have been pleased to take of my labors, had it been early, had been kind; but it has been delayed till I am indifferent, and cannot enjoy it; till I am solitary, and cannot impart it; till I am known, and do not want [need] it. I hope it is no very cynical asperity not to confess obligations where no benefit has been received, or to be unwilling that the public should consider me as owing that to a patron, which Providence has enabled me to do for myself.

Having carried on my work thus far with so little obligation to any favorer of learning, I shall not be disappointed though I should conclude it, if less be possible, with less; for I have been long wakened from that dream of hope, in which I once boasted myself with so much exultation, my Lord,

> your lordship's most humble,
> most obedient servant,
> *Sam: Johnson.*

To James Macpherson [perpetrator of the so-called Ossian poems]

Mr. James Macpherson—

I received your foolish and impudent note. Whatever insult is offered me I will do my best to repel, and what I cannot do for myself, the law will do for me. I will not desist from detecting what I think a cheat, from any fear of the menaces of a ruffian.

You want me to retract. What shall I retract? I thought your book an imposture from the beginning. I think it upon yet surer reasons an imposture still. For this opinion I give the public my reasons, which I here dare you to refute.

But however I may despise you, I reverence truth, and if you can prove the genuineness of the work I will confess it. Your rage I defy, your abilities since your Homer are not so formidable, and what I have heard of your morals disposes me to pay regard not to what you shall say, but to what you can prove.

You may print this if you will.

Sam: Johnson.

Jan. 20, 1775.

Excerpt from a letter to Mrs. Thrale, October 27, 1777

Some, when they write to their friends, are all affection; some are wise and sententious; some strain their powers for effects of gaiety; some write news; and some write secrets; but to make a letter without affection, without wisdom, without gaiety, without news, and without a secret, is, doubtless, the great epistolic art.

Excerpt from THE IDLER, *No. 32. Saturday, November 25, 1758*

Vulgar and inactive minds confound familiarity with knowledge, and conceive themselves informed of the whole nature of things when they are shown their form or told their use; but the speculatist who is not content with superficial views, harasses himself with fruitless curiosity, and still as he inquires more perceives only that he knows less.

Excerpts from the preface to A DICTIONARY OF THE ENGLISH LAN-
GUAGE, *1755*

It is the fate of those who toil at the lower employments of life to be rather driven by the fear of evil, than attracted by the prospect of good; to be exposed to censure, without hope of praise; to be disgraced by miscarriage, or punished for neglect, where success would have been without applause, and diligence without reward.

Among these unhappy mortals is the writer of dictionaries, whom mankind have considered, not as the pupil, but as the slave of science, the pioneer [in the Roman army, according to Gibbon, a laborer who did not fight] of literature, doomed only to remove rubbish and clear obstructions from the paths through which Learning and Genius press forward to conquest and glory, without bestowing a smile on the humble drudge that facilitates their progress. Every other author may aspire to praise; the lexicographer can only hope to escape reproach, and even this negative recompense has been yet granted to very few.

I have, notwithstanding this discouragement, attempted a dictionary of the English language, which, while it was employed in the cultivation of every species of literature, has itself been hitherto neglected; suffered to spread, under the direction of chance, into wild exuberance; resigned to the tyranny of time and fashion; and exposed to the corruptions of ignorance and caprices of innovation.

When I took the first survey of my undertaking, I found our speech copious without order, and energetic without rules: wherever I turned my view, there was perplexity to be disentangled and confusion to be regulated; choice was to be made out of boundless variety, without any established principle of selection; adulterations were to be detected, without a settled test of purity; and modes of expression to be rejected or received, without the

suffrages of writers of classical reputation or acknowledged
authority.

Having therefore no assistance but from general grammar,
I applied myself to the perusal of our writers; and, noting whatever might be of use to ascertain or illustrate any word or phrase,
accumulated in time the materials of a dictionary, which, by degrees, I reduced to method, establishing to myself, in the progress
of the work, such rules as experience and analogy suggested to me;
experience, which practice and observation were continually increasing; and analogy, which, though in some words obscure, was
evident in others.

*Opening paragraph of preface to Johnson's edition of Shake-
speare, 1765*

That praises are without reason lavished on the dead, and that the
honors due only to excellence are paid to antiquity, is a complaint
likely to be always continued by those who, being able to add
nothing to truth, hope for eminence from the heresies of paradox;
or those who, being forced by disappointment upon consolatory
expedients, are willing to hope from posterity what the present
age refuses, and flatter themselves that the regard which is yet
denied by envy will be at last bestowed by time.

EDWARD GIBBON [1737–1794]

Excerpts from THE HISTORY OF THE DECLINE AND FALL OF THE
ROMAN EMPIRE, *1776, Volume I, Chapter 1*

The principal conquests of the Romans were achieved under the
republic; and the emperors, for the most part, were satisfied with
preserving those dominions which had been acquired by the policy

of the senate, the active emulation of the consuls, and the martial enthusiasm of the people. The seven first centuries were filled with a rapid succession of triumphs; but it was reserved for Augustus to relinquish the ambitious design of subduing the whole earth, and to introduce a spirit of moderation into the public councils. Inclined to peace by his temper and situation, it was easy for him to discover that Rome, in her present exalted situation, had much less to hope than to fear from the chance of arms; and that, in the prosecution of remote wars, the undertaking became every day more difficult, the event more doubtful, and the possession more precarious and less beneficial. The experience of Augustus added weight to these salutary reflections, and effectually convinced him that, by the prudent vigor of his counsels, it would be easy to secure every concession which the safety or the dignity of Rome might require from the most formidable barbarians. Instead of exposing his person and his legions to the arrows of the Parthians, he obtained, by an honorable treaty, the restitution of the standards and prisoners which had been taken in the defeat of Crassus.

Happily for the repose of mankind, the moderate system recommended by the wisdom of Augustus was adopted by the fears and vices of his immediate successors. Engaged in the pursuit of pleasure, or in the exercise of tyranny, the first Caesars seldom showed themselves to the armies or to the provinces; nor were they disposed to suffer that those triumphs which *their* indolence neglected should be usurped by the conduct and valor of their lieutenants. The military fame of a subject was considered as an insolent invasion of the imperial prerogative; and it became the duty, as well as interest, of every Roman general to guard the frontiers intrusted to his care, without aspiring to conquests which might have proved no less fatal to himself than to the vanquished barbarians.

The only accession which the Roman empire received during the first century of the Christian era was the province of Britain.

In this single instance the followers of Caesar and Augustus were persuaded to follow the example of the former, rather than the precept of the latter. The proximity of its situation to the coast of Gaul seemed to invite their arms; the pleasing, though doubtful, intelligence of a pearl-fishery attracted their avarice; and as Britain was viewed in the light of a distinct and insulated world, the conquest scarce formed any exception to the general system of continental measures. After a war of about forty years, undertaken by the most stupid [Claudius], maintained by the most dissolute [Nero], and terminated by the most timid of all the emperors [Domitian], the far greater part of the island submitted to the Roman yoke. The various tribes of Britain possessed valor without conduct, and the love of freedom without the spirit of union. They took up arms with savage fierceness; they laid them down, or turned them against each other, with wild inconstancy; and while they fought singly, they were successively subdued. Neither the fortitude of Caractacus, nor the despair of Boadicea, nor the fanaticism of the Druids, could avert the slavery of their country, or resist the steady progress of the imperial generals, who maintained the national glory, when the throne was disgraced by the weakest or the most vicious of mankind. At the very time when Domitian, confined to his palace, felt the terrors which he inspired, his legions, under the command of the virtuous Agricola, defeated the collected force of the Caledonians at the foot of the Grampian hills; and his fleets, venturing to explore an unknown and dangerous navigation, displayed the Roman arms round every part of the island. The conquest of Britain was considered as already achieved; and it was the design of Agricola to complete and insure his success by the easy reduction of Ireland, for which, in his opinion, one legion and a few auxiliaries were sufficient. The western isle might be improved into a valuable possession, and the Britons would wear their chains with less reluctance, if the prospect and example of freedom was on every side removed from before their eyes.

But the superior merit of Agricola soon occasioned his removal from the government of Britain; and forever disappointed this rational, though extensive, scheme of conquest. Before his departure the prudent general had provided for security as well as for dominion. He had observed that the island is almost divided into two unequal parts by the opposite gulfs, or, as they are now called, the Friths of Scotland. Across the narrow interval of about forty miles he had drawn a line of military stations, which was afterwards fortified, in the reign of Antoninus Pius, by a turf rampart, erected on foundations of stone. This wall of Antoninus, at a small distance beyond the modern cities of Edinburgh and Glasgow, was fixed as the limit of the Roman province. The native Caledonians preserved, in the northern extremity of the island, their wild independence, for which they were not less indebted to their poverty than to their valor. Their incursions were frequently repelled and chastised, but their country was never subdued. The masters of the fairest and most wealthy climates of the globe turned with contempt from gloomy hills assailed by the winter tempest, from lakes concealed in a blue mist, and from cold and lonely heaths, over which the deer of the forest were chased by a troop of naked barbarians.

Such was the state of the Roman frontiers, and such the maxims of imperial policy, from the death of Augustus to the accession of Trajan.

෴

EDMUND BURKE [1729–1797]

Excerpt from SPEECH ON CONCILIATION WITH THE COLONIES, *March 22, 1775*

My hold of the colonies is in the close affection which grows from common names, from kindred blood, from similar privileges, and equal protection. These are the ties which, though light as air, are as strong as links of iron. Let the colonies always keep the idea of their civil rights associated with your government; they will cling and grapple to you, and no force under heaven will be of power to tear them from their allegiance. But let it be once understood that your government may be one thing and their privileges another, that these two things may exist without any mutual relation—the cement is gone, the cohesion is loosened, and everything hastens to decay and dissolution. As long as you have the wisdom to keep the sovereign authority of this country as the sanctuary of liberty, the sacred temple consecrated to our common faith, wherever the chosen race and sons of England worship Freedom they will turn their faces towards you. The more they multiply, the more friends you will have; the more ardently they love liberty, the more perfect will be their obedience. Slavery they can have anywhere. It is a weed that grows in every soil. They may have it from Spain; they may have it from Prussia. But, until you become lost to all feeling of your true interest and your natural dignity, freedom they can have from none but you. This is the commodity of price, of which you have the monopoly. This is the true Act of Navigation, which binds to you the commerce of the colonies, and through them secures to you the wealth of the world. Deny them this participation of freedom, and you break that sole bond which originally made, and must still preserve, the unity of the Empire. Do not entertain so weak an imagination as that your registers and your bonds, your affidavits and your sufferances, your cockets and your clearances are what form the great securities of your commerce. Do not dream that your letters of office, and your instructions, and your suspending clauses are the things that hold together the great contexture of the mysterious whole. Dead instruments, passive tools as they are, it is the spirit of the English communion that gives all their life and efficacy to them. It is the spirit of the English Constitution, which, infused through the mighty mass, pervades, feeds, unites, invigorates, vivifies every part of the Empire, even down to the minutest member.

Is it not the same virtue which does everything for us here in England? Do you imagine, then, that it is the Land Tax Act which raises your revenue? that it is the annual vote in the Committee of Supply which gives you your army? or that it is the Mutiny Bill which inspires it with bravery and discipline? No! surely no! It is the love of the people; it is their attachment to their government, from the sense of the deep stake they have in such a glorious institution, which gives you your army and your navy, and infuses into both that liberal obedience without which your army would be a base rabble and your navy nothing but rotten timber.

All this, I know well enough, will sound wild and chimerical to the profane herd of those vulgar and mechanical politicians who have no place among us, a sort of people who think that nothing exists but what is gross and material, and who therefore, far from being qualified to be directors of the great movement of empire, are not fit to turn a wheel in the machine. But to men truly initiated and rightly taught, these ruling and master principles, which, in the opinion of such men as I have mentioned, have no substantial existence, are in truth everything, and all in all. Magnanimity in politics is not seldom the truest wisdom; and a great empire and little minds go ill together. If we are conscious of our station and glow with zeal to fill our place as becomes our situation and ourselves, we ought to auspicate all our public proceedings on America with the old warning of the Church, *Sursum corda!* [Lift up your hearts!] We ought to elevate our minds to the greatness of that trust to which the order of Providence has called us. By adverting to the dignity of this high calling, our ancestors have turned a savage wilderness into a glorious empire, and have made the most extensive and the only honorable conquests, not by destroying but by promoting the wealth, the number, the happiness of the human race. Let us get an American revenue as we have got an American empire. English privileges have made it all that it is; English privileges alone will make it all it can be.

In full confidence of this unalterable truth, I now *(quod felix faustumque sit)* [may it be fruitful and fortunate] lay the first stone of the temple of peace; and I move you

"That the colonies and plantations of Great Britain in North America, consisting of fourteen separate governments, and containing two millions and upwards of free inhabitants, have not had the liberty and privilege of electing and sending any knights and burgesses or others to represent them in the high court of Parliament."

THOMAS PAINE [1737–1809]

First two paragraphs of THE AMERICAN CRISIS, *December 23, 1776*

These are the times that try men's souls: the summer soldier and the sunshine patriot will, in this crisis, shrink from the service of his country; but he that stands it Now, deserves the love and thanks of man and woman. Tyranny, like hell, is not easily conquered; yet we have this consolation with us, that the harder the conflict, the more glorious the triumph. What we obtain too cheap, we esteem too lightly:—'Tis dearness only that gives everything its value. Heaven knows how to put a proper price upon its goods; and it would be strange indeed, if so celestial an article as FREEDOM should not be highly rated. Britain, with an army to enforce her tyranny, has declared that she has a right (not only to) TAX but "to BIND *us in* ALL CASES WHATSOEVER," and if being *bound in that manner*, is not slavery, then there is not such a thing as slavery upon earth. Even the expression is impious, for so unlimited a power can belong only to God.

Whether the Independence of the Continent was declared too soon, or delayed too long, I will not now enter into as an argument; my own simple opinion is, that had it been eight months earlier, it would have been much better. We did not make a proper use of last winter, neither could we, while we were in a dependent state. However, the fault, if it were one, was all our own; we have none to blame but ourselves. But no great deal is lost yet; all that Howe has been doing for this month past, is rather a ravage than a conquest, which the spirit of the Jersies[2] a year ago would have quickly repulsed, and which time and a little resolution will soon recover.

❧

THOMAS BABINGTON MACAULAY [1800–1859]

Paragraph on the Restoration, from essay on Milton, 1825

Then came those days, never to be recalled without a blush, the days of servitude without loyalty and sensuality without love, of dwarfish talents and gigantic vices, the paradise of cold hearts and narrow minds, the golden age of the coward, the bigot, and the slave. The King cringed to his rival that he might trample on his people, sank into a viceroy of France, and pocketed, with complacent infamy, her degrading insults, and her more degrading gold. The caresses of harlots, and the jests of buffoons, regulated the policy of the state. The government had just ability enough to deceive, and just religion enough to persecute. The principles of liberty were the scoff of every grinning courtier, and the Anathema Maranatha of every fawning dean. In every high place, worship was paid to Charles and James, Belial and Moloch; and England propitiated those obscene and cruel idols with the blood

2 What is now New Jersey was originally two colonies, East Jersey and West Jersey.

of her best and bravest children. Crime succeeded to crime, and disgrace to disgrace, till the race accursed of God and man was a second time driven forth, to wander on the face of the earth, and to be a byword and a shaking of the head to the nations. [This refers to the Revolution of 1688, which drove James II out of England and replaced him with William and Mary.]

☙

P. T. BARNUM [1810–1891]

STRUGGLES AND TRIUMPHS, *1888, first two paragraphs and last two paragraphs of Chapter 25*

I now come to a series of events which, all things considered, constitute one of the most remarkable experiences of my life—an experience which brought me much pain and many trials; which humbled my pride and threatened me with hopeless financial ruin; and yet, nevertheless, put new blood in my veins, fresh vigor in my action, warding off all temptation to rust in the repose which affluence induces, and developed, I trust, new and better elements of manliness in my character. This trial carried me through a severe and costly discipline, and now that I have passed through it and have triumphed over it, I can thank God for sending it upon me, though I feel no special obligations to the human instruments employed in the severe chastening.

When the blow fell upon me, I thought that I could never recover; the event has shown, however, that I have gained both in character and fortune, and what threatened, for years, to be my ruin, has proved one of the most fortunate happenings of my career. The "Bull Run" of my life's battle was a crushing defeat, which, unknown to me at the time, only presaged the victories which were to follow. . . .

Yet, these new lessons conveyed the old, old story. There

were those who had fawned upon me in my prosperity, who now jeered at my adversity; people whom I had specially favored, made special efforts to show their ingratitude; papers which, when I had the means to make it an object for them to be on good terms with me, overloaded me with adulation, now attempted to overwhelm me with abuse; and then the immense amount of moralizing over the "instability of human fortunes," and especially the retributive justice that is sure to follow "ill-gotten gains," which my censors assumed to be the sum and substance of my honorably acquired and industriously worked-for property. I have no doubt that much of this kind of twaddle was believed by the twaddlers to be sincere; and thus my case was actual capital to certain preachers and religious editors who were in want of fresh illustrations wherewith to point their morals.

As for myself, I was in the depths, but I did not despond. I was confident that with energetic purpose and divine assistance I should, if my health and life were spared, get on my feet again; and events have since fully justified and verified the expectation and the effort.

Exercises

1. Some pompous ass whom you know is going to be awarded a prize for pomposity—though of course those who selected him don't call it that. Think of yourself as the toastmaster at a dinner in his honor, and write an appropriate speech, in Gibbon's best manner, to be delivered when you present the prize. Then think of yourself as the recipient of the prize, and write an appropriate acceptance speech in Barnum's best manner. Don't let either speech run on, however, for more than two pages. Be lavish with such abstractions as "integrity," "humility," "selfless devotion," "self-sacrifice," "courage," "dedication," "service," etc. Don't on any account use the word "pomposity" or any other un-

flattering term; write speeches that could actually be delivered and applauded.

2. You are a speech-writer for the president of your college or university. Write a two-page "Charge to the Graduates," in the manner of Dr. Johnson, for delivery at the next commencement exercises. Avoid any idea that isn't a cliché. Try to make the speech nothing but an unintermitted series of neatly balanced, well-turned clichés.

Varieties of Poetic Prose

*The affectionate husband of his admiring
and devoted wife, he had created an
imaginary beloved; had attributed to her
the authorship of all his books that had any
talent, and though habitually a sober
man, I have known him to get drunk,
and at the height of his intoxication,
when most men speak the truth, to
attribute his state to remorse for
having been unfaithful to Fiona
Macleod.*

YEATS ON WILLIAM SHARP
in The Trembling of the Veil, IV. 18

OLIVER WENDELL HOLMES, SR., says that writing verse is an activity of inferior minds and that poets don't do it. This, from the author of such great poems in verse as "The One-Hoss Shay" and "The Chambered Nautilus," can only be taken as an expression of modesty. Surely he exaggerates. Of course it is true that not all verse is poetry, and equally true that not all poetry is verse; but lest we abandon all definition and slip into anarchy, let us remember that writing poetic prose is an activity of all too many inferior minds and that poets don't do it. Poets write poetry. Whether they use verse or prose, they write poetry. And inferior minds, whether they use prose or verse, don't write poetry.

It is very easy to write bad poetic prose. Rather than do that, it would be better not to write at all—and a much more difficult achievement. Listen to this, from Chapter I of "Fiona Macleod's" *Pharais* (1895):

> It was midway in the seventh month of her great joy that the child moved, while a rapture leaped to her heart, within the womb of Lora, daughter of the dead Norman Maclean, minister of Inisron, in the Outer Isles.
>
> On that same eve the cruel sorrow came to her that had lain waiting in the dark place beyond the sunrise.
>
> Alastair, her so dearly beloved, had gone, three days earlier, by the Western Isles steamer, to the port of Greenock, thence to fare to Glasgow, to learn from a great professor of medicine con-

cerning that which so troubled him—both by reason of what the islesmen whispered among themselves, and for what he felt of his own secret pain and apprehension.

That's a pretty fancy way to say that Lora was waiting for her husband to come back from Glasgow, where he had gone—pardon me, I mean whither he had fared—to find out if the insanity that had afflicted his father and grandfather was hereditary. The combination of a steamer and a professor of medicine with "eve," "the dark place beyond the sunrise" and "that which so troubled him"—the combination of modern matters of fact with phony antiquities of diction—makes this passage not poetic but ridiculous. And the first sentence trails off into anticlimax on anticlimax. As Dr. Johnson said of Macpherson's "Ossianic" poems, "Sir, a man might write such stuff for ever, if he would *abandon* his mind to it."

To write good poetic prose is correspondingly difficult. In our day the older modes would seem to be good only for humor, for pastiche or parody, not for serious writing. A poet in prose today must work out his own idiom, as Nabokov and Beckett have done. The poetic styles of Nabokov and Beckett are not imitable. They depend on visual images, on personal vocabularies and attitudes, that are characteristic of their authors and of no one else; in order to develop a poetic style of your own you too must be a poet: you must be able to put your very physiology into it. What Proust said about style in writing—that it is like color in painting, the expression of a way of seeing that is peculiar to one person—is especially true of any style that aspires to poetry now. The old forms have been imitated so often, and are now so easy to imitate, that they probably cannot be used for anything original.

This doesn't mean that the masterpieces of poetic prose in traditional forms are not masterpieces or that they are not still valid. The expression of a forceful mind remains forceful; the expression of a poetic mind remains poetic; they are not devalued by the failure of their imitators.

Among pre-literate peoples, the preservation of important facts, ideas and beliefs from generation to generation required that they be put in memorizable form; the earliest written records of almost all peoples are therefore in verse of one kind or another, with strongly marked rhythms, alliterations and metaphors as aids to memory. Agricultural, medical and astronomical information, for example, was preserved in verse—for the same reason that we say

> *A pint's a pound*
> *The world around,*

and

> *Red in the morning,*
> *Sailors take warning,*

and

> I *before* E,
> *Except after* C,
> *Or when sounded like* A,
> *As in* NEIGHBOR *and* WEIGH.

If some inspired poet should work the nine exceptions to this last rule into a rhyming or rhythmical or alliterative pattern, we could undoubtedly remember them a great deal more easily than we can now.

But even when such mnemonic patterns preserve misinformation—as primitive medical records undoubtedly do—they carry a force of conviction that mere unpatterned prose doesn't. We feel that they *must* be true, because our whole body responds to them, participates in them, rocks, swings, sways and vibrates—however imperceptibly—in harmony and agreement with them.

That is to say, they are aesthetically pleasing. But aesthetic pleasure is not always or necessarily sub-intellectual. Verses that are mere sound without sense do often give us pleasure—"Lilla-bulero" or "Lillibulero," for example, which you will find in

Tristram Shandy, IX, 19—but more often we are pleased by the interplay of ideas and sounds, and sometimes by the play of ideas alone. The ancient skaldic poems had extremely complicated alliterative, metrical and grammatical patterns that violated the normal word order as freely as Mallarmé was to violate normal French word order in the nineteenth century; but they also played games with the meanings of words—with metaphors—which are pleasing even in the plainest prose translation. One tells, for example, of a warrior who in a time of famine had to barter his arrows for some herrings. As he did so, he said, "Thus I exchange the leaping herrings of the bow for the flashing arrows of the sea." That inversion, quite aside from the charm of its visual images—its leaping arrows and flashing fish—is a bit of magic. The poet, if not the warrior, triumphs over the situation. The poet's hearers doubtless triumphed too—they shared his triumph over words, if over nothing else—and we, in this far distant time and place, also suffer with the warrior and triumph with the poet.

For poetry is magic. It is not wisdom, it is not morality, it is not common sense. It is magic. And that is a gift that either we have or we don't have. But even the most inspired poet, if he wants to make his readers feel anything of his inspiration—his breathing, his taking magical power from the air—must learn his craft and develop his art, as the old skald who sang about the warrior had done. And those of us who are not poets, but who want to write good prose, can also profit by learning the techniques of prose poetry.

It has been said that God foresaw the translation of the Bible into English under royal auspices in 1611, and had therefore filled England with great writers. However that may be, the King James version is a great piece of English writing. The first chapter of Genesis is magnificent poetry. Observe its rhythmic repetitions: "And God said, . . . And God said, . . . And God said, . . ." "And

it was so. . . . And it was so. . . . And it was so. . . ." "And God saw
that it was good. . . . And God saw that it was good. . . . And God
saw that it was good. . . ." "And the evening and the morning were
the first day. . . . And the evening and the morning were the
second day. . . ." "And God made. . . . And God created. . . ."
"And God blessed them. . . . And God blessed them. . . ." Short,
simple, clear, clean sentences; simple images—light, darkness, land,
water, plants, animals, man, woman; and a strong, simple rhythm.

Lafcadio Hearn's poetry depends less on the repetition of themes
than on the profusion of brightly colored visual images—green,
gold, red, tiles, lacquer, silk, molten metal, embroidery of pearls
and flowers. There is also onomatopoeia: the sounds of the bell,
the muttering and roar of the fires, etc. And there is also a very
careful choice of words that are smooth and pleasant to hear:
words full of flowing *l*'s and *r*'s and murmuring *m*'s and *n*'s, rather
than words like *dig* and *kick* and *cat*, which stop the voice.

In Oscar Wilde's story the Biblical repetitions are an obvious influence. His visual images, however, are those of a self-conscious
aestheticism rather than those of nature. Yeats, in *The Trembling
of the Veil* IV.2 (1927), says that Wilde began "The Doer of
Good" as a simple story, and offers a conjecture as to why he put
it into fancy language:

> When in London for my play [*The Land of Heart's Desire*] I
> had asked news from an actor who had seen him constantly. "He
> is in deep melancholy," was the answer. "He says that he tries
> to sleep away as much of life as possible, only leaving his bed at
> two or three in the afternoon, and spending the rest of the day
> at the Café Royal. He has written what he calls the best short
> story in the world, and will have it that he repeats to himself on
> getting out of bed and before every meal, 'Christ came from a
> white plain to a purple city, and as He passed through the first
> street, He heard voices overhead, and saw a young man lying

drunk upon a window-sill. "Why do you waste your soul in drunkenness?" He said. "Lord, I was a leper and you healed me, what else can I do?" A little further through the town He saw a young man following a harlot, and said, "Why do you dissolve your soul in debauchery?" and the young man answered, "Lord, I was blind, and You healed me, what else can I do?" At last in the middle of the city He saw an old man crouching, weeping upon the ground, and when He asked why he wept, the old man answered, "Lord, I was dead and You raised me into life, what else can I do but weep?" ' "

Wilde published that story a little later, but spoiled it with the verbal decoration of his epoch, and I have to repeat it to myself as I first heard it, before I can see its terrible beauty. I no more doubt its sincerity than I doubt that his parade of gloom, all that late rising, and sleeping away his life, that elaborate playing with tragedy, was an attempt to escape from an emotion by its exaggeration. He had three successful plays running at once; he had been almost poor, and now, his head full of Flaubert, found himself with ten thousand [pounds] a year:— "Lord, I was dead, and You raised me into life, what else can I do but weep?" A comedian, he was in the hands of those dramatists who understand nothing but tragedy.

But however sincere the emotion behind it, the story as Wilde published it gives an effect of artificiality and play-acting. The youthful Joyce, reviewing a book of sincere but badly written patriotic verse, said, "A man who writes a book cannot be excused by his good intentions, or by his moral character; he enters into a region where there is question of the written word." In "The Doer of Good" the written word lacks what Joyce in the same review called "literary sincerity."

Francis W. Bain is a much neglected writer, and it is his own fault. He taught economics at Oxford; he wrote technical papers on bullion, bimetallism, tariffs, etc.; he wrote a life of the wicked Queen

Christina of Sweden, justifying all her murders and other crimes by the doctrine that divine right is by definition unlimited; he wrote books deploring Darwinism and representative government and the shortening of the fourteen-hour work day; he found the last Czar of Russia too liberal for his taste; he wrote two novels, whose quality is indicated by their titles: *José: A Spanish Romance*, and *Dmitri: A Romance of Old Russia*. So far so bad.

But then he went to India as headmaster of a school at Poona for the sons of British colonial officials, and the change of scene or of occupation or of reading matter—or of all these—or of something else—awakened a sleeping talent in him. He learned Sanskrit; he read many Sanskrit novellas, and between 1898 and 1919 he wrote thirteen novellas of the same kind, each an exquisite little masterpiece. He passed them off as translations, with phony learned footnotes and in some cases with a cock-and-bull story of how he had got the manuscript. He fooled all the Sanskrit scholars and philologists and comparative mythologists; they praised his work in their books and professional journals, and hoped that he would soon publish the Sanskrit originals. The only people who doubted at first, strangely enough, were the hack reviewers for the daily papers. But when he could not produce the originals, the doubts spread; and when he finally admitted the hoax, the admission ruined him. He died overwhelmed with the contempt of the self-righteous: of hack reviewers and embarrassed scholars. Today he is still all but unknown. But he was a good writer of poetic prose; now and then he sinks into bathos, but as a rule his rhythms are almost Biblical in their simplicity; his images, though simple and natural, give an effect of richness by their profusion; and—a miracle—that sour old man, when he posed as a translator, turned out to have a delightful sense of humor.

The appeal of Sir Thomas Malory's prose is largely the appeal of the antique: of medieval idioms and locutions. This is the kind of thing Joyce parodies in the passage from *Ulysses* in this chapter.

Joyce's own poetry in *Finnegans Wake* will be apparent to your ear if you read it aloud. "What can't be coded can be decorded if an ear aye seize what no eye ere grieved for," he says. His description of the river goddess is full of images of water and wetness and flowing, and of the names of rivers and streams, many of which themselves mean "river" or "stream" or "water." His vocabulary, blending elements from at least nineteen languages, serves him to make a dream language for the dream of the human race. Joyce himself has said that the language of *Finnegans Wake* is "basically English"; certainly its syntax is that of standard English. The words, as I have indicated in the Introduction, are strange not because they lack meaning but because the meanings cluster all too thickly. I have included the passage on Anna Livia Plurabelle because it is poetry, because I love it, and because it shows what a supreme genius can do when he has absolute mastery of language. But I do not advise anyone who is not a linguist to try to imitate *Finnegans Wake*. There could be no sillier mistake than to substitute for this rich multiplicity of meanings and forms a mere jumble of meaningless sounds and formless groups of letters. Read the passage and discover as much of its semantic richness as you can. The more you discover, the more you will be encouraged to write carefully—with what Milton called wanton heed and giddy cunning.

The name Isak Dinesen was the pen name of the late Baroness Karen Blixen of Denmark. She set out to be a painter, but soon discovered that her true métier was fiction; and since more people read English than Danish, she wrote in English. Vladimir Nabokov also writes in English, as well as in French and in his native Russian. English is one of the most difficult languages to learn, and these are two of the very small number of continental Europeans who have learned to write it better than most native English or American writers. Others are Joseph Conrad, Valery Larbaud and Thorstein Veblen. I include Veblen because, though he was born in Wisconsin and grew up in Minnesota, he spent his childhood and most of his youth in small, isolated communities of immigrant Norwegian farmers, learned English as a second language, and spoke it with an accent all his life. But he was one of the best American stylists—as we shall see in the last chapter.

Isak Dinesen was not quite a serious writer. She had a rather cheap imagination. In the passage quoted here, for example, the sentence about the dhow's secret load and the two sentences following it are full of schmaltzy abstractions of a kind that were the stock in trade of Rider Haggard: "secret load," "stir," "great forces," "slumbering countries," "dream," "something had happened to the world," "the soul of it," "by some magic." And such Dinesen stories as "The Roads Around Pisa" and "A Consolatory Tale" are full of play-acting and glamor in the most elegant manner of Somerset Maugham, the very model of a distinguished butler.

Vladimir Nabokov is a much better writer in every respect. Every detail of the passage quoted here—a typical passage—is concrete and particular, from the meerschaum penholder to the interlaced arches. Moreover, in this story about children, these are details that a child would notice with joy. The story is pure poetry. Every line of it is pure poetry.

But I think the best poet of our time, at least in English—and he writes in French as well—is Samuel Beckett. The description of evening quoted here from *Malone Dies* deals with a mass of people, not as a thing in itself—a mass of mud or a flow of lava or a mob in whose single purpose the individuality that marks humanity is lost—and not as clearly defined individuals either, but as a mass without coherence made up of lonely nondescript individual men and women. Their individuality is indicated not by their appearance or their qualities but only by the fact that they suffer individually; and the evening through which they move—the details of which we see in such vivid concreteness—reflects the desolation of heart that seems to be the only mark of their humanity. Beckett is the poet of desolation. I say "the poet" in the same sense that medieval philosophers, speaking of Aristotle, said "the philosopher."

THE KING JAMES BIBLE [1611]

Genesis, Chapter 1

In the beginning God created the heaven and the earth.

And the earth was without form, and void; and darkness was upon the face of the deep. And the spirit of God moved upon the face of the waters.

And God said, Let there be light: and there was light.

And God saw the light, that it was good: and God divided the light from the darkness.

And God called the light Day, and the darkness he called Night. And the evening and the morning were the first day.

And God said, Let there be a firmament in the midst of the waters, and let it divide the waters from the waters.

And God made the firmament, and divided the waters which were under the firmament from the waters which were above the firmament: and it was so.

And God called the firmament Heaven. And the evening and the morning were the second day.

And God said, Let the waters under the heaven be gathered together unto one place, and let the dry land appear: and it was so.

And God called the dry land Earth; and the gathering together of the waters called he Seas: and God saw that it was good.

And God said, Let the earth bring forth grass, the herb yielding seed, and the fruit tree yielding fruit after his kind, whose seed is in itself, upon the earth: and it was so.

And the earth brought forth grass, and herb yielding seed after his kind, and the tree yielding fruit, whose seed was in itself, after his kind: and God saw that it was good.

And the evening and the morning were the third day.

And God said, let there be lights in the firmament of the heaven to divide the day from the night; and let them be for signs, and for seasons, and for days, and years;

And let them be for lights in the firmament of the heaven to give light upon the earth: and it was so.

And God made two great lights; the greater light to rule the day, and the lesser light to rule the night: he made the stars also.

And God set them in the firmament of the heaven to give light upon the earth,

And to rule over the day and over the night, and to divide the light from the darkness: and God saw that it was good.

And the evening and the morning were the fourth day.

And God said, Let the waters bring forth abundantly the moving creature that hath life, and fowl that may fly above the earth in the open firmament of heaven.

And God created great whales, and every living creature that moveth, which the waters brought forth abundantly, after their kind, and every winged fowl after his kind: and God saw that it was good.

And God blessed them, saying, Be fruitful, and multiply, and fill the waters in the seas, and let fowl multiply in the earth.

And the evening and the morning were the fifth day.

And God said, Let the earth bring forth the living creature after his kind, cattle, and creeping thing, and beast of the earth after his kind: and it was so.

And God made the beast of the earth after his kind, and

every thing that creepeth upon the earth after his kind: and God saw that it was good.

And God said, Let us make man in our image, after our likeness: and let them have dominion over the fish of the sea, and over the fowl of the air, and over the cattle, and over all the earth, and over every creeping thing that creepeth upon the earth.

So God created man in his own image, in the image of God created he him; male and female created he them.

And God blessed them, and God said unto them, Be fruitful, and multiply, and replenish the earth, and subdue it: and have dominion over the fish of the sea, and over the fowl of the air, and over every living thing that moveth upon the earth.

And God said, Behold, I have given you every herb bearing seed, which is upon the face of all the earth, and every tree, in the which is the fruit of a tree yielding seed; to you it shall be for meat.

And to every beast of the earth, and to every fowl of the air, and to every thing that creepeth upon the earth, wherein there is life, I have given every green herb for meat: and it was so.

And God saw every thing that he had made, and, behold, it was very good. And the evening and the morning were the sixth day.

LAFCADIO HEARN [1850–1904]

"The Soul of the Great Bell," from SOME CHINESE GHOSTS, *1887*

She hath spoken, and her words still resound in his ears.
HAO-KHIEOU-TOKUAN: CHAPTER 9

The water-clock marks the hour in the Ta-chung sz'—in the Tower of the Great Bell: now the mallet is lifted to smite the lips of the metal monster—the vast lips inscribed with Buddhist texts from the sacred "Fa-hwa-King," from the chapters of the holy

"Ling-yen-King"! Hear the great bell responding!—how mighty her voice, though tongueless!—KO-NGAI! All the little dragons on the high-tilted eaves of the green roofs shiver to the tips of their gilded tails under that deep wave of sound; all the porcelain gargoyles tremble on their carven perches; all the hundred little bells of the pagodas quiver with desire to speak. KO-NGAI! All the green-and-gold tiles of the temple are vibrating; the wooden goldfish above them are writhing against the sky; the uplifted finger of Fo shakes high over the heads of the worshipers through the blue fog of incense! KO-NGAI!—What a thunder tone was that! All the lacquered goblins on the palace cornices wriggle their firecolored tongues! And after each huge shock, how wondrous the multiple echo and the great golden moan and, at last, the sudden sibilant sobbing in the ears when the immense tone faints away in broken whispers of silver—as though a woman should whisper, "Hiai!" Even so the great bell hath sounded every day for well-nigh five hundred years—Ko-Ngai: first with stupendous clang, then with silver murmuring of "Hiai!" And there is not a child in all the many-colored ways of the old Chinese city who does not know the story of the great bell—who cannot tell you why the great bell says Ko-Ngai and Hiai!

Now, this is the story of the great bell in the Ta-chung sz', as the same is related in the "Pe-Hiao-Tou-Choue," written by the learned Yu-Pao-Chen, of the City of Kwang-chau-fu.

Nearly five hundred years ago the Celestially August, the Son of Heaven, Yong-Lo, of the "Illustrious," or Ming, dynasty, commanded the worthy official Kouan-Yu that he should have a bell made of such size that the sound thereof might be heard for one hundred *li*. And he further ordained that the voice of the bell should be strengthened with brass, and deepened with gold, and sweetened with silver; and that the face and the great lips of it should be graven with blessed sayings from the sacred books, and that it should be suspended in the centre of the imperial capital, to sound through all the many-colored ways of the City of Pe-King.

Therefore the worthy mandarin Kouan-Yu assembled all the master-moulders and the renowned bellsmiths of the empire, and all men of great repute and cunning in foundry work; and they measured the materials for the alloy, and treated them skill-fully, and prepared the moulds, the fires, the instruments, and the monstrous melting-pot for fusing the metal. And they labored exceedingly, like giants—neglecting only rest and sleep and the comforts of life; toiling both night and day in obedience to Kouan-Yu, and striving in all things to do the behest of the Son of Heaven.

But when the metal had been cast, and the earthen mould separated from the glowing casting, it was discovered that, despite their great labor and ceaseless care, the result was void of worth; for the metals had rebelled one against the other—the gold had scorned alliance with the brass, the silver would not mingle with the molten iron. Therefore the moulds had to be once more pre-pared, and the fires rekindled, and the metal remelted, and all the work tediously and toilsomely repeated. The Son of Heaven heard, and was angry, but spake nothing.

A second time the bell was cast, and the result was even worse. Still the metals obstinately refused to blend one with the other; and there was no uniformity in the bell, and the sides of it were cracked and fissured, and the lips of it were slagged and split asunder; so that all the labor had to be repeated even a third time, to the great dismay of Kouan-Yu. And when the Son of Heaven heard these things, he was angrier than before; and sent his mes-senger to Kouan-Yu with a letter upon lemon-colored silk, and sealed with the Seal of the Dragon, containing these words:

> From the Mighty Yong-Lo, the Sublime Tait-Sung, the Celestial and August—whose reign is called "Ming"—to Kouan-Yu the Fuh-yin: Twice thou hast betrayed the trust we have deigned graciously to place in thee; if thou fail a third time in fulfilling

our command, thy head shall be severed from thy neck. Tremble, and obey!

Now, Kouan-Yu had a daughter of dazzling loveliness, whose name—Ko-Ngai—was ever in the mouths of poets, and whose heart was even more beautiful than her face. Ko-Ngai loved her father with such love that she had refused a hundred worthy suitors rather than make his home desolate by her absence; and when she had seen the awful yellow missive, sealed with the Dragon-Seal, she fainted away with fear for her father's sake. And when her senses and her strength returned to her, she could not rest or sleep for thinking of her parent's danger, until she had secretly sold some of her jewels, and with the money so obtained had hastened to an astrologer, and paid him a great price to advise her by what means her father might be saved from the peril impending over him. So the astrologer made observations of the heavens, and marked the aspect of the Silver Stream (which we call the Milky Way), and examined the signs of the Zodiac—the Hwangtao, or Yellow Road—and consulted the table of the Five Hin, or Principles of the Universe, and the mystical books of the alchemists. And after a long silence, he made answer to her, saying: "Gold and brass will never meet in wedlock, silver and iron never will embrace, until the flesh of a maiden be melted in the crucible; until the blood of a virgin be mixed with the metals in their fusion." So Ko-Ngai returned home sorrowful at heart; but she kept secret all that she had heard, and told no one what she had done.

At last came the awful day when the third and last effort to cast the great bell was to be made; and Ko-Ngai, together with her waiting-woman, accompanied her father to the foundry, and they took their places upon a platform overlooking the toiling of the moulders and the lava of liquefied metal. All the workmen wrought their tasks in silence; there was no sound heard but the muttering of the fires. And the muttering deepened into a roar like the roar of typhoons approaching, and the blood-red lake of metal slowly brightened like the vermilion of a sunrise, and the vermilion was transmuted into a radiant glow of gold, and the gold whitened blindingly, like the silver face of a full moon. Then the workers ceased to feed the raving flame, and all fixed their eyes upon the eyes of Kouan-Yu; and Kouan-Yu prepared to give the signal to cast.

But ere he lifted his finger, a cry caused him to turn his head; and all heard the voice of Ko-Ngai sounding sharply sweet as a bird's song above the great thunder of the fires—"For thy sake, O my Father!" And even as she cried, she leaped into the white flood of metal; and the lava of the furnace roared to receive her, and spattered monstrous flakes of flame to the roof, and burst over the verge of the earthen crater, and cast up a whirling fountain of many-colored fires, and subsided quakingly, with lightnings and with thunders and with mutterings.

Then the father of Ko-Ngai, wild with his grief, would have leaped in after her, but that strong men held him back and kept firm grasp upon him until he had fainted away and they could bear him like one dead to his home. And the serving-woman of Ko-Ngai, dizzy and speechless for pain, stood before the furnace, still holding in her hands a shoe, a tiny, dainty shoe, with embroidery of pearls and flowers—the shoe of her beautiful mistress that was. For she had sought to grasp Ko-Ngai by the foot as she leaped, but had only been able to clutch the shoe, and the pretty shoe came off in her hand; and she continued to stare at it like one gone mad.

But in spite of all these things, the command of the Celestial and August had to be obeyed, and the work of the moulders to be finished, hopeless as the result might be. Yet the glow of the metal seemed purer and whiter than before; and there was no sign of the beautiful body that had been entombed therein. So the ponderous casting was made; and lo! when the metal had become cool, it was found that the bell was beautiful to look upon, and perfect in form, and wonderful in color above all other bells. Nor was there any trace found of the body of Ko-Ngai; for it had been totally absorbed by the precious alloy, and blended with the well-blended brass and gold, with the intermingling of the silver and the iron. And when they sounded the bell, its tones were found to be deeper and mellower and mightier than the tones of any other bell—reaching even beyond the distance of one hundred *li*, like a pealing of summer thunder; and yet also like some vast voice uttering a name, a woman's name—the name of Ko-Ngai!

And still, between each mighty stroke there is a long low moaning heard; and ever the moaning ends with a sound of sobbing and of complaining, as though a weeping woman should murmur, "Hiai!" And still, when the people hear that great golden moan they keep silence; but when the sharp, sweet shuddering comes in the air, and the sobbing of "Hiai!" then, indeed, do all the Chinese mothers in all the many-colored ways of Pe-King whisper to their little ones: "Listen! That is Ko-Ngai crying for her shoe! That is Ko-Ngai calling for her shoe!"

It has nothing to do with style, but look up the story of the death of the Greek philosopher Empedocles.

❧

OSCAR WILDE [1854–1900]

"The Doer of Good," from A HOUSE OF POMEGRANATES, *1891*

It was night-time, and He was alone.

And He saw afar off the walls of a round city, and went towards the city.

And when He came near He heard within the city the tread of the feet of joy, and the laughter of the mouth of gladness, and the loud noise of many lutes. And He knocked at the gate and certain of the gate-keepers opened to Him.

And He beheld a house that was of marble, and had fair pillars of marble before it. The pillars were hung with garlands, and within and without there were torches of cedar. And He entered the house.

And when He had passed through the hall of chalcedony and the hall of jasper, and reached the long hall of feasting, He saw lying on a couch of sea-purple one whose hair was crowned with red roses and whose lips were red with wine.

And He went behind him and touched him on the shoulder, and said to him:

"Why do you live like this?"

And the young man turned round and recognised Him, and made answer, and said: "But I was a leper once, and you healed me. How else should I live?"

And He passed out of the house and went again into the street.

And after a little while He saw one whose face and raiment were painted and whose feet were shod with pearls. And behind her came slowly, as a hunter, a young man who wore a cloak of two colours. Now the face of the woman was as the fair face of an idol, and the eyes of the young man were bright with lust.

And He followed swiftly, and touched the hand of the young man, and said to him: "Why do you look at this woman and in such wise?"

And the young man turned round and recognised Him, and said: "But I was blind once, and you gave me sight. At what else should I look?"

And He ran forward and touched the painted raiment of the woman, and said to her: "Is there no other way to walk save the way of sin?"

And the woman turned round and recognised Him, and laughed, and said: "But you forgave me my sins, and the way is a pleasant way."

And He passed out of the city.

And when He passed out of the city, He saw, seated by the roadside, a young man who was weeping.

And He went towards him and touched the long locks of his hair, and said to him: "Why are you weeping?"

And the young man looked up and recognised Him, and made answer: "But I was dead once, and you raised me from the dead. What else should I do but weep?"

&ⷮ

FRANCIS W. BAIN [1863–1940]

"*The Story of the Creation of Woman*," *from* A DIGIT OF THE MOON, *1898*

In the beginning, when Twashtri came to the creation of woman, he found that he had exhausted his materials in the making of man, and that no solid elements were left. In this dilemma, after profound meditation, he did as follows. He took the rotundity of the moon, and the curves of creepers, and the clinging of tendrils, and the trembling of grass, and the slenderness of the reed, and the bloom of flowers, and the lightness of leaves, and the tapering of the elephant's trunk, and the glances of deer, and the clustering of rows of bees, and the joyous gaiety of sunbeams, and the weeping of clouds, and the fickleness of the winds, and the timidity of the hare, and the vanity of the peacock, and the softness of the

parrot's bosom, and the hardness of adamant, and the sweetness
of honey, and the cruelty of the tiger, and the warm glow of fire,
and the coldness of snow, and the chattering of jays, and the coo-
ing of the "kokila," and the hypocrisy of the crane, and the fidelity
of the "chakrawaka"; and compounding all these together, he made
woman, and gave her to man.[1] But after one week, man came to
him and said: Lord, this creature that you have given me makes my
life miserable. She chatters incessantly, and teases me beyond en-
durance, never leaving me alone; and she requires incessant attention, and takes all my time up, and cries about nothing, and is always idle; and so I have come to give her back again, as I cannot
live with her. So Twashtri said: Very well: and he took her back.
Then after another week, man came again to him, and said: Lord,
I find that my life is very lonely since I gave you back that creature. I remember how she used to dance and sing to me, and look
at me out of the corner of her eye, and play with me, and cling to
me; and her laughter was music, and she was beautiful to look at,
and soft to touch: so give her back to me again. So Twashtri said:
Very well: and gave her back again. Then after only three days,
man came back to him again, and said: Lord, I know not how it
is; but after all, I have come to the conclusion that she is more of a
trouble than a pleasure to me: so please take her back again. But
Twashtri said: Out on you! Be off! I will have no more of this.
You must manage how you can. Then man said: But I cannot live
with her. And Twashtri replied: Neither could you live without
her. And he turned his back on man, and went on with his work.
Then man said: What is to be done? For I cannot live either with
or without her.

[1] Hindu poets see a resemblance between rows of bees and eye-glances. The
"kokila" is the Indian cuckoo. The crane is a byword for inward villainy
and sanctimonious exterior. The "chakrawaka," or Brahmany drake, is
fabled to pass the night sorrowing for the absence of his mate and she for
him.—Bain's notes.

☙

SIR THOMAS MALORY [1405?–1471]

LE MORTE D'ARTHUR, *Book 21, Chapter 1, Written about 1470*

How Sir Mordred presumed and took on him to be king of England, and would have married the Queen, his father's wife

As Sir Mordred was ruler of all England, he did do make letters as though that they came from beyond the sea; and the letters specified that King Arthur was slain in battle with Sir Lancelot. Wherefore Sir Mordred made a parliament and called the lords together, and there he made them to choose him king. And so was he crowned at Canterbury, and held a feast there fifteen days; and afterward he drew him unto Winchester. And there he took the Queen Guinevere, and said plainly that he would wed her which was his uncle's wife and his father's wife. And so he made ready for the feast, and a day prefixed that they should be wedded; wherefore Queen Guinevere was passing heavy. But she durst not discover her heart, but spake fair, and agreed to Sir Mordred's will.

Then she desired of Sir Mordred for to go to London, to buy all manner of things that longed unto the wedding. And because of her fair speech Sir Mordred trusted her well enough, and gave her leave to go. And so, when she came to London, she took the Tower of London; and suddenly in all haste possible she stuffed it with all manner of victual, and well garnished it with men, and so kept it. Then when Sir Mordred wist and understood how he was beguiled, he was passing wroth, out of measure. And, a short tale for to make, he went and laid a mighty siege about the Tower of London, and made many great assaults thereat, and threw many great engines unto them, and shot great guns. But all might not prevail Sir Mordred, for Queen Guinevere would never, for fair speech nor for foul, would never trust to come in his hands again.

Then came the Bishop of Canterbury, the which was a noble clerk and an holy man, and thus he said to Sir Mordred: "Sir, what will ye do? Will ye first displease God and sithen shame yourself and all knighthood? Is not King Arthur your uncle, no father but your mother's brother, and on her himself King Arthur begat you upon his own sister? Therefore how may you wed your father's wife? Sir," said the noble clerk, "leave this opinion, or I shall curse you with book and bell and candle."

"Do thou thy worst!" said Sir Mordred. "Wit thou well I shall defy thee!"

"Sir," said the Bishop, "and wit you well I shall not fear me to do that me ought to do. Also, where ye noise where my lord Arthur is slain, and that is not so, and therefore ye will make a foul work in this land."

"Peace, thou false priest," said Sir Mordred, "for and thou chafe me any more, I shall make strike off thy head."

So the Bishop departed and did the cursing in the most orgulous way that might be done. And then Sir Mordred sought the Bishop of Canterbury, for to have slain him. Then the Bishop fled, and took part of his goods with him, and went nigh unto Glastonbury; and there he was a priest hermit in a chapel, and lived in poverty and in holy prayers. For well he understood that mischievous war was at hand. Then Sir Mordred sought on Queen Guinevere by letters and sonds, and by fair means and foul means, for to have her to come out of the Tower of London; but all this availed not, for she answered him shortly, openly and privily, that she had liefer slay herself than be married with him.

Then came word to Sir Mordred that King Arthur had araised the siege for Sir Lancelot, and he was coming homeward with a great host, to be avenged upon Sir Mordred; wherefore Sir Mordred made write writs to all the barony of this land, and much people drew to him. For then was the common voice among them that with Arthur was none other life than war and strife, and with Sir Mordred was great joy and bliss. Thus was Sir Arthur depraved and evil said of. And many there were that King Arthur had made up of nought, and given them lands, might not then say him a good word.

Lo, ye all Englishmen, see ye not what a mischief here was? For he that was the most king and knight of the world, and most loved the fellowship of noble knights, and by him they were all upholden, now might not these Englishmen hold them content with him. Lo, thus was the old custom and usage of this land; and also men say that we of this land have not yet lost nor forgotten that custom and usage. Alas, this is a great default of us Englishmen, for there may no thing please us no term.

And so fared the people at that time: they were better pleased with Sir Mordred than they were with King Arthur; and much people drew unto Sir Mordred, and said they would abide with him for better and for worse. And so Sir Mordred drew with a great host to Dover, for there he heard say that Sir Arthur would arrive, and so he thought to beat his own father from his lands; and the most party of all England held with Sir Mordred, the people were so newfangle.

༺༻

JAMES JOYCE [1882–1941]
Excerpt from ULYSSES, *1922, Chapter 12*

In Inisfail the fair there lies a land, the land of holy Michan. There rises a watchtower beheld of men afar. There sleep the mighty dead as in life they slept, warriors and princes of high renown. A pleasant land it is in sooth of murmuring waters, fishful streams where sport the gunnard, the plaice, the roach, the halibut, the gibbed haddock, the grilse, the dab, the brill, the flounder, the mixed coarse fish generally and other denizens of the aqueous kingdom too numerous to be enumerated. In the mild breezes of the west and of the east the lofty trees wave in different directions their first class foliage, the wafty sycamore, the Lebanonian cedar, the exalted planetree, the eugenic eucalyptus and other ornaments of the arboreal world with which that region is thoroughly well supplied. Lovely maidens sit in close proximity to the roots of the lovely trees singing the most lovely songs while they play with all kinds of lovely objects as for example golden ingots, silvery fishes, crans of herrings, drafts of eels, codlings, creels of fingerlings, purple seagems and playful insects. And heroes voyage from afar to woo them, from Eblana to Slievemargy, the peerless princes of unfettered Munster and of Connacht the just and of smooth sleek Leinster and of Cruachan's land and of Armagh the splendid and of the noble district of Boyle, princes, the sons of kings.

And there rises a shining palace whose crystal glittering roof is seen by mariners who traverse the extensive sea in barks built expressly for that purpose and thither come all herds and fatlings and first fruits of that land for O'Connor Fitzsimon takes toll of them, a chieftain descended from chieftains. Thither the extremely large wains bring foison of the fields, flaskets of cauliflowers, floats of spinach, pineapple chunks, Rangoon beans, strikes of tomatoes, drums of figs, drills of Swedes, spherical potatoes and tallies of iridescent kale, York and Savoy, and trays of onions, pearls of the earth, and punnets of mushrooms and custard marrows and fat vetches and bere and rape and red green yellow brown russet sweet big bitter ripe pomellated apples and chips of strawberries and sieves of gooseberries, pulpy and pelurious, and strawberries fit for princes and raspberries from their canes.

Excerpt from FINNEGANS WAKE, *1939. Part of a description of the river goddess Anna Livia Plurabelle (the Liffey River)*

First she let her hair fal and down it flussed to her feet its teviots winding coils. Then, mothernaked, she sampood herself with gala-water and fraguant pistania mud, wupper and lauar, from crown to sole. Next she greesed the groove of her keel, warthes and wears and mole and itcher, with antifouling butterscatch and turfentide and serpenthyme and with leafmould she ushered round prunella isles and eslats dun, quincecunct, allover her little mary. Peeld gold of waxwork her jellybelly and her grains of incense anguille bronze. And after that she wove a garland for her hair. She pleated it. She plaited it. Of meadowgrass and riverflags, the bulrush and waterweed, and of fallen griefs of weeping willow. Then she made her bracelets and her anklets and her armlets and a jetty amulet for necklace of clicking cobbles and pattering pebbles and rumbledown rubble, richmond and rehr, of Irish rhunerhinerstones and shellmarble bangles. That done, a dawk of smut to her airy ey, Annushka Lutetiavitch Pufflovah, and the lellipos cream to her lippeleens and the pick of the paintbox for her pommettes, from strawbirry reds to extra violates, and she sendred her boudeloire maids to His Affluence, Cilegia Grande and Kirschie Real, the two chirsines, with respecks from his missus, seepy and sewery, and a request might she passe of him for a minnikin. A call to pay and light a taper, in Brie-on-Arrosa, back in a sprizzling. The cock striking mine, the stalls bridely sign, there's Zambosy waiting for Me! She said she wouldn't be half her length away. Then, then, as soon as the lump his back was turned, with her mealiebag slang over her shulder, Anna Livia, oysterface, forth of her bassein came.

ॐ

ISAK DINESEN [1885–1962]

First three paragraphs of "The Dreamers," in SEVEN GOTHIC TALES, *1934*

On a full-moon night of 1863 a dhow was on its way from Lamu to Zanzibar, following the coast about a mile out.

She carried full sails before the monsoon, and had in her a freight of ivory and rhino-horn. This last is highly valued as an aphrodisiac, and traders come for it to Zanzibar from as far as

China. But besides these cargoes the dhow also held a secret load, which was about to stir and raise great forces, and of which the slumbering countries which she passed did not dream.

This still night was bewildering in its deep silence and peace, as if something had happened to the world; as if the soul of it had been, by some magic, turned upside down. The free monsoon came from far places, and the sea wandered on under its sway, on her long journey, in the face of the dim luminous moon. But the brightness of the moon upon the water was so clear that it seemed as if all the light in the world were in reality radiating from the sea, to be reflected in the skies. The waves looked solid, as if one might safely have walked upon them, while it was into the vertiginous sky that one might sink and fall, into the turbulent and unfathomable depths of silvery worlds, of bright silver or dull and tarnished silver, forever silver reflected within silver, moving and changing, towering up, slowly and weightless.

✍

VLADIMIR NABOKOV [1899–   ]

   Last three paragraphs of "First Love," in NABOKOV'S DOZEN, *1958.*
   "First Love" was written in 1948.

Among the trivial souvenirs acquired at Biarritz before leaving, my favorite was not the small bull of black stone and not the sonorous sea shell but something which now seems almost symbolic—a meerschaum penholder with a tiny peephole of crystal in its ornamental part. One held it quite close to one's eye, screwing up the other, and when one had got rid of the shimmer of one's own lashes, a miraculous photographic view of the bay and of the line of cliffs ending in a lighthouse could be seen inside.

And now a delightful thing happens. The process of recreating that penholder and the microcosm in its eyelet stimulates my memory to a last effort. I try again to recall the name of Colette's dog—and, sure enough, along those remote beaches, over the glossy evening sands of the past, where each footprint slowly fills up with sunset water, here it comes, here it comes, echoing and vibrating: Floss, Floss, Floss!

Colette was back in Paris by the time we stopped there for a day before continuing our homeward journey; and there, in a fawn park under a cold blue sky, I saw her (by arrangement between our mentors, I believe) for the last time. She carried a hoop and a short stick to drive it with, and everything about her was extremely proper and stylish in an autumnal, Parisian, *tenue-de-ville-pour-fillettes* [town-clothes-for-little-girls] way. She took from her governess and slipped into my brother's hand a farewell present, a box of sugar-coated almonds, meant, I knew, solely for me; and instantly she was off, tap-tapping her glinting hoop through light and shade, around and around a fountain choked with dead leaves near which I stood. The leaves linger in my memory with the leather of her shoes and gloves, and there was, I remember, some detail in her attire (perhaps a ribbon on her Scottish cap, or the pattern of her stockings) that reminded me then of the rainbow spiral in a glass marble. I still seem to be holding that wisp of iridescence, not knowing exactly where to fit it, while she runs with her hoop ever faster around me and finally dissolves among the slender shadows cast on the graveled path by the interlaced arches of its low looped fence.

SAMUEL BECKETT [1906–   ]

Excerpt from MALONE DIES, *1956*

Since morning he has been here and now it is evening. The tugs, their black funnels striped with red, tow to their moorings the

last barges, freighted with empty barrels. The water cradles already the distant fires of the sunset, orange, rose and green,
quenches them in its ruffles and then in trembling pools spreads
them bright again. His back is turned to the river, but perhaps
it appears to him in the dreadful cries of the gulls that evening
assembles, in paroxysms of hunger, round the outflow of the
sewers, opposite the Bellevue Hotel. Yes, they too, in a last
frenzy before night and its high crags, swoop ravening about the
offal. But his face is towards the people that throng the streets at
this hour, their long day ended and the whole long evening before
them. The doors open and spew them out, each door its contingent.
For an instant they cluster in a daze, huddled on the sidewalk or in
the gutter, then set off singly on their appointed ways. And even
those who know themselves condemned, at the outset, to the same
direction, for the choice of directions at the outset is not great, take
leave of one another and part, but politely, with some polite ex-
cuse, or without a word, for they all know one another's little
ways. And God help him who longs, for once, in his recovered
freedom, to walk a little way with a fellow-creature, no matter
which, unless of course by a merciful chance he stumble on one
in the same plight. Then they take a few paces happily side by side,
then part, each one muttering perhaps, Now there will be no holding him. At this hour then erotic craving accounts for the majority
of couples. But these are few compared to the solitaries pressing
forward through the throng, obstructing the access to places of
amusement, bowed over the parapets, propped against vacant walls.
But soon they come to the appointed place, at home or at some
other home, or abroad, as the saying is, in a public place, or in a
doorway in view of possible rain. And the first to arrive have seldom long to wait, for all hasten towards one another, knowing how
short the time in which to say all the things that lie heavy on the
heart and conscience and to do all the things they have to do together, things one cannot do alone. So there they are for a few

hours in safety. Then the drowsiness, the little memorandum book with its little special pencil, the yawned goodbyes.

Exercises

1. Recount the deeds of some godlike politician, local, state, national, or foreign, in the manner of Genesis 1. Cut them off after two pages or less.

2. Describe an academic procession, and all the other folderol of commencement exercises, in the manner of Malory. Cut it off after two pages or less.

3. Rewrite a story from *Astounding Science Fiction* in the manner of Isak Dinesen. Cut if off after two pages or less.

4. Rewrite a story from *Playboy* in the manner of Francis W. Bain. Cut it off after two pages or less.

At this stage of the game, don't try to imitate Beckett or Nabokov.

RABELAISIAN STYLES

Rabelais is the huge mask of ancient comedy detached from the Greek proscenium, the bronze made flesh, henceforth a living human face, but still enormous, coming to laugh at us among us and with us.

VICTOR HUGO
William Shakespeare

⟨❧⟩ THE AGE THAT DISCOVERED America also produced Rabelais. What an age that was! Before the light of common day we have the brief but glorious glory of the dawn. When since the Renaissance have we had such another blaze of literary brilliance? Consider an uneven dozen of major figures only:

Dante (1265–1321)
Petrarch (1304–1374)
Boccaccio (1313–1375)
Chaucer (c. 1340–1400)
Erasmus (1466 or 1469–1536)
Rabelais (1483 or 1494–1553?)[1]
Ronsard (1524–1585)
Tasso (1544–1595)
Cervantes (1547–1616)
Shakespeare (1564–1616)
Jonson (1573?–1637)
Milton (1608–1674)

Consider particularly those four good-natured story-tellers, Boccaccio, Chaucer, Erasmus and Rabelais: four brilliant celebrants of the warmth of life: and consider most particularly

[1] For a brief summary of the arguments about the date of Rabelais' birth, see the Garnier Classics edition of his complete works, I, i, note 1. There is no record of his death. After April 1553 he simply disappears.

Rabelais, perhaps the most brilliant, certainly the lustiest and most joyful of the four.

Victor Hugo called him "the Aeschylus of eatables, who made that great discovery, the belly." In 1532 he published *Pantagruel: The Horrible and Frightful Feats and Prowesses of the Very Renowned Pantagruel, King of the Dipsodes*, and in 1534 *The Very Horrific Life of the Great Gargantua, Father of Pantagruel, King of the Dipsodes: A Book Full of Pantagruelism.* In 1546 and 1552 he published two further volumes of Pantagruel's adventures; in 1562, nine years after the last record of his life, a fifth volume appeared, and in 1564 an expanded version of the fifth volume; for several reasons besides their late appearance, the authenticity of these last two is doubtful.

But we are not concerned with Rabelais' bibliography, or with the details of his career as begging friar, monk, secular priest, doctor, professor of medicine, and hospital administrator. For our purposes, the essential point is that he was a Renaissance humanist, full of enthusiasm for everything that contributes to human enjoyment, fulfillment and development; everybody who has a heart and a brain and an appetite must love him as the father of all roaring, roistering, boistering, bustering, laughing, stamping, stumping, thumping, jumping, plumping, bumping, abounding, astounding, resounding, redounding, surrounding, eating, drinking, glass-clinking writers. He dedicates *Gargantua* to all good drinkers: "for, in the composing of this masterly book, I never lost nor bestowed any more, nor any other time, than what was appointed to serve me for taking of my bodily refection, that is, whilst I was eating and drinking." Those of us who have some tincture of Greek (a language Rabelais taught himself and loved to show off) will know that Dipsodes are Thirsty Fellows; and Rabelais himself assures us that the name Pantagruel means Allthirst. He calls his philosophy Pantagruelism; the quintessence of it, he says, is to be a good Pantagruelist: that is, "to live in peace, joy, health, always eating and drinking and making merry," and moreover to have "certain gaiety of spirit, preserved by scorn of fortuitous things."

His main characters are giants of nature, his subject is abundant nature, his style is nature overflowing. Pantagruel's all-welcoming Renaissance thirst has no limit: he wants not only to eat and drink but also to know everything, do everything, enjoy everything, without restraint. He knows that the appetite for knowledge and experience grows with knowledge and experience: "He who eats salt beef can find the wine without a candle, though it were hid in the bottom of a collier's sack."

Rabelais' belief that whatever is natural is good and whatever is not natural is bad can of course be rebutted, in principle and in detail, on many grounds—the great questions being Why? and What is natural? Does ice cream occur in nature? But is it unnatural to like ice cream? Ants do occur in nature, and there are people who enjoy eating them—with or without a chocolate coating; is their appetite unnatural? Certainly a person who enjoys ice cream is in no position to say so. The difficulty of distinguishing nature from custom is well known; and Rabelais was on the side of charity. The bad thing about this point of view is that all kinds of crimes and vices, including sadism, slavery and murder, have been defended on the ground that they are "natural"; that is what I meant by the first sentence of this paragraph. The learned, thoughtful and slightly pedantic Gustave Lanson said in the first edition of his *Histoire de la Littérature Française*, "Rabelais is not profound; we must venture to say it"; but in the eleventh edition he added this footnote: "I would not venture to say it now. I am not now fully persuaded that it takes greater depth of mind to imagine a system of metaphysics than to accept life and make a philosophy that corresponds to it. Refusing to build a system of metaphysics does not necessarily denote superficial thinking. Neither idealism nor reason requires the support of metaphysics. In short, a courageous optimism, clear-sighted and practical, which doesn't insult life but applies itself to making life better, is quite as valuable as pessimistic beliefs or subtle speculations." This of course is no licence for anti-intellectualism, an arrogantly pessimistic attitude; even less does it condone a supine acquiescence in everything that is—nothing could be less Rabelaisian than that. Plato and his followers regretted that the mind had a body; on a much lower level of artistry, D. H. Lawrence and his followers regretted that the body had a mind; Rabelais regretted neither. He favored everything that encouraged their harmonious development, and opposed everything that discouraged such development.

He was first translated into English in 1653 by the fantastical Sir Thomas Urquhart (1611–1660?), whose version of the first three books remains by far the best: that is to say, the most Rabelaisian; but the companion translation of the fourth and fifth books by Peter Motteux (c. 1660–1718) is Rabelaisian too and remains far better than any other. This fat jolly book by these two roaring Rabelaisians has become a classic of English prose. Directly or indirectly, it has had a strong influence on such widely different writers as Fielding, Smollett, Swift, Sterne, Joyce, Thomas Wolfe and Dylan Thomas.

But the style that bears Rabelais' name was not invented by him alone. It was practiced before him with great gusto by the Italian poets Luigi Pulci (1432–1484) and Teofilo Folengo (1496–1544), and by the anonymous French author of *The Great and Inestimable Chronicles of the Huge and Enormous Giant Gargantua* (1532), which Rabelais freely acknowledged as the immediate inspiration for his own work. The Rabelaisian style was also practiced by Shakespeare, Thomas Nash (1567–1600), Thomas Dekker (1570?–1632) and others who died long before Urquhart began his translation and who may or may not have read Rabelais in French. Dekker's reference to Gargantua in *The Shoemaker's Holiday* (1600) indicates that the name was familiar to London theatergoers, most of whom probably did not read French. But the Rabel-aisian style was a natural, appropriate, practically inevitable style to express the enthusiasm of Renaissance men—men who, as Hippolyte Taine said in his *History of English Literature*, "were seeing gold sparkle and hearing silk rustle for the first time."

Its predominant features are a love of lists and synonyms—a refusal to use one word where twenty will do—and a vocabulary that knows no embarrassment. "Rabelais has no taste," says Lanson: in his exuberance he says many things that are not said and uses many words that are not used in polite conversation. Cardinal Jean du Bellay, a friend and protector of Rabelais, refused to have as a guest at his table anyone who had not read "The Book," as he called Rabelais' works; but the University of Paris banned "The Book," and it is unlikely that any modern Department of English would use a textbook of writing that presented Rabelais unexpur-gated. In view of the difficulty of finding passages of any length that do not contain obscenities, I have therefore replaced the obscenities with little dots.

But if one way to frustrate the naughtiness of naughty readers is to change the text, another is to leave it unchanged: an easy trick at least as old as Gibbon, who quoted accounts of ancient Roman carryings-on in the original Latin. In the third passage from Rabelais in this chapter most of the obscenities are in inkhorn Latin, and I have let them stand.

For the meaning of "inkhorn," see Albert C. Baugh's *History of the English Language* (Appleton-Century-Crofts, 1935), pp. 266–269, or any other good book of this kind. During the Renaissance not only gold and silk but also the pleasures of literature became generally available to middle-class men for the first time; in order to get at the literature of the past, as well as for their professional purposes, they studied Latin and Greek with great avidity: Rabelais and Erasmus went at Greek the way a hungry man goes at a beefsteak. Like many men in all times and places, many men of Renaissance Europe liked to display their new possessions, and many did so with tasteless extravagance. Those who had some newly acquired Latin or Greek often sprinkled their speech and writing with it; sometimes the sprinkling was so thick that the effect was unintentionally funny; even funnier was their Anglicized or Gallicized Latin; Baugh gives a horrendous example, and the third selection from Rabelais in this chapter gives another. All writers of term papers should take this selection to heart.

❧

FRANÇOIS RABELAIS [1483 or 1494–1553?]

THE WORKS OF RABELAIS, *Book I, Chapter 25, slightly expurgated*

At that time, which was the season of vintage, in the beginning of harvest, when the country shepherds were set to keep the vines, and hinder the starlings from eating up the grapes: as some cake-bakers of Lerné happened to pass along the broad highway, driving unto the city ten or twelve horses loaded with cakes, the said shepherds courteously intreated them to give them some for their money, as the price then ruled in the market. For here it is to be remarked, that it is a celestial food to eat for breakfast hot fresh cakes with grapes, especially the frail clusters, the great red grapes, muscadine, the verjuice grape, and the luskard. . . .

The cake-bakers were in nothing inclinable to their request; but which was worse, did injure [insult] them most outrageously, calling them prating gablers, lickorous gluttons, freckled bittors, mangy rascals, . . . scoundrels, drunken roysters, sly knaves, drowsy loiterers, slapsauce fellows, slabberdegullion druggels, lubbardly louts, cousening foxes, ruffian rogues, paltry customers, sycophant varlets, drawlatch hoydons, flouting milk-sops, jeering companions, staring clowns, forlorn snakes, ninny lobcocks, scurvey sneaksbies, fondling fips, base loons, saucy coxcombs, idle lusks, scoffing braggards, noddy meacocks, blockish grutnols, doddipol joltheads, jobbernol goosecaps, foolish loggerheads, slutch calf-lollies, grout-head gnatsnappers, lob-dotterels, gaping changelings, codshead loobies, woodcock slangams, ninny-hammer flycatchers, noddipeak simpletons, turgy gut, . . . shepherds, and other such defamatory epithets, saying further, that it was not for them to eat of those dainty cakes, but might very well content themselves with the coarse unraunged bread, or to eat of the great brown household loaf. To which provoking words, one amongst them called Forgier (an honest fellow of his person, and a notable springall) made answer very calmly thus: "How long is it since you have got horns, that you are become so proud? Indeed, formerly, you were wont to give us some freely, and will you not now let us have some for our money? This is not the part of good neighbours, neither do we serve you thus when you come hither to buy our good corn [grain], whereof you make your cakes and buns. Besides that, we should have given you to the bargain some of our grapes, but, *by his zounds*, you may chance to repent it, and possibly have need of us another time, when we shall use you after the like manner, and therefore remember it."

Then Marquet, a prime man in the confraternity of the cake-bakers, said unto him, "Yea, Sir, thou art pretty well crest-risen this morning, thou didst eat yesternight too much millet and bolymong; come hither, sirrah, come hither, I will give thee some cakes." Whereupon Forgier, dreading no harm, in all simplicity went towards him, and drew a sixpence out of his leather satchel, thinking that Marquet would have sold him some of his cakes; but instead of cakes, he gave him with his whip such a rude lash overthwart his legs, that the marks remained; then would have fled away, but Forgier cried out as loud as he could, "O! Murder, murder, help, help, help, help"; and in the meantime threw a great cudgel after him, which he carried under his arm, wherewith he hit him in the coronal joint of the head, upon the crotophic artery of the right side thereof, so forcibly, that Marquet fell down from his mare, more like a dead than a living man.

Meanwhile, the farmers and country swains that were watching their walnuts near to that place, came running with their great poles and long staves, and laid such load on these cake-bakers, as if they had been to thresh upon green rye. The other shepherds and shepherdesses, hearing the lamentable shout of Forgier, came with their slings and slackies following them, and throwing great stones at them, as thick as hail. At last, these overtook them, and took from them about four or five dozen of their cakes: Nevertheless, they paid for them the ordinary price, and gave them over and above one hundred eggs [bumps], and three baskets full of mulberries [bruises]. Then did the cake-bakers help to get Marquet mounted upon his mare again, who was most shrewdly wounded; and forthwith they returned to Lerné, changing the resolution they had to go to Pareille, threatening very sharp and boisterously the cowherds, shepherds, and farmers of Sevilé and Sinays. This done, the shepherds and shepherdesses made merry with these cakes and fine grapes, and sported themselves together at the sound of the pretty small pipe, scoffing and laughing at those vain-glorious cake-bakers, who had that day met with mischief for want of crossing themselves with a good hand in the morning. Nor did they forget to apply to Forgier's leg some fair great, red, and medicinal grapes, and so handsomely dressed it and bound it up, that it was quickly cured.

THE WORKS OF RABELAIS, *Book II, Chapter 3, slightly expurgated*

When Pantagruel was born, there was none more astonished and perplexed than was his father Gargantua: for, on the one side seeing his wife Badebec dead, and on the other side his son Pantagruel born, so fair and so goodly, *he knew not what to say, nor what to do*; and the doubt, that troubled his brain, was to know whether he should *cry* for the death of his wife, or *laugh* for the joy of his son: he was on either side choaked with sophistical arguments; for he framed them very well in *modo & figura* [according to the categories of Aristotelian logic], but he could not resolve them, remaining pestered and entangled by this means, like a mouse catched in a trap, or a kite snared in a gin. "Shall I weep?" said he: "yes. For why? my so good wife is dead, who was the most *this*, the most *that*, that ever was in the world; never shall I see her, never shall I recover such another; it is unto me an inestimable loss! O my good God, what had I done, that thou shouldest thus punish me? Why didst thou not take me away before her, seeing for me to live, without her, is but to languish? Ah! Badebec, Badebec, my minion [*mignonne*], my dear heart, my pigsney, my duck, my honey, my *little coney* (yet it hath in circumference full six acres, three rods, five poles, four yards, two feet, one inch and a half of good woodland measure), my tender Peggy, my . . . , my . . . , my . . . , never shall I see thee! Ah! poor Pantagruel, thou hast lost thy good mother, thy sweet nurse, thy well-beloved lady! O false death, how injurious and despightful hast thou been to me! how malicious and outrageous have I found thee, in taking her from me, my well-beloved wife, who should, of right, have been immortal!"

With these words he did cry like a cow; but on a sudden fell a laughing like a calf, when Pantagruel came into his mind. "Ha! my little son," said he, "my childilolly, fedlifondy, dandlichucky, my . . . , my pretty rogue: O how jolly thou art, and how much I am bound to my gracious God, that hath been pleased to bestow on me a son so fair, so spriteful, so lively, so smiling, so pleasant, and so gentle. *Ho, ho, ho, ho,* how glad I am! let us drink, *ho,* and put away melancholy: bring of the best: rinse the glasses; lay the cloth; drive out these dogs; blow this fire; light candles; shut that door there; cut this bread in sippets for brewis [little pieces for soup]; send away these poor folks; give them what they ask; hold my gown; I will strip myself into my doublet, *en cuerpo* [an abbreviation of the Spanish idiom *en cuerpo de camisa*, in shirtsleeves], to make the gossips merry, and keep them company."

As he spoke this, he heard the litanies and momentos of the priests that carried his wife to be buried; which dashed all his merriment again, and he was suddenly ravished another way, saying "Lord God, must I again *contrist* [sadden] myself? This grieves me; I am no longer young; I grow old; the weather is dangerous; I am sick; I faint away. By the faith of a gentleman, it were better to *cry* less, and *drink* more.

"My wife is dead, well, by G—— (*da jurandi*) [pardon my swearing] I shall not raise her again by my crying: she is well; she is in paradise at least, if she be no higher: she prayeth to God for us; she is happy; she is above the sense of our miseries, nor can our calamities reach her. What though she be dead, must not we also die? The same debt, which she hath paid, hangs over our heads; nature will require it of us, and we must all of us, some day, taste of the same sauce: let her pass then, and the Lord preserve the survivors, for I must now cast about how to get another wife. But I will tell you what you shall do," said he to the midwives "(where be they? good folks, I cannot see you),[2] go to my wife's interment, and I will the while *rock* my son; for I find myself strangely altered, and in danger of falling sick; but drink one good draught first; you will be the better for it, believe me, upon my honour." They, at his request, went to her burial and funeral obsequies: in the meanwhile, poor Gargantua staying at home, and willing to have somewhat in remembrance of her to be engraven upon her tomb, made this epitaph, in the manner as followeth:

2 He has tears in his eyes.

Dead is the noble Badebec,
Who had a face like a rebec;[3]
    A Spanish body, and a belly
Of Swisserland;[4] *she died, I tell ye,*
In child-birth; pray to God that her
He pardon wherein she did err.
Here lies her body, which did live
Free from all vice, as I believe;
    And did decease at my bed-side,
    The year and day in which she died.[5]

THE WORKS OF RABELAIS, *Book II, Chapter 6, slightly expurgated*

[Compare Horace's treatment of Crispinus in Jonson's *The Poetaster*, Act V, Scene iii, *1601.*]

Upon a certain day, I know not when, Pantagruel walking, after supper, with some of his fellow-students, without that gate of the city through which we enter on the road to Paris, encountered with a young handsome spruce scholar, that was coming upon the very same way; and, after they had saluted one another, asked him thus: "My friend, from whence comest thou now?" The scholar answered him, "From the *alme, inclyte* and celebrate academy, which is *vocitated Lutetia.*" "What is the meaning of this?" said Pantagruel to one of his men. "It is," answered he, "from Paris." "Thou comest from Paris, then," said Pantagruel; "and how do you spend your time there, you, my masters, the students of Paris?" The *scholar* answered, "We *transfretate* the *sequan* at the *dilucal* and *crepuscul*; we *deambulate* by the *compites* and *quadrives* of the

---

[3] A medieval stringed instrument, a predecessor of the cello, whose head was often ornamented with a carving of a jolly human face.
[4] A slim, elegant body but a hearty appetite.
[5] This feeble joke was already old in Rabelais' time.

urb; we *despumate* the *latial verbocination*; and like *verisimilarie amorabons*, we *captat* the benevolence of the *omnijugal, omniform* and *omnigenal foeminine sex*; upon certain *diecules* we *invisat* the *lupanares*, and in a *venerian extase inculcate* our *veretres*, into the *penitissime recesses* of the *pudends* of these *amicabilissim meretricules*: then do we *cauponisate* in the *meritory taberns* of the *pineapple*, the *castle, the magdalene*, and the *mule*, goodly *vervecine spatules performinated* with *petrosile*: and if by fortune there be rarity, or penury of *pecune* in our *marsupies*; and that they be exhausted of *ferruginean* metal for the shot, we *dimit* our *codices*, and *oppignerat* our vestments, whilst we *prestolate* the coming of the *tabellaries* from the *penates*, and *patriotic lares*." To which Pantagruel answered, "What devilish language is this? By the Lord, I think thou art some kind of heretic." "My Lord, no," said the scholar; "for *libentissimally*, as soon as it *illucesceth* any *minutle* slice of the day, I *demigrate* into one of these so well *architected* minsters, and there *irrorating* myself with fair *lustral* water, I mumble off little parcels of some *missick precation* of our *sacrificals*; and *submurmurating* my *horary precules*, I *elevate* and *absterg* my *anime* from its nocturnal *inquinations*. I *revere* the *olympicols*; I *latrially venere* the *supernal astripotent*; I *dilige* and *redame* my *proxims*; I observe the *decalogical precepts*; and, according to the *facultatule* of my *vires*, I do not *discede* from them one breadth of an *unguicule*; nevertheless it is *veriform*, that because *Mammona* doth not *supergurgitate* anything in my *locules*, that I am somewhat *rare* and *lent* to *supererrogate* the *elemosynes* to those *egents* that *ostially queritate* their *stipe*."

"Prut, tut," said Pantagruel, "what doth this fool mean to say? I think he is upon the forging of some *diabolical* tongue, and that, inchanter-like, he would *charm* us." To whom one of his men said, "Without doubt, sir, this fellow would counterfeit the language of the Parisians; but he doth only flay the Latin, imagining, by so doing, that he doth mightily pindarize it in most eloquent terms, and strongly conceiteth himself to be therefore a great orator in the French, because he disdaineth the common manner of speaking." To which Pantagruel said, "Is it true?" The scholar answered, "My worshipful lord, my *genie* is not *apt nate* to that which this *flagitious nebulon* saith, to *excoriate* the *cuticle* of our *vernacular Gallick*; but *viceversally* I *gnave opere*, and by *veles* and *rames enite* to *locupletate* it with the *Latinicome* redundance." "By G——," said Pantagruel, "I will teach you to speak: but first come hither, and tell me whence thou art?" To this the scholar answered: "The *primeval origin* of my *aves* and *ataves* was *indigenary* of the *Lemovick* regions, where *requiesceth* the *corpor* of the *hagiotat* St. Martial." "I understand thee very well," said Pantagruel, "when all comes to all, thou art a Limousin, and thou wilt here, by thy affected speech, counterfeit the Parisians. Well now, come hither; I must shew thee a new trick, and handsomely give thee one fling." With this he took him by the throat, saying to him, "Thou flayest the Latin; but by St. John, I will make thee flay the fox, for I will now flay thee alive." Then began the poor Limousin to cry: "Haw, gwid maaster! haw, Laord, my halp, and St. Marshaw! haw, I am worried: haw, my thropple, the bean of my cragg is bruk: haw, for Guaad's seck, lawt me lean, mawster; waw, waw, waw." "Now," said Pantagruel, "thou speakest naturally"; and so let him go: for the poor Limousin had. . . . "Then," said Pantagruel, "St. Alipantin, what civette? Foh, fah; to the devil with this turnip-eater. How he stinks!" And so let him depart. But this hug of Pantagruel's was such a terror to him all the days of his life, and he had such a thirst upon him, that he would often cry out that Pantagruel held him by the throat. And after some few years he died a Rowland death;[6] a work of divine vengeance, shewing us that which saith the philosopher,[7] and Aulus Gellius, *that it becometh us to speak according to the common language*;

---

[6] According to a popular tradition, the knight Roland died of thirst.
[7] Aristotle.

and that we should, as said Octavian Augustus, shun all strange words, with as much care as pilots of ships avoid the rocks in the sea.

❧

WILLIAM SHAKESPEARE [1564–1616]

KING HENRY IV, PART I, *c. 1597. Excerpt from Act I, Scene ii*

(London. An apartment of the Prince of Wales. Enter the Prince and Falstaff.)

FALSTAFF: Now, Hal, what time of day is it, lad?

PRINCE: Thou art so fat-witted, with drinking of old sack and unbuttoning thee after supper and sleeping upon benches after noon, that thou hast forgotten to demand that truly which thou wouldst truly know. What a devil hast thou to do with the time of the day? Unless hours were cups of sack, and minutes capons, and clocks the tongues of bawds, and dials the signs of leaping-houses, and the blessed sun himself a fair hot wench in flame-coloured taffeta, I see no reason why thou shouldst be so superfluous[8] to demand the time of day.

FALSTAFF: Indeed, you come near me now, Hal; for we that take purses go by the moon and the seven stars, and not by Phoebus, he, "that wandering knight so fair." And, I prithee, sweet wag, when thou art king, as, God save thy grace,— majesty, I should say, for grace thou wilt have none,—

PRINCE: What, none?

FALSTAFF: No, by my troth, not so much as will serve to be pro- logue to an egg and butter.

PRINCE: Well, how then? come, roundly, roundly.

[8] An inkhorn term for overflowing or eager.

FALSTAFF: Marry then, sweet wag, when thou art king, let not us that are squires of the night's body be called thieves of the day's beauty: let us be Diana's foresters, gentlemen of the shade, minions of the moon; and let men say we be men of good government, being governed, as the sea is, by our noble and chaste mistress the moon, under whose countenance we steal.

PRINCE: Thou sayest well, and it holds well too; for the fortune of us that are the moon's men doth ebb and flow like the sea, being governed, as the sea is, by the moon. As, for proof, now: a purse of gold most resolutely snatched on Monday night and most dissolutely spent on Tuesday morning; got with swearing "Lay by" and spent with crying "Bring in"; now in as low an ebb as the foot of the ladder, and by and by in as high a flow as the ridge of the gallows.

FALSTAFF: By the Lord, thou sayest true, lad. And is not my hostess of the tavern a most sweet wench?

PRINCE: As the honey of Hybla, my old lad of the castle. And is not a buff jerkin a most sweet robe of durance?

FALSTAFF: How now, how now, mad wag! what, in thy quips and thy quiddities? what a plague have I to do with a buff jerkin?

PRINCE: Why, what a pox have I to do with my hostess of the tavern?

FALSTAFF: Well, thou hast called her to a reckoning many a time and oft.

PRINCE: Did I ever call for thee to pay thy part?

FALSTAFF: No; I'll give thee thy due, thou hast paid all there.

PRINCE: Yea, and elsewhere, so far as my coin would stretch; and where it would not, I have used my credit.

FALSTAFF: Yea, and so used it that, were it not here apparent that thou art heir apparent—But, I prithee, sweet wag, shall there be gallows standing in England when thou art king? and resolution thus fobbed as it is with the rusty curb of old father antic the law? Do not thou, when thou art king, hang a thief.

PRINCE: No; thou shalt.

FALSTAFF: Shall I? O rare! By the Lord, I'll be a brave judge.

PRINCE: Thou judgest false already: I mean, thou shalt have the hanging of the thieves and so become a rare hangman.

FALSTAFF: Well, Hal, well; and in some sort it jumps with my humour as well as waiting in the court, I can tell you.

PRINCE: For obtaining of suits?

FALSTAFF: Yea, for obtaining of suits, whereof the hangman hath no lean wardrobe. 'Sblood, I am as melancholy as a gib cat or a lugged bear.

PRINCE: Or an old lion, or a lover's lute.

FALSTAFF: Yea, or the drone of a Lincolnshire bagpipe.

PRINCE: What sayest thou to a hare, or the melancholy of Moor-ditch?

FALSTAFF: Thou hast the most unsavoury similes, and art indeed the most comparative, rascalliest, sweet young prince. But, Hal, I prithee, trouble me no more with vanity. I would to God thou and I knew where a commodity of good names were to be bought. An old lord of the council rated me the other day in the street about you, sir, but I marked him not; and yet he talked very wisely, but I regarded him not; and yet he talked wisely, and in the street too.

PRINCE: Thou didst well; for wisdom cries out in the streets, and no man regards it.

FALSTAFF: O, thou hast damnable iteration, and art indeed able to corrupt a saint. Thou hast done much harm upon me, Hal; God forgive thee for it! Before I knew thee, Hal, I knew nothing; and now am I, if a man should speak truly, little better than one of the wicked. I must give over this life, and I will give it over: by the Lord, an I do not, I am a villain: I'll be damned for never a king's son in Christendom.

PRINCE: Where shall we take a purse tomorrow, Jack?

FALSTAFF: 'Zounds, where thou wilt, lad; I'll make one; an I do not, call me villain and baffle me.

PRINCE: I see a good amendment of life in thee; from praying to purse-taking.

FALSTAFF: Why, Hal, 'tis my vocation, Hal; 'tis no sin for a man to labour in his vocation.

~~~

THOMAS DEKKER [1570?–1632]

Excerpt from THE SHOEMAKER'S HOLIDAY, *1600, Act I, Scene i*

(Scene: A Street in London. Enter Simon Eyre, master shoe-maker; his wife, Margery; Hodge, Firk and Ralph, his work-ers; and Ralph's bride, Jane.)

EYRE: Leave whining, leave whining! Away with this whimpering, this puling, these blubbering tears, and these wet eyes! I'll get thy husband discharged, I warrant thee, sweet Jane; go to!

HODGE: Master, here be the captains.

EYRE: Peace, Hodge; husht, ye knave, husht!

FIRK: Here be the cavaliers and the colonels, master.

EYRE: Peace, Firk; peace, my fine Firk! Stand by with your pishery-pashery, away! I am a man of the best presence; I'll speak to them, an they were Popes.—Gentlemen, captains, colonels, commanders! Brave men, brave leaders, may it please you to give me audience. I am Simon Eyre, the mad shoemaker of Tower Street; this wench with the mealy mouth that will never tire is my wife, I can tell you; here's Hodge, my man and my foreman; here's Firk, my fine firking journey-man, and this is blubbered Jane. All we come to be suitors for this honest Ralph. Keep him at home, and as I am a true shoemaker and a gentleman of the Gentle Craft, buy spurs yourselves, and I'll find ye boots these seven years.

MARGERY: Seven years, husband?

EYRE: Peace, midriff, peace! I know what I do. Peace!

FIRK: Truly, master cormorant, you shall do God good service to let Ralph and his wife stay together. She's a young new-married woman; if you take her husband away from her a night, you undo her; she may beg in the daytime; for he's as good a workman at a prick and an awl, as any is in our trade.

JANE: O let him stay, else I shall be undone.

FIRK: Ay, truly, she shall be laid at one side like a pair of old shoes else, and be occupied for no use.

LACY: Truly, my friends, it lies not in my power:
The Londoners are pressed, paid, and set forth
By the lord mayor, I cannot change a man.

HODGE: Why then you were as good be a corporal as a colonel, if you cannot discharge one good fellow; and I tell you true, I think you do more than you can answer, to press a man within a year and a day of his marriage.

EYRE: Well said, melancholy Hodge; gramercy, my fine foreman.

MARGERY: Truly, gentlemen, it were ill done for such as you, to stand so stiffly against a poor young wife; considering her case, she is new-married, but let that pass: I pray, deal not roughly with her; her husband is a young man, and but newly entered, but let that pass.

EYRE: Away with your pishery-pashery, your pols and your edi-pols! Peace, midriff; silence, Cicely Bumtrinket! Let your head speak.

FIRK: Yea, and the horns too, master.

EYRE: Too soon, my fine Firk, too soon! Peace, scoundrels! See you this man? Captains, you will not release him? Well, let him go; he's a proper shot; let him vanish! Peace, Jane, dry up thy tears, they'll make his powder dankish. Take him, brave men; Hector of Troy was an hackney to him, Hercules and Termagant scoundrels, Prince Arthur's Roundtable—by the Lord of Ludgate—ne'er fed such a tall, such a dapper swordsman; by the life of Pharaoh, a brave resolute swordsman! Peace, Jane! I say no more, mad knaves.

FIRK: See, see, Hodge, how my master raves in commendation of Ralph.

HODGE: Ralph, th'art a gull, by this hand, an thou goest not.

ASKEW: I am glad, good master Eyre, it is my hap
To meet so resolute a soldier.
Trust me, for your report and love to him,
A common slight regard shall not respect him.

LACY: Is thy name Ralph?

RALPH: Yes, sir.

LACY: Give me thy hand;
Thou shalt not want, as I am a gentleman.
Woman, be patient; God, no doubt, will send
Thy husband safe again; but he must go,
His country's quarrel says it shall be so.

HODGE: Th'art a gull, by my stirrup, if thou dost not go. I will not have thee strike thy gimlet into these weak vessels; prick thine enemies, Ralph.

෨෩

LAURENCE STERNE [1713–1768]

TRISTRAM SHANDY, *1760, Book I, Chapters 1–5*

CHAPTER I

I wish either my father or my mother, or indeed both of them, as they were in duty both equally bound to it, had minded what they were about when they begot me; had they duly considered how much depended upon what they were then doing;—that not only the production of a rational Being was concerned in it, but that possibly the happy formation and temperature of his body, perhaps his genius and the very cast of his mind;—and, for aught they knew to the contrary, even the fortunes of his whole house might take their turn from the humours and dispositions which were then uppermost;—Had they duly weighed and considered all this, and proceeded accordingly,—I am verily persuaded I should have made a quite different figure in the world, from that in which the reader is likely to see me.—Believe me, good folks, this is not so inconsiderable a thing as many of you may think it; —you have all, I dare say, heard of the animal spirits, as how they are transfused from father to son, etc. etc.—and a great deal to that purpose:—Well, you may take my word, that nine parts in ten of a man's sense or his nonsense, his successes and miscarriages in this world depend upon their motions and activity, and the different tracts and trains you put them into, so that when they are once set a-going, whether right or wrong, 'tis not a halfpenny matter, —away they go clattering like hey-go mad; and by treading the same steps over and over again, they presently make a road of it, as plain and as smooth as a garden-walk, which, when they are once used to, the Devil himself sometimes shall not be able to drive them off it.

"Pray, my Dear," quoth my mother, "have you not forgot to wind up the clock?"——"Good G—!" cried my father, making an exclamation, but taking care to moderate his voice at the same time,—"Did ever woman, since the creation of the world, interrupt a man with such a silly question?" Pray, what was your father saying?—Nothing.

CHAPTER 2

—Then, positively, there is nothing in the question that I can see, either good or bad.—Then, let me tell you, Sir, it was a very

unseasonable question at least,—because it scattered and dispersed
the animal spirits, whose business it was to have escorted and gone
hand in hand with the Homunculus, and conducted him safe to
the place destined for his reception.

The Homunculus, Sir, in however low and ludicrous a light
he may appear, in this age of levity, to the eye of folly or prejudice;
—to the eye of reason in scientific research, he stands confessed—
a Being guarded and circumscribed with rights.—The minutest
philosophers who, by the bye, have the most enlarged understand-
ings, (their souls being inversely as their enquiries) shew us incon-
testably, that the Homunculus is created by the same hand,—en-
gendered in the same course of nature,—endowed with the same
locomotive powers and faculties with us:—That he consists as we
do, of skin, hair, fat, flesh, veins, arteries, ligaments, nerves, cartilages, bones, marrow, brains, glands, genitals, humours, and artic-
ulations;—is a Being of as much activity,—and, in all senses of the
word, as much and as truly our fellowcreature as my Lord Chancellor of England.—He may be benefited,—he may be injured,—
he may obtain redress;—in a word, he has all the claims and rights
of humanity, which Tully, Puffendorf, or the best ethic writers
allow to arise out of that state and relation.

Now, dear Sir, what if any accident had befallen him in his
way alone!—or that, through terror of it, natural to so young a
traveller, my little Gentleman had got to his journey's end miser-
ably spent;—his muscular strength and virility worn down to a
thread;—his own animal spirits ruffled beyond description,—and
that in this sad disordered state of nerves, he had lain down a prey
to sudden starts, or a series of melancholy dreams and fancies, for
nine long, long months together.—I tremble to think what a foun-
dation had been laid for a thousand weaknesses both of body and
mind, which no skill of the physician or the philosopher could ever
afterwards have set thoroughly to rights.

CHAPTER 3

To my uncle Mr. Toby Shandy do I stand indebted for the pre-
ceding anecdote, to whom my father, who was an excellent natural
philosopher, and much given to close reasoning upon the smallest
matters, had oft, and heavily complained of the injury; but once
more particularly, as my uncle Toby well remembered, upon his
observing a most unaccountable obliquity, (as he called it) in my
manner of setting up my top, and justifying the principles upon
which I had done it,—the old gentleman shook his head, and in a
tone more expressive by half of sorrow than reproach,—he said
his heart all along foreboded, and he saw it verified in this, and
from a thousand other observations he had made upon me, That
I should neither think nor act like any other man's child:—"But
alas!" continued he, shaking his head a second time, and wiping
away a tear which was trickling down his cheeks, "My Tristram's
misfortunes began nine months before ever he came into the
world."

—My mother, who was sitting by, looked up,—but she knew
no more than her backside what my father meant,—but my uncle,
Mr. Toby Shandy, who had been often informed of the affair,—
understood him very well.

CHAPTER 4

I know there are readers in the world, as well as many other good
people in it, who are no readers at all,—who find themselves ill at
ease, unless they are let into the whole secret from first to last, of
everything which concerns you.

It is in pure compliance with this humour of theirs, and from
a backwardness in my nature to disappoint any one soul living,
that I have been so very particular already. As my life and opinions
are likely to make some noise in the world, and if I conjecture
right, will take in all ranks, professions, and denominations of men

whatever,—be no less read than the *Pilgrim's Progress* itself—and in the end, prove the very thing which Montaigne dreaded his Essays should turn out, that is, a book for a parlour-window;—I find it necessary to consult every one a little in his turn; and therefore must beg pardon for going on a little further in the same way: For which cause, right glad I am, that I have begun the history of myself in the way I have done; and that I am able to go on, tracing every thing in it, as Horace says, *ab Ovo*.

Horace, I know does not recommend this fashion altogether: But that gentleman is speaking only of an epic poem or a tragedy; —(I forget which,)—besides, if it was not so, I should beg Mr. Horace's pardon;—for in writing what I have set about, I shall confine myself neither to his rules, nor to any man's rules that ever lived.

To such, however, as do not choose to go so far back into these things, I can give no better advice, than that they skip over the remaining part of this chapter; for I declare beforehand, 'tis wrote only for the curious and inquisitive.

—————————————Shut the door———————————

I was begot in the night, betwixt the first Sunday and the first Monday in the month of March, in the year of our Lord one thousand seven hundred and eighteen. I am positive I was,—But how I came to be so very particular in my account of a thing which happened before I was born, is owing to another small anecdote known only in our own family, but now made public for the better clearing up this point.

My father, you must know, who was originally a Turkey merchant, but had left off business for some years, in order to retire to, and die upon, his paternal estate in the county of ———, was, I believe, one of the most regular men in everything he did, whether 'twas matter of business, or matter of amusement, that ever lived. As a small specimen of this extreme exactness of his, to which he was in truth a slave,—he had made it a rule for many years of his life—on the first Sunday-night of every month throughout the whole year,—as certain as ever the Sunday-night came,—to wind up a large house-clock, which we had standing on the back-stairs head, with his own hands:—And being somewhere between fifty and sixty years of age at the time I have been speaking of,—he had likewise gradually brought some other little family concernments to the same period, in order, as he would often say to my uncle Toby, to get them all out of the way at one time, and be no more plagued and pestered with them the rest of the month.

It was attended with but one misfortune, which, in a great measure, fell upon myself, and the effects of which I fear I shall carry with me to my grave; namely, that from an unhappy association of ideas, which have no connection in nature, it so fell out at length, that my poor mother could never hear the said clock wound up,—but the thoughts of some other things unavoidably popped into her head—and *vice versâ*:—Which strange combination of ideas, the sagacious Locke, who certainly understood the nature of these things better than most men, affirms to have produced more wry actions than all other sources of prejudice whatsoever.

But this by the bye.

Now it appears by a memorandum in my father's pocket-book, which now lies upon the table, "That on Lady-day, which was on the 25th of the same month in which I date my geniture, —my father set out upon his journey to London, with my eldest brother Bobby, to fix him at Westminster school"; and, as it appears from the same authority, "That he did not get down to his wife and family till the second week in May following,"—it brings the thing almost to a certainty. However, what follows in the beginning of the next chapter, puts it beyond all possibility of doubt.

—But pray, Sir, What was your father doing all December, —January, and February?—Why, Madam,—he was all that time afflicted with a Sciatica.

CHAPTER 5

On the fifth day of November, 1718, which to the era fixed on, was as near nine calendar months as any husband could in reason have expected,—was I Tristram Shandy, Gentleman, brought forth into this scurvy and disastrous world of ours.—I wish I had been born in the Moon, or in any of the planets, (except Jupiter or Saturn, because I never could bear cold weather) for it could not well have fared worse with me in any of them (though I will not answer for Venus) than it has in this vile, dirty planet of ours, —which, o' my conscience, with reverence be it spoken, I take to be made up of the shreds and clippings of the rest;—not but the planet is well enough, provided a man could be born in it to a great title or to a great estate; or could any how contrive to be called up to public charges, and employments of dignity or power; —but that is not my case;—and therefore every man will speak of the fair as his own market has gone in it;—for which cause I affirm it over again to be one of the vilest worlds that ever was made;—for I can truly say, that from the first hour I drew my breath in it, to this, that I can now scarce draw it at all, for an asthma I got in skating against the wind in Flanders;—I have been the continual sport of what the world calls Fortune; and though I will not wrong her by saying, She has ever made me feel the weight of any great or signal evil;—yet with all the good temper in the world, I affirm it of her, that in every stage of my life, and at every turn and corner where she could get fairly at me, the ungracious duchess has pelted me with a set of as pitiful misadventures and cross accidents as ever small Hero sustained.

☙

HERMAN MELVILLE [1819–1891]

MOBY DICK, *1851, Chapter 40*

HEADS OR TAILS

"De balena vero sufficit, si rex habeat caput, et regina caudam."[9]

BRACTON, *l. 3, c. 3.*

Latin from the books of the Laws of England, which taken along with the context, means, that of all whales captured by anybody on the coast of that land, the King, as Honorary Grand Harpooneer, must have the head, and the Queen be respectfully presented with the tail. A division which, in the whale, is much like halving an apple; there is no intermediate remainder. Now as this law, under a modified form, is to this day in force in England; and as it offers in various respects a strange anomaly touching the general law of Fast and Loose-Fish, it is here treated of in a separate chapter, on the same courteous principle that prompts the English railways to be at the expense of a separate car, specially reserved for the accommodation of royalty. In the first place, in curious proof of the fact that the above-mentioned law is still in force, I proceed to lay before you a circumstance that happened within the last two years.

It seems that some honest mariners of Dover, or Sandwich, or some one of the Cinque Ports, had after a hard chase succeeded in killing and beaching a fine whale which they had originally descried afar off from the shore. Now the Cinque Ports are partially or somehow under the jurisdiction of a sort of policeman or beadle, called a Lord Warden. Holding the office directly from the crown, I believe, all the royal emoluments incident to the Cinque Port

[9] "As for the whale, if the king have the head and the queen the tail, nothing more really need be said."

territories become by assignment his. By some writers this office is called a sinecure. But not so. Because the Lord Warden is busily employed at times in fobbing his perquisites; which are his chiefly by virtue of that same fobbing of them.

Now when these poor sun-burnt mariners, bare-footed, and with their trowsers rolled high up on their eely legs, had wearily hauled their fat fish high and dry, promising themselves a good £150 from the precious oil and bone; and in fantasy sipping rare tea with their wives, and good ale with their cronies, upon the strength of their respective shares; up steps a very learned and most Christian and charitable gentleman, with a copy of Blackstone under his arm; and laying it upon the whale's head, he says —"Hands off! this fish, my masters, is a Fast-Fish. I seize it as the Lord Warden's." Upon this the poor mariners in their respectful consternation—so truly English—knowing not what to say, fall to vigorously scratching their heads all round; meanwhile ruefully glancing from the whale to the stranger. But that did in nowise mend the matter, or at all soften the hard heart of the learned gentleman with the copy of Blackstone. At length one of them, after long scratching about for his ideas, made bold to speak.

"Please, sir, who is the Lord Warden?"

"The Duke."

"But the Duke had nothing to do with taking this fish?"

"It is his."

"We have been at great trouble, and peril, and some expense, and is all that to go to the Duke's benefit; we getting nothing at all for our pains but our blisters?"

"It is his."

"Is the Duke so very poor as to be forced to this desperate mode of getting a livelihood?"

"It is his."

"I thought to relieve my old bed-ridden mother by part of my share of this whale."

"It is his."

"Won't the Duke be content with a quarter or a half?"

"It is his."

In a word, the whale was seized and sold, and his Grace the Duke of Wellington received the money. Thinking that viewed in some particular lights, the case might by a bare possibility in some small degree be deemed, under the circumstances, a rather hard one, an honest clergyman of the town respectfully addressed a note to his Grace, begging him to take the case of those unfortunate mariners into full consideration. To which my Lord Duke in substance replied (both letters were published) that he had already done so, and received the money, and would be obliged to the reverend gentleman if for the future he (the reverend gentleman) would decline meddling with other people's business. Is this the still militant old man, standing at the corners of the three kingdoms, on all hands coercing alms of beggars?

It will readily be seen that in this case the alleged right of the Duke to the whale was a delegated one from the Sovereign. We must needs inquire then on what principle the Sovereign is originally invested with that right. The law itself has already been set forth. But Plowdon gives us the reason for it. Says Plowdon, the whale so caught belongs to the King and Queen, "because of its superior excellence." And by the soundest commentators this has ever been held a cogent argument in such matters.

But why should the King have the head, and the Queen the tail? A reason for that, ye lawyers!

In his treatise on "Queen-Gold," or Queen-pin-money, an old King's Bench author, one William Prynne, thus discourseth: "Ye tail is ye Queen's, that ye Queen's wardrobe may be supplied with ye whalebone." Now this was written at a time when the black limber bone of the Greenland or Right Whale was largely used in ladies' bodices. But this same bone is not in the tail; it is in the head, which is a sad mistake for a sagacious lawyer like

Prynne. But is the Queen a mermaid, to be presented with a tail? An allegorical meaning may lurk here.

There are two royal fish so styled by the English law writers —the whale and the sturgeon; both royal property under certain limitations, and nominally supplying the tenth branch of the crown's ordinary revenue. I know not that any other author has hinted of the matter; but by inference it seems to me that the sturgeon must be divided in the same way as the whale, the King receiving the highly dense and elastic head peculiar to that fish, which, symbolically regarded, may possibly be humorously grounded upon some presumed congeniality. And thus there seems a reason in all things, even in law.

JAMES JOYCE [1882–1941]

Excerpt from ULYSSES, *1922, Chapter 7*

Our travellers reached the rustic hostelry and alighted from their palfreys.

—Ho, varlet! cried he, who by his mien seemed the leader of the party. Saucy knave! To us!

So saying he knocked loudly with his swordhilt upon the open lattice.

Mine host came forth at the summons girding him with his tabard.

—Give you good den, my masters, said he with an obsequious bow.

—Bestir thyself, sirrah! cried he who had knocked. Look to our steeds. And for ourselves give us of your best for ifaith we need it.

—Lackaday, good masters, said the host, my poor house has but a bare larder. I know not what to offer your lordships.

—How now, fellow? cried the second of the party, a man of pleasant countenance, so servest thou the king's messengers, Master Taptun?

An instantaneous change overspread the landlord's visage.

—Cry you mercy, gentlemen, he said humbly. An you be the king's messengers (God shield His Majesty!) you shall not want for aught. The king's friends (God bless His Majesty!) shall not go afasting in my house I warrant me.

—Then about! cried the traveller who had not spoken, a lusty trencherman by his aspect. Hast aught to give us?

—What say you, good masters, to a squab pigeon pasty, some collops of venison, a saddle of veal, widgeon with crisp hog's bacon, a boar's head with pistachios, a bason of jolly custard, a medlar tansy and a flagon of old Rhenish?

—Gadzooks! cried the last speaker. That likes me well. Pistachios!

—Aha! cried he of the pleasant countenance. A poor house and a bare larder, quotha! 'Tis a merry rogue.

Exercises

1. Describe in the manner of Rabelais an encounter with a jive-talker, or with a professor of sociology.

2. Describe in the manner of Rabelais a student rally protesting the dismissal of a popular teacher or the cancellation of a speech by a controversial public figure.

Confine your exuberance to two pages, unless you make a list that extends it beyond reason.

SOME VICTORIAN STYLES

*And there are other memories, more recent:
the house where lived the thundering and
growling prophet of the Hero [Carlyle]. (A
curse has fallen on it: it has become a museum.)
But all the houses around it are still living. . . .*

*They are living, but there is about them
such a wish for peace and quiet that it seems
that in this corner of the city abysses of silence
separate all objects one from another, even the
closest. In the eighteenth century, pottery was
made here; now, with infinite care, the
inhabitants cultivate a precious thing, silence.
Here, everything is apart from everything else:
the gardens, the city trees with their coating of
damp soot, the chapels, the hospitals, the cab
rank, all these things exist noiselessly, without
a sound to call their activity to the attention of
the passer-by. Everything is solitary and
discreet; even the colors are quiet, and have to
be looked at more attentively than elsewhere;
and only very close, and only on sunny days,
can one see that the bridge, swung between its
high pillars like a double garland from one bank
to the other, is painted green. And the river is
indistinguishable from the fog except as a dim
glow of silver or of copper, according to
the time of day. . . .*

VALERY LARBAUD
Beauté, Mon Beau Souci, 1920

꧁ VIRGINIA WOOLF, an excellent minor novelist who strained her talent in vain efforts to be a major one, was perhaps at her best as a critic. Certainly she was bookish; her minor but exquisite novel *Orlando* (1928), which she called a biography, is more than anything else a glittering diadem of critical diamonds, with which may her head be enhaloed forever. How's that for schmaltzy? "Critical diamonds," indeed! Have you ever seen a critical diamond? That is the worst kind of fancy journalese, worthy of a staff book reviewer for *The New York Times*. And what unpragmatic emptiness, what mere bombastic vanity, is the clause "with which may her head be enhaloed forever"! The series begun with "novel" and continued with "biography" should have been concluded, simply and appropriately, with "book of criticism." But I momentarily lost my sense of propriety and my sense of silliness, being carried away by emotion—for I love Virginia Woolf. I love particularly the end of Chapter 4 of *Orlando*, and the beginning of Chapter 5. At the end of Chapter 4 she tells how, with the first stroke of midnight on December 31, 1799, Orlando noticed in the clear and sparkling sky a small cloud behind the dome of St. Paul's; and how it spread rapidly until by the time the twelfth stroke sounded all England was blanketed with impenetrable fog: "The eighteenth century was over; the nineteenth century had begun." At the beginning of Chapter 5 she tells how the clear, light air and brilliant sunshine of the eighteenth century gave way to the clinging mists, dripping walls and insistent mildew of the nineteenth:

> Thus, stealthily and imperceptibly, none marking the exact day or hour of the change, the constitution of England was altered and nobody knew it. Everywhere the effects were felt. The hardy country gentleman, who had sat down gladly to a meal of ale and beef in a room designed, perhaps by the brothers Adam, with classic dignity, now felt chilly. Rugs appeared, beards were grown and trousers fastened tight under the instep. The chill which he felt in his legs he soon transferred to his house; furniture was muffled; walls and tables were covered too. Then a change of diet became essential. The muffin was invented, and the crumpet. Coffee supplanted the after-dinner port, and, as coffee led to a drawing-room in which to drink it, and a drawing-room to glass cases, and glass cases to artificial flowers, and artificial flowers to mantelpieces, and mantelpieces to pianofortes, and pianofortes to drawing-room ballads, and drawing-room ballads (skipping a stage or two) to innumerable little dogs, mats, and antimacassars, the home—which had become extremely important—was completely altered.
>
> Outside the house—it was another effect of the damp— ivy grew in unparalleled profusion. Houses that had been of bare stone were smothered in greenery. No garden, however formal its original design, lacked a shrubbery, a wilderness, a maze. What light penetrated to the bedrooms where children were born was naturally of an obfusc green and what light penetrated to the drawing-rooms where grown men and women lived came through curtains of brown and purple plush. But the change did not stop at outward things. The damp struck within. Men felt the chill in their hearts; the damp in their minds. In a desperate effort to snuggle their feelings into some sort of warmth one subterfuge was tried after another. Love, birth, and death were all swaddled in a variety of fine phrases. The sexes drew further and further apart. No open conversation was tolerated. Evasions and concealments were assiduously practised on both

sides. And just as the ivy and the evergreen rioted in the damp earth outside, so did the same fertility show itself within. The life of the average woman was a succession of childbirths. She married at nineteen and had fifteen or eighteen children by the time she was thirty; for twins abounded. Thus the British Empire came into existence; and thus—for there is no stopping damp; it gets into the inkpot as it gets into the woodwork— sentences swelled, adjectives multiplied, lyrics became epics, and little trifles that had been essays a column long were now encyclopaedias in ten or twenty volumes.

In the passages that follow we shall see some of the grotesque and swollen forms taken by some of the sentences of some of the Victorians, and try to feel our way through the mists that rose from them. Mark Twain, recounting his dangerous experiences as a steamboat pilot on the often fogbound Mississippi, said, "A gray mist would tangle the head of the oldest man that ever lived."

Of course Mrs. Woolf exaggerates, and we must not take her metaphor as anything more than a metaphor. *Orlando* is after all a work of imaginative humor, not of literal truth. Not all Victorian writers were turgid and swollen in their prose; many of them, such as John Stuart Mill, Herbert Spencer and Charles Darwin, wrote with a fine dry clarity and exactitude; but we don't customarily think of these as "Victorians." This fact indicates the prevalent subjectivity with which we use the term.

Victoria lived from 1819 to 1901, and was Queen of England from 1837 to 1901. The Oxford English Dictionary defines a Victorian as "a person who lived in or has the characteristics typical of the reign of Queen Victoria," but it doesn't say what those characteristics are; certainly, with regard to writers, the only objective thing we can say is that a Victorian writer was a writer who wrote between 1837 and 1901. In terms of chronology, the witty Oscar Wilde (1854–1900) was at least as much a Victorian as the earnest Alfred Tennyson (1809–1892); the agnostic Thomas

Henry Huxley (1825–1895) was at least as much a Victorian as the undoubting Thomas Carlyle (1795–1881); the tripping W. S. Gilbert (1836–1911) was at least as much a Victorian as the tramping Rudyard Kipling (1865–1936); and that ineffable bowdlerizer Dr. Thomas Bowdler (1754–1825) was not a Victorian at all.

But we hardly ever use the term in its merely chronological sense. Tennyson's *Idylls of the King*, Fitzgerald's version of *The Rubáiyát of Omar Khayyám*, Darwin's *The Origin of Species* and Mill's *On Liberty* were all published in 1859; when we apply the adjective "Victorian" to the first of these books but not to the other three, we designate by it a state of mind rather than a period of time. That is to say, of all the states of mind that existed during the period from 1837 to 1901, we have chosen one to call "Victorian," to the exclusion of all others; and of all the styles in which writers wrote between 1837 and 1901, we have chosen a few with certain features in common to call "Victorian." These styles, as we might expect, are the ones with the most obviously imitable features; in this chapter, therefore, and for no other reason, I shall respect the cliché notion that equates Victorianism with harrumphing, borborygmic and eructant bombast.

What we call the Victorian attitude was Queen Victoria's own attitude. Because of her position as the leader of society it had more influence than it could possibly have achieved on its merits, which were at best almost invisible. Her favorite pieces of music by Gilbert's partner Sir Arthur Sullivan were "Onward Christian Soldiers" and "The Lost Chord"; she told him that a man who could write such magnificent serious music shouldn't waste his time and talent writing comic operas; when he sat at her piano one evening and played and sang

> *I am the monarch of the sea,*
> *The ruler of the Queen's Navee,*

she chilled his blood by saying, "We are not amused"; and what are we to think of the intellect or taste of a woman who in all seriousness called piano legs "piano limbs"?

What we call the Victorian styles are the styles that that woman liked.

By 1901 most adults of intellect and taste had had enough of Queen Victoria's attitude, and of the styles it encouraged; a reaction against them had already begun, and in 1918 the ironic anti-Victorianism of many late Victorians achieved perfect expression in Lytton Strachey's delightful *Eminent Victorians*. Mrs. Woolf (1882–1941) was a lifelong friend and admirer of Strachey (1880–1932)—in fact, she had at one time been engaged to marry him—and there can be no doubt that each helped the other outgrow the period they had outlived. We still share their view of the period—a partial view that omits many clear thinkers and many wanderings into clarity by thinkers who walked by preference in fog.

The contradictions of the Victorian period are plainly evident in the close personal friendship of Carlyle and Mill, who differed radically (look up this word) in their social attitudes, and whose literary styles embody the difference. Mill, recommending in his autobiography the scholastic logic he had studied under his father's direction, said, "I am persuaded that nothing, in modern education, tends so much, when properly used, to form exact thinkers, who attach a precise meaning to words and propositions, and are not imposed on by vague, loose, or ambiguous terms." But Carlyle called logicians "logic-choppers," and dismissed the study of social and economic facts as "the dismal science." He preferred exhortation; he was a great thrower-around of vague, loose, and ambiguous terms.

It was easy to be imposed on by the hortatory Victorians, for they cultivated an imposing manner. Their orchestration ran to brasses and kettledrums. Carlyle put on the title page of *Past and Present*, as epigraph, Schiller's resounding line, "Life is earnest"; Longfellow added, "Let us then be up and doing," and "Excelsior!" and Tennyson changed Dante's Ulysses, a conscience-less adventurer (*Inferno*, XXVI), into a Victorian yachtsman who has had one drink too many. The image that floats before my eyes is a blend of Sir Thomas Lipton, Commander Schweppes, Colonel Finger-Lickin' Good, and Lord Alfred himself.

I said a couple of paragraphs back that some foggy Victorian writers occasionally wandered into clarity. There is a corollary: even the clearest writers of the Victorian age sometimes wandered into the prevailing fog and got involved in tortuous inversions and clumsy interpolations. John Stuart Mill, for example, in the admirably clear *On Liberty* (1859), says, "The time, it is to be hoped, is gone by, when any defence would be necessary of the 'liberty of the press' as one of the securities against corrupt or tyrannical government. . . . and, speaking generally, it is not, in constitutional countries, to be apprehended, that the government, whether completely responsible to the people or not, will often attempt to control the expression of opinion, except when in doing so it makes itself the organ of the general intolerance of the public." And Anthony Trollope, who wrote the travel-book *North America* (1862) in good simple journalistic prose, not journalese, nevertheless got twisted around backwards in the art gallery at West Point: "There were some copies from well-known works of art of very high excellence, when the age is taken into account of those by whom they were done."

"When any defence would be necessary of"! "When the age is taken into account of"! "It is not, in constitutional countries, to be apprehended"! Such squirming indirection just isn't English! Perhaps this clumsiness was due to what Mrs. Woolf called the obfusc light of the period. Personally I think it was due to an epidemic Victorian cold in the head. Henry James, as, in due course, we, I, looking, how disconsolately and, indeed, I think I may add, distractedly, soever, somewhat ahead, do now, albeit with a heart that may, all things considered, be termed, to say the least, heavy, in good faith, promise you, shall see, had, at the end of the period, a cold that developed, I think it would not, on balance, be excessive to say, into pneumonia.

Let us therefore drily and soberly analyze some of the drippier Victorian styles. This term does not apply to the passages from *Bleak House,* which represent Dickens at the height of his genius; it does apply to the chapter from *The Old Curiosity Shop.*

☙

THOMAS CARLYLE [1795–1881]

Excerpts from PAST AND PRESENT, *1843, Book I, Chapter 2, "The Sphinx"*

Foolish men imagine that because judgment for an evil thing is delayed, there is no justice, but an accidental one, here below. Judgment for an evil thing is many times delayed some day or two, some century or two, but it is sure as life, it is sure as death! In the centre of the world-whirlwind, verily now as in the oldest days, dwells and speaks a God. The great soul of the world is *just.* O brother, can it be needful now, at this late epoch of experience, after eighteen centuries of Christian preaching for one thing, to remind thee of such a fact; which all manner of Mahometans, old Pagan Romans, Jews, Scythians and heathen Greeks, and indeed more or less all men that God made, have managed at one time to see into; nay which thou thyself, till "redtape" strangled the inner life of thee, hadst once some inkling of: That there *is* justice here below; and even, at bottom, that there is nothing else but justice! Forget that, thou hast forgotten all. Success will never more attend thee: how can it now? Thou hast the whole Universe against thee. No more success: mere sham-success, for a day and days; rising ever higher,—towards its Tarpeian Rock [a cliff from which the ancient Romans threw traitors]. . . .

In this God's-world, with its wild-whirling eddies and mad foam-oceans, where men and nations perish as if without law, and judgment for an unjust thing is sternly delayed, dost thou think that therefore there is no justice? It is what the fool hath said in his heart. It is what the wise, in all times, were wise because they denied, and knew forever not to be. I tell thee again, there is nothing else but justice. One strong thing I find here below: the just thing, the true thing. My friend, if thou hadst all the artillery of Woolwich [formerly an arsenal and a school where cadets were trained for the Royal Artillery] trundling at thy back in support of an unjust thing; and infinite bonfires visibly waiting ahead of thee, to blaze centuries long for thy victory on behalf of it,—I would advise thee to call halt, to fling down thy baton, and say, "In God's name, No!" Thy "success"? Poor devil, what will thy success amount to? If the thing is unjust, thou hast not succeeded; no, not though bonfires blazed from North to South, and bells rang, and editors wrote leading-articles, and the just thing lay trampled out of sight, to all mortal eyes an abolished and anni-hilated thing! Success? In a few years thou wilt be dead and dark, —all cold, eyeless, deaf; no blaze of bonfires, ding-dong of bells or leading-articles visible or audible to thee again at all forever: What kind of success is that!—

Here we have a prize exam-ple of what Mrs. Woolf was talking about: the Victorian tur-gidity at its worst. This rhodomontade might be recited with equal conviction by representatives of all sides in any controversy. What makes it empty is the fact that the word "justice" is not defined in terms of any particular kind of action. Only when we know what concrete actions a man considers just do we know what he means when he utters the word "justice"; and unless our use of such a word clearly implies acts of certain kinds, and precludes acts of certain other kinds, it is vague, loose, and ambiguous. We could never guess, from the passage we have just read, that Carlyle was a defender of slavery in America, an apologist for the serfdom that followed the Norman conquest of England, an opponent of every effort to legislate some improvement in the cruel conditions of labor in Victorian England (which in fact were not improved except by legislation), and an authoritarian who in the most explicit terms condemned representative government and personal freedom. Only when he gets down to such particular cases do we see what he means by "justice." He thinks it would be unjust, for example, for Parliament to interpose legal restraints between any Victorian manufacturer and the little children who worked fourteen hours a day for him. "Think, how were it, stoodst thou suddenly in his shoes!" he says. The mingling of archaisms such as "thou," "thy" and "thee" with modern clichés such as "redtape" and "in his shoes" is one of the things that make Carlyle all but unreadable today. The subjunctive "how were it," the interjected "Nay," and such odd hyphenizations as "sham-success" and "God's-world" contribute to the total effect of bombastic fakery.

From Book III, Chapter 11, "Labour"

For there is a perennial nobleness, and even sacredness, in Work. Were he never so benighted, forgetful of his high calling, there is always hope in a man that actually and earnestly works: in Idleness alone is there perpetual despair. Work, never so Mammonish-mean, *is* in communication with Nature; the real desire to get Work done will itself lead one more and more to truth, to Nature's appointments and regulations, which are truth.

The latest Gospel in this world is, Know thy work and do it.

"Know thyself": long enough has that poor "self" of thine tormented thee; thou wilt never get to "know" it, I believe! Think it not thy business, this of knowing thyself; thou art an unknowable individual: know what thou canst work at; and work at it, like a Hercules! That will be thy better plan.

It has been written, "an endless significance lies in Work"; a man perfects himself by working. Foul jungles are cleared away, fair seedfields rise instead, and stately cities; and withal the man himself first ceases to be a jungle and foul unwholesome desert thereby. Consider how, even in the meanest sorts of Labour, the whole soul of a man is composed into a kind of real harmony, the instant he sets himself to work! Doubt, Desire, Sorrow, Remorse, Indignation, Despair itself, all these like helldogs lie beleaguering the soul of the poor dayworker, as of every man: but he bends himself with free valour against his task, and all these are stilled, all these shrink murmuring far off into their caves. The man is now a man. The blessed glow of Labour in him, is it not as purifying fire, wherein all poison is burnt up, and of sour smoke itself there is made bright blessed flame!

Destiny, on the whole, has no other way of cultivating us. A formless Chaos, once set it *revolving*, grows round and ever rounder; ranges itself, by mere force of gravity, into strata, spherical courses; is no longer a Chaos, but a round compacted World. What would become of the Earth, did she cease to revolve? In the poor old Earth, so long as she revolves, all inequalities, irregularities disperse themselves; all irregularities are incessantly becoming regular. Hast thou looked on the Potter's wheel, —one of the venerablest objects; old as the prophet Ezechiel and far older? Rude lumps of clay, how they spin themselves up, by mere quick whirling, into beautiful circular dishes. And fancy the most assiduous Potter, but without his wheel; reduced to make dishes, or rather amorphous botches, by mere kneading and baking! Even such a Potter were Destiny, with a human soul that would rest and lie at ease, that would not work and spin! Of an idle unrevolving man the kindest Destiny, like the most assiduous Potter without wheel, can bake and knead nothing other than a botch; let her spend on him what expensive colouring, what gilding and enamelling she will, he is but a botch. Not a dish; no, a bulging, kneaded, crooked, shambling, squint-cornered, amorphous botch,—a mere enamelled vessel of dishonour! Let the idle think of this.

Blessed is he who has found his work; let him ask no other blessedness. He has a work, a life-purpose; he has found it, and will follow it! How, as a free-flowing channel, dug and torn by noble force through the sour mud-swamp of one's existence, like an ever-deepening river there, it runs and flows;—draining off the sour festering water, gradually from the root of the remotest grass-blade; making, instead of pestilential swamp, a green fruitful meadow with its clear-flowing stream. How blessed for the meadow itself, let the stream and *its* value be great or small! Labour is Life: from the inmost heart of the Worker rises his god-given Force, the sacred celestial Life-essence breathed into him by Almighty God; from his inmost heart awakens him to all nobleness,—to all knowledge, "self-knowledge" and much else, as soon as Work fitly begins. Knowledge? The knowledge that will hold good in working, cleave thou to that; for Nature herself accredits that, says Yea to that. Properly thou hast no other knowledge but what thou hast got by working: the rest is all yet a hypothesis of knowledge; a thing to be argued of in schools, a thing floating in the clouds, in endless logic-vortices, till we try it and fix it. "Doubt, of whatever kind, can be ended by Action alone."

Carlyle is brilliantly parodied by Joyce in Chapter 14 of *Ulysses*. See pages 201–203, and compare the passage quoted there with the passage you have just read.

CHARLES DICKENS [1812–1870]

Excerpts from THE MUDFOG PAPERS, *1880, Chapter 1 (first published in* BENTLEY'S MISCELLANY, *1837)*

Mudfog is a pleasant town—a remarkably pleasant town—situated in a charming hollow by the side of a river, from which river, Mudfog derives an agreeable scent of pitch, tar, coals, and rope-yarn, a roving population in oil-skin hats, a pretty steady influx of drunken bargemen, and a great many other maritime advantages. There is a good deal of water about Mudfog, and yet it is not exactly the sort of town for a watering-place, either. Water is a perverse sort of element at the best of times, and in Mudfog it is particularly so. In Winter, it comes oozing down the streets and tumbling over the fields,—nay, rushes into the very cellars and kitchens of the houses, with a lavish prodigality that might well be dispensed with; but in the hot summer weather it *will* dry up, and turn green: and, although green is a very good colour in its way, especially in grass, still it certainly is not becoming to water; and it cannot be denied that the beauty of Mudfog is rather impaired, even by this trifling circumstance. Mudfog is a healthy place —very healthy;—damp, perhaps, but none the worse for that. It's quite a mistake to suppose that damp is unwholesome: plants thrive best in damp situations, and why shouldn't men? The inhabitants of Mudfog are unanimous in asserting that there exists not a finer race of people on the face of the earth; here we have an indisputable and veracious contradiction of the vulgar error at once. So, admitting Mudfog to be damp, we distinctly state that it is salubrious. . . .

Now there happened to be in Mudfog, as somehow or other there does happen to be, in almost every town in the British dominions, and perhaps in foreign dominions too—we think it very likely, but, being no great traveller, cannot distinctly say—there happened to be, in Mudfog, a merry-tempered, pleasant-faced, good-for-nothing sort of vagabond, with an invincible dislike to manual labour, and an unconquerable attachment to strong beer and spirits, whom everybody knew, and nobody, except his wife, took the trouble to quarrel with, who inherited from his ancestors the appellation of Edward Twigger, and rejoiced in the *sobriquet* of Bottle-nosed Ned. He was drunk upon the average once a day, and penitent upon an equally fair calculation once a month; and when he was penitent, he was invariably in the very last stage of maudlin intoxication. He was a ragged, roving, roaring kind of fellow, with a burly form, a sharp wit, and a ready head, and could turn his hand to anything when he chose to do it. He was by no means opposed to hard labour on principle, for he would work away at a cricket-match by the day together,—running, and catching, and batting, and bowling, and revelling in toil which would exhaust a galley-slave. He would have been invaluable to a fire-office; never was a man with such a natural taste for pumping engines, running up ladders, and throwing furniture out of two-pair-of-stairs' windows: nor was this the only element in which he was at home; he was a humane society in himself, a portable drag, an animated life-preserver, and had saved more people, in his time, from drowning, than the Plymouth life-boat, or Captain Manby's apparatus. With all these qualifications, notwithstanding his dissipation, Bottle-nosed Ned was a general favourite; and the authorities of Mudfog, remembering his numerous services to the population, allowed him in return to get drunk in his own way, without the fear of stocks, fine, or imprisonment. He had a general license, and he showed his sense of the compliment by making the most of it.

Excerpt from BLEAK HOUSE, *1853, Chapter 1, "In Chancery"*

London. Michaelmas Term lately over, and the Lord Chancellor sitting in Lincoln's Inn Hall. Implacable November weather. As much mud in the streets, as if the waters had but newly retired from the face of the earth, and it would not be wonderful to meet a Megalosaurus, forty feet long or so, waddling like an elephantine lizard up Holborn Hill. Smoke lowering down from chimney-pots, making a soft black drizzle, with flakes of soot in it as big as full-grown snowflakes—gone into mourning, one might imagine, for the death of the sun. Dogs, undistinguishable in mire. Horses, scarcely better; splashed to their very blinkers. Foot passengers, jostling one another's umbrellas, in a general infection of ill-temper, and losing their foot-hold at street-corners, where tens of thousands of other foot-passengers have been slipping and sliding since the day broke (if this day ever broke), adding new deposits to the crust upon crust of mud, sticking at those points tenaciously to the pavement, and accumulating at compound interest.

Fog everywhere. Fog up the river, where it flows among green aits [islets] and meadows; fog down the river, where it rolls defiled among the tiers of shipping, and the waterside pollutions of a great (and dirty) city. Fog on the Essex marshes, fog on the Kentish heights. Fog creeping into the cabooses of collier-brigs; fog lying out on the yards [spars], and hovering in the rigging of great ships; fog drooping on the gunwales of barges and small boats. Fog in the eyes and throats of ancient Greenwich pensioners, wheezing by the firesides of their wards; fog in the stem and bowl of the afternoon pipe of the wrathful skipper, down in his close cabin; fog cruelly pinching the toes and fingers of his shivering little 'prentice boy on deck. Chance people on the bridges peeping over the parapets into a nether sky of fog, with fog all round them, as if they were up in a balloon, and hanging in the misty clouds.

Gas looming through the fog in divers places in the streets, much as the sun may, from the spongy fields, be seen to loom by husbandman and ploughboy. Most of the shops lighted two hours before their time—as the gas seems to know, for it has a haggard and unwilling look.

The raw afternoon is rawest, and the dense fog is densest, and the muddy streets are muddiest, near that leaden-headed old obstruction, appropriate ornament for the threshold of a leaden-headed old corporation [city government]: Temple Bar. And hard by Temple Bar, in Lincoln's Inn Hall, at the very heart of the fog, sits the Lord High Chancellor in his High Court of Chancery.

Never can there come fog too thick, never can there come mud and mire too deep, to assort with the groping and floundering condition which this High Court of Chancery, most pestilent of hoary sinners, holds, this day, in the sight of heaven and earth.

On such an afternoon, if ever, the Lord High Chancellor ought to be sitting here—as here he is—with a foggy glory round his head, softly fenced in with crimson cloth and curtains, addressed by a large advocate with great whiskers, a little voice, and an interminable brief, and outwardly directing his contemplation to the lantern in the roof, where he can see nothing but fog. On such an afternoon, some score of members of the High Court of Chancery bar ought to be—as here they are—mistily engaged in one of the ten thousand stages of an endless cause, tripping one another up on slippery precedents, groping knee-deep in technicalities, running their goat-hair and horse-hair warded heads against walls of words, and making a pretence of equity with serious faces, as players might. On such an afternoon, the various solicitors in the cause, some two or three of whom have inherited it from their fathers, who made a fortune by it, ought to be—as are they not?—ranged in a line, in a long matted well (but you might look in vain for Truth at the bottom of it), between the registrar's red table and the silk gowns [the Queen's Counsel], with bills, cross-bills, answers, rejoinders, injunctions, affidavits, issues, references to masters, masters' reports, mountains of costly nonsense, piled before them. Well may the court be dim, with wasting candles here and there; well may the fog hang heavy in it, as if it would never get out; well may the stained glass windows lose their colour, and admit no light of day into the place; well may the uninitiated from the streets, who peep in through the glass panes in the door, be deterred from entrance by its owlish aspect, and by the drawl languidly echoing to the roof from the padded dais where the Lord High Chancellor looks into the lantern that has no light in it, and where the attendant wigs are all stuck in a fog-bank! This is the Court of Chancery; which has its decaying houses and its blighted lands in every shire; which has its worn-out lunatic in every madhouse, and its dead in every churchyard; which has its ruined suitor, with his slipshod heels and thread-bare dress, borrowing and begging through the round of every man's acquaintance; which gives to monied might, the means abundantly of wearying out the right; which so exhausts finances, patience, courage, hope; so overthrows the brain and breaks the heart; that there is not an honourable man among its practitioners who would not give—who does not often give—the warning, "Suffer any wrong that can be done you, rather than come here!" . . .

Excerpt from Chapter 2, "In Fashion"

. . . Sir Leicester Dedlock is only a baronet, but there is no mightier baronet than he. His family is as old as the hills, and infinitely more respectable. He has a general opinion that the world might get on without hills, but would be done up without Dedlocks. He would on the whole admit Nature to be a good idea (a little low, perhaps, when not enclosed with a park-fence), but an idea dependent for its execution on your great county families. He is a gentleman of strict conscience, disdainful of all littleness and meanness [stinginess], and ready, on the shortest notice, to die any death you may please to mention rather than give occasion for the least impeachment of his integrity. He is

an honorable, obstinate, truthful, high-spirited, intensely preju-
diced, perfectly unreasonable man.

Sir Leicester is twenty years, full measure, older than my
Lady. He will never see sixty-five again, nor perhaps sixty-six,
nor yet sixty-seven. He has a twist of the gout now and then, and
walks a little stiffly. He is of a worthy presence, with his light
grey hair and whiskers, his fine shirt-frill, his pure white waistcoat,
and his blue coat with bright buttons always buttoned. He is ceremonious, stately, most polite on every occasion to my Lady, and
holds her personal attractions in the highest estimation. His gal-
lantry to my Lady, which has never changed since he courted her,
is the one little touch of romantic fancy in him.

Indeed, he married her for love. A whisper still goes about,
that she had not even family; howbeit, Sir Leicester had so much
family that perhaps he had enough, and could dispense with any
more. But she had beauty, pride, ambition, insolent resolve, and
sense enough to portion out a legion of fine ladies. Wealth and
station, added to these, soon floated her upward; and for years,
now, my Lady Dedlock has been at the centre of the fashionable
intelligence, and at the top of the fashionable tree.

How Alexander wept when he had no more worlds to conquer, everybody knows—or has some reason to know by this time,
the matter having been rather frequently mentioned. My Lady
Dedlock, having conquered *her* world, fell, not into the melting,
but rather into the freezing mood. An exhausted composure, a
worn-out placidity, an equanimity of fatigue not to be ruffled by
interest or satisfaction, are the trophies of her victory. She is perfectly well-bred. If she could be translated to Heaven to-morrow,
she might be expected to ascend without any rapture.

She has beauty still, and, if it be not in its heydey, it is not yet
in its autumn. She has a fine face—originally of a character that
would be rather called very pretty than handsome, but improved
into classicality by the acquired expression of her fashionable state.

Her figure is elegant, and has the effect of being tall. Not that she is so, but that "the most is made," as the Honourable Bob Stables has frequently asserted upon oath, "of all her points." The same authority observes, that she is perfectly got up; and remarks, in commendation of her hair especially, that she is the best-groomed woman in the whole stud.

With all her perfections on her head, my Lady Dedlock has come up from her place in Lincolnshire (hotly pursued by the fashionable intelligence), to pass a few days at her house in town previous to her departure for Paris, where her Ladyship intends to stay some weeks, after which her movements are uncertain. And at her house in town, upon this muddy, murky afternoon, presents himself an old-fashioned old gentleman, attorney-at-law, and eke solicitor of the High Court of Chancery, who has the honour of acting as legal adviser of the Dedlocks, and has as many cast-iron boxes in his office with that name outside, as if the present baronet were the coin of the conjuror's trick, and were constantly being juggled through the whole set. Across the hall, and up the stairs, and along the passages, and through the rooms, which are very brilliant in the season and very dismal out of it—Fairy-land to visit, but a desert to live in—the old gentleman is conducted, by a Mercury in powder [a footman in a powdered wig], to my Lady's presence.

The old gentleman is rusty to look at, but is reputed to have made good thrift out of aristocratic marriage settlements and aristocratic wills, and to be very rich. He is surrounded by a mysterious halo of family confidences; of which he is known to be the silent depository. There are noble Mausoleums rooted for centuries in retired glades of parks, among the growing timber and the fern, which perhaps hold fewer noble secrets than walk abroad among men, shut up in the breast of Mr. Tulkinghorn. He is of what is called the old school—a phrase generally meaning any school that seems never to have been young—and wears knee

breeches tied with ribbons, and gaiters or stockings. One peculiar-
ity of his black clothes, and of his black stockings, be they silk or
worsted, is, that they never shine. Mute, close, irresponsive to any
glancing light, his dress is like himself. He never converses, when
not professionally consulted. He is found sometimes, speechless
but quite at home, at corners of dinner-tables in great country
houses, and near doors of drawing-rooms, concerning which the
fashionable intelligence is eloquent: where everybody knows him,
and where half the Peerage stops to say "How do you do, Mr.
Tulkinghorn?" he receives these salutations with gravity, and
buries them along with the rest of his knowledge.

Sir Leicester Dedlock is with my Lady, and is happy to see
Mr. Tulkinghorn. There is an air of prescription about him which
is always agreeable to Sir Leicester; he receives it as a kind of tribute. He likes Mr. Tulkinghorn's dress; there is a kind of tribute
in that too. It is eminently respectable, and likewise, in a general
way, retainer-like. It expresses, as it were, the steward of the
legal mysteries, the butler of the legal cellar, of the Dedlocks.

Has Mr. Tulkinghorn any idea of this himself? It may be so,
or it may not; but there is this remarkable circumstance to be
noted in everything associated with my Lady Dedlock as one of
a class—as one of the leaders and representatives of her little world.
She supposes herself to be an inscrutable Being, quite out of the
reach and ken of ordinary mortals—seeing herself in her glass,
where indeed she looks so. Yet, every dim little star revolving about
her, from her maid to the manager of the Italian Opera, knows her
weaknesses, prejudices, follies, haughtinesses, and caprices; and
lives upon as accurate a calculation and as nice [exact] a measure
of her moral nature, as her dressmaker takes of her physical pro-
portions. Is a new dress, a new custom, a new singer, a new dancer,
a new form of jewellery, a new dwarf or giant, a new chapel, a new
anything, to be set up? There are deferential people, in a dozen
callings, whom my Lady Dedlock suspects of nothing but pros-

tration before her, who can tell you how to manage her as if she were a baby; who do nothing but nurse her all their lives; who, humbly affecting to follow with profound subservience, lead her and her whole troop after them; who, in hooking one, hook all and bear them off, as Lemuel Gulliver bore away the stately fleet of the majestic Lilliput. [Dickens nods here; see Chapter 5 of *Gulliver's Travels*, Book I.] "If you want to address our people, sir," say Blaze and Sparkle the jewellers—meaning by our people, Lady Dedlock and the rest—"you must remember that you are not dealing with the general public; you must hit our people in their weakest place, and their weakest place is such a place." "To make this article go down, gentlemen," say Sheen and Gloss the mercers, to their friends the manufacturers, "you must come to us, because we know where to have [how to take advantage of] the fashionable people, and we can make it fashionable." "If you want to get this print upon the tables of my high connexion, sir," says Mr. Sladdery the librarian [the book dealer], "or if you want to get this dwarf or giant into the houses of my high connexion, sir, or if you want to secure to this entertainment, the patronage of my high connexion, sir, you must leave it, if you please, to me; for I have been accustomed to study the leaders of my high connexion, sir; and I may tell you, without vanity, that I can turn them round my finger,"—in which Mr. Sladdery, who is an honest man, does not exaggerate at all.

Therefore, while Mr. Tulkinghorn may not know what is passing in the Dedlock mind at present, it is very possible that he may.

"My Lady's cause has been again before the Chancellor, has it, Mr. Tulkinghorn?" says Sir Leicester, giving him his hand.

"Yes. It has been on again to-day," Mr. Tulkinghorn replies; making one of his quiet bows to my Lady, who is on a sofa near the fire, shading her face with a hand-screen.

"It would be useless to ask," says my Lady, with the dreariness of the place in Lincolnshire still upon her, "whether anything has been done."

"Nothing that *you* would call anything, has been done to-day," replies Mr. Tulkinghorn.

"Nor ever will be," says my Lady.

Sir Leicester has no objection to an interminable Chancery suit. It is a slow, expensive, British, constitutional kind of thing. To be sure, he has not a vital interest in the suit in question, her part in which was the only property my Lady brought him; and he has a shadowy impression that for his name—the name of Dedlock—to be in a cause, and not in the title of that cause, is a most ridiculous accident. But he regards the Court of Chancery, even if it should involve an occasional delay of justice and a trifling amount of confusion, as a something, devised in conjunction with a variety of other somethings, by the perfection of human wisdom, for the eternal settlement (humanly speaking) of everything. And he is upon the whole of a fixed opinion, that to give the sanction of his countenance to any complaints respecting it, would be to encourage some person in the lower classes to rise up somewhere—like Wat Tyler.

"As a few fresh affidavits have been put upon the file," says Mr. Tulkinghorn, "and as they are short, and as I proceed upon the troublesome principle of begging leave to possess my clients with any new proceedings in a cause"; cautious man Mr. Tulkinghorn, taking no more responsibility than necessary; "and further, as I see you are going to Paris; I have brought them in my pocket."

(Sir Leicester was going to Paris too, by the bye, but the delight of the fashionable intelligence was in his Lady.)

Mr. Tulkinghorn takes out his papers, asks permission to place them on a golden talisman of a table at my Lady's elbow, puts on his spectacles, and begins to read by the light of a shaded lamp.

"In Chancery. Between John Jarndyce—"

My Lady interrupts, requesting him to miss as many of the formal horrors as he can.

Mr. Tulkinghorn glances over his spectacles, and begins again lower down. My Lady carelessly and scornfully abstracts her attention. Sir Leicester in a great chair looks at the fire, and appears to have a stately liking for the legal repetitions and pro-lixities, as ranging among the national bulwarks. It happens that the fire is hot, where my Lady sits; and that the hand-screen is more beautiful than useful, being priceless but small. My Lady, changing her position, sees the papers on the table—looks at them nearer—looks at them nearer still—asks impulsively:

"Who copied that?"

Mr. Tulkinghorn stops short, surprised by my Lady's ani-mation and her unusual tone.

"Is it what you people call law-hand?" she asks, looking full at him in her careless way again, and toying with her screen.

"Not quite. Probably"—Mr. Tulkinghorn examines it as he speaks—"the legal character which it has, was acquired after the original hand was formed. Why do you ask?"

"Anything to vary this detestable monotony. O, go on, do!"

Mr. Tulkinghorn reads again. The heat is greater, my Lady screens her face. Sir Leicester dozes, starts up suddenly, and cries, "Eh? What do you say?"

"I say I am afraid," says Mr. Tulkinghorn, who had risen hastily, "that Lady Dedlock is ill."

"Faint," my Lady murmurs, with white lips, "only that; but it is like the faintness of death. Don't speak to me. Ring, and take me to my room."

Mr. Tulkinghorn retires into another chamber; bells ring, feet shuffle and patter, silence ensues. Mercury at last begs Mr. Tulkinghorn to return.

"Better now," quoth Sir Leicester, motioning the lawyer to sit down and read to him alone. "I have been quite alarmed. I never knew my Lady swoon before. But the weather is extremely trying—and she really has been bored to death down at our place in Lincolnshire."

Trollope wrote flawless minor novels; Dickens wrote flawed great ones. The jocular tone of "quoth," in the paragraph immediately above, for example, is a flaw because it is out of place; and there are larger and more serious flaws in *Bleak House*—which, however, should not deter us and need not detain us, for *Bleak House* is one of the greatest novels, and pointing out its flaws is as vain as it is easy. It is like pointing out Shakespeare's anachronisms: they just don't matter. Like all great writers, Dickens transcended his age: to call him a Victorian is like calling Swift an eighteenth-century writer, or Thoreau a New Englander, or Milton a Puritan, or Melville a romantic: the designation is accurate as far as it goes, but it doesn't go very far.

Dickens transcended his age by growing beyond its forms. The passages I have quoted from *The Mudfog Papers* are far and away the best in that deservedly forgotten book; the superiority of those from *Bleak House* shows how much Dickens grew between 1837 and 1853. He began to grow immediately, with *The Pickwick Papers* (1837), which surpassed *The Mudfog Papers* as much in variety of interest and depth of understanding as in geographical range; and by the sixteenth year of Victoria's reign Dickens was in the twentieth century. Nobody who is not a Dickens specialist, or who is not at least taking a graduate course in Dickens, reads *The Mudfog Papers* now; *The Pickwick Papers* and certain other novels of his, such as *Hard Times, Our Mutual Friend* and *The Old Curiosity Shop*, we enjoy chiefly as antiques —as examples of Victorian writing and to some extent as portrayals of Victorian life; but we read *Bleak House* as we would read a novel of our own time, because it continues to speak to us with as much pertinence as it spoke to its original readers. It pertains to our life as it pertained to theirs. The detail of life has changed since 1853, but its essence has not; and in *Bleak House* Dickens has not only recorded the detail of Victorian life but has also caught the essence of life that his age shared with ours. *Bleak House* is a great symbolic novel, as *Don Quixote* is a great symbolic novel. We don't read *Don Quixote* in order to learn about Life In Early Seventeenth-Century Spain, or in order to sneer at romances we haven't read; we read it because the adventures of the mad knight and his ridiculously sane squire are symbolic of our own experience; and just as Don Quixote's misconception of the windmill symbolizes the eternal and continuing misconception of new economic forces and new social arrangements by those who live in romantic dreams of the past, so the fog that chills the hearts and limits the vision of the Dedlocks, Tulkinghorns, Chadbands and Skimpoles in *Bleak House* still chills and makes purblind their counterparts in our own day. Kafka acknowledged a deep indebtedness to Dickens.

How thin is the mere literal fog of *The Mudfog Papers* by comparison with the richly symbolic fog of *Bleak House*—the former a mere ordinary ground-clinging cloud of mere ordinary water vapor, the latter an outward concomitant of an inward obfuscation! Oscar Wilde also was to associate the two kinds of dimness: "London is full of fogs and serious people," he was to say, "but it is impossible to tell whether the fogs make the serious people or the serious people make the fogs." Some pages back I said that perhaps much Victorian prose was clumsy because of the obfusc light of the period; but I see now that it would be more consistent with the main thesis of this book to believe that the light was obfusc because the prose was clumsy. This is at least a more hopeful view, for we can do something about our prose.

Dickens sheds light. He leads us into the High Court of Chancery by way of Temple Bar, an imposing structure which in the middle ages had marked the limits of the city's jurisdiction outside its walls but which long ago ceased to serve any purpose and is now merely an "obstruction" in the busiest part of the city. A lesser writer would have taken us straight into the courtroom without mentioning such a seeming irrelevancy; Dickens, by bluntly using the word "obstruction" for this monument of the past, and by observing that the obstruction is an appropriate ornament at the entrance to the headquarters of the city government, makes the irrelevancy relevant—or, as we say, symbolic. In so doing he anticipates such twentieth-century symbolic novelists as Rilke, Joyce, Kafka and Broch. That bar is what Joyce would have called an "epiphany"—a detail of fact that symbolizes a whole way of thinking and living, a whole culture even.

To be sure, Dickens lacked the necessary confidence in his readers to let the symbols speak for themselves, as twentieth-century writers do. He felt a need to state explicitly that the Court of Chancery was "at the very heart of the fog," that the fog and mud were appropriate to "the groping and floundering condition" of the court, that the Chancellor had "a foggy glory round his head"—for all the world like MacFlecknoe's—and that when he looked toward a conventional source of light he could see "nothing but fog." Such explicit pointing out of the connections deprives the reader of the pleasure of discovering them for himself—or, if he doesn't discover them, of somehow feeling their effect. But even so, this writing is more modern than "Victorian." That was what I meant when I said that in *Bleak House* Dickens transcended his age.

In the conscious use of symbolism Dickens was not by any means alone or even foremost among the great novelists of his century; Hawthorne, Melville, Twain, Zola, Balzac, Flaubert, James, Conrad, Gogol, Tolstoy, Dostoyevsky—they all had depths beneath their surfaces, they all experimented with techniques that were to reach the fullest development in the works of twentieth-

[166]

century masters. There were of course many novelists in the
nineteenth century—as there are in the twentieth—whose works
afford no more than meets the eye; but they come and go and
have no lasting interest. Eden Phillpotts, Hugh Walpole, Compton
Mackenzie and E. M. Delafield came and were widely read and
highly regarded by hack reviewers and went and are forgotten.
Is the surface all? The surface alone is nothing. Where now is
Miss Peanut Butter of 1956?

That Dickens was a superb technician, who was not content
merely to do better what had been done well by many before him,
we can demonstrate by pointing out another detail in which he
anticipated the great innovators of the twentieth century.

> Mr. Tulkinghorn reads again. The heat is greater, my Lady
> screens her face. Sir Leicester dozes, starts up suddenly, and
> cries, "Eh? What do you say?"
>
> "I say I am afraid," says Mr. Tulkinghorn, who had risen
> hastily, "that Lady Dedlock is ill."

This major ellipsis—this deliberate omission of Mr. Tulkinghorn's
statement the first time he utters it, together with the omission
of any such helpful narration as "Lady Dedlock turned pale, and
seemed about to faint. Mr. Tulkinghorn, alarmed, rose hastily to
his feet and exclaimed, . . ."—this major ellipsis, which forces the
reader to participate in creating the scene, and also makes him
share Sir Leicester's surprise, takes him into the heart of the incident instead of merely telling him about it. Observe also that Mr.
Tulkinghorn's rising is quite properly relegated to a subordinate
clause, the proper place for any such merely incidental act; and
that the clause is inserted before the end of the sentence, thus
holding in suspense and thereby emphasizing the main idea, "Lady
Dedlock is ill." A less accomplished writer than Dickens might
have put it this way: " 'I say I am afraid that Lady Dedlock is ill,'

says Mr. Tulkinghorn, rising hastily to his feet." To his feet, in- deed! To what else? This is a flat-footed anticlimax.

But Dickens went through a long development before he achieved such economy and such power. He had not yet achieved them in *The Old Curiosity Shop* (1841); for, though it is full of symbols, its language is the language of Victorian sentimentality, pure, unmitigated, and almost unbelievable. My grandmother used to crochet little baskets, pink, white, blue, and stiffen them with sugar-water; when I read *The Old Curiosity Shop* those little baskets float in my mind's eye, and I can still taste them. What I am saying is that no technical device can be depended on as a formula for good writing. In the chapter I shall quote, everything foreshadows and symbolizes Little Nell's death, which will not occur for another nineteen chapters: the little house where she takes up her last residence, the old Bachelor, the churchyard itself most obviously of all; but the language is such that a modern reader can only smile. The content, accordingly, is no longer what Dick- ens intended. Paul Valéry, that contemptible moral Babbitt, says somewhere, "Where others see form, I see content." I hate to admit it, but in such matters Valéry is right. That is to say, he agrees with me.

THE OLD CURIOSITY SHOP, *1841*, *Chapter 52*

After a long time, the schoolmaster appeared at the wicketgate of the churchyard, and hurried towards them, jingling in his hand, as he came along, a bundle of rusty keys. He was quite breathless with pleasure and haste when he reached the porch, and at first could only point towards the old building which the child had been contemplating so earnestly.

"You see those two old houses," he said at last.

"Yes, surely," replied Nell. "I have been looking at them nearly all the time you have been away."

"And you would have looked at them more curiously yet, if you could have guessed what I have to tell you," said the friend. "One of those houses is mine."

Without saying any more, or giving the child time to reply, the schoolmaster took her hand, and, his honest face quite radiant with exultation, led her to the place of which he spoke.

They stopped before its low arched door. After trying several of the keys in vain, the schoolmaster found one to fit the huge lock, which turned back, creaking, and admitted them into the house.

The room into which they entered was a vaulted chamber once nobly ornamented by cunning architects, and still retaining, in its beautiful groined roof and rich stone tracery, choice remnants of its ancient splendour. Foliage carved in the stone, and emulating the mastery of Nature's hand, yet remained to tell how many times the leaves outside had come and gone, while it lived on unchanged. The broken figures supporting the burden of the chimney-piece, though mutilated, were still distinguishable for what they had been—far different from the dust without—and showed sadly by the empty hearth, like creatures who had outlived their kind, and mourned their own too slow decay.

In some old time—for even change was old in that old place —a wooden partition had been constructed in one part of the chamber to form a sleeping-closet, into which the light was admitted at the same period by a rude window, or rather niche, cut in the solid wall. This screen, together with two seats in the broad chimney, had at some forgotten date been part of the church or convent; for the oak, hastily appropriated to its present purpose, had been little altered from its former shape, and presented to the eye a pile of fragments of rich carving from old monkish stalls.

An open door leading to a small room or cell, dim with the light that came through leaves of ivy, completed the interior of this portion of the ruin. It was not quite destitute of furniture. A few strange chairs, whose arms and legs looked as though they had dwindled away with age; a table, the very spectre of its race; a great old chest that had once held records in the church, with other quaintly fashioned domestic necessaries, and store of firewood for the winter, were scattered around, and gave evident tokens of its occupation as a dwelling-place at no very distant time.

The child looked around her, with that solemn feeling with which we contemplate the work of ages that have become but drops of water in the great ocean of eternity. The old man had followed them, but they were all three hushed for a space, and drew their breath softly, as if they feared to break the silence even by so slight a sound.

"It is a very beautiful place!" said the child, in a low voice.

"I almost feared you thought otherwise," returned the schoolmaster. "You shivered when we first came in, as if you felt it cold or gloomy."

"It was not that," said Nell, glancing round with a slight shudder. "Indeed, I cannot tell you what it was, but when I saw the outside, from the church porch, the same feeling came over me. It is its being so old and grey perhaps."

"A peaceful place to live in, don't you think so?" said her friend.

"Oh, yes," rejoined the child, clasping her hands earnestly. "A quiet, happy place—a place to live and learn to die in!" She would have said more, but that the energy of her thoughts caused her voice to falter, and come in trembling whispers from her lips.

"A place to live, and learn to live, and gather health of mind and body in," said the schoolmaster; "for this old house is yours."

"Ours!" cried the child.

"Ay," returned the schoolmaster gaily, "for many a merry year to come, I hope. I shall be a close neighbour—only next door —but this house is yours."

Having now disburdened himself of his great surprise, the schoolmaster sat down, and drawing Nell to his side, told her how he had learnt that that ancient tenement had been occupied for a very long time by an old person, nearly a hundred years of age, who kept the keys of the church, opened and closed it for the serv- ices, and showed it to strangers; how she had died not many weeks ago, and nobody had yet been found to fill the office; how, learning all this in an interview with the sexton, who was confined to his bed by rheumatism, he had been bold to make mention of his fellow-traveller, which had been so favourably received by that high authority, that he had taken courage, acting on his advice, to propound the matter to the clergyman. In a word, the result of his exertions was that Nell and her grandfather were to be carried before the last-named gentleman next day; and, his approval of their conduct and appearance reserved as a matter of form, that they were already appointed to the vacant post.

"There's a small allowance of money," said the schoolmaster. "It is not much, but still enough to live upon in this retired spot. By clubbing our funds together, we shall do bravely; no fear of that."

"Heaven bless and prosper you!" sobbed the child.

"Amen, my dear," returned her friend cheerfully; "and all of us, as it will, and has, in leading us through sorrow and trouble to this tranquil life. But we must look at *my* house now. Come!"

They repaired to the other tenement; tried the rusty keys as before; at length found the right one; and opened the worm-eaten door. It led into a chamber, vaulted and old, like that from which they had come, but not so spacious, and having only one other little room attached. It was not difficult to divine that the other house was of right the schoolmaster's, and that he had chosen for himself the least commodious, in his care and regard for them. Like the adjoining habitation, it held such old articles of furniture as were absolutely necessary, and had its stack of fire-wood.

To make these dwellings as habitable and full of comfort as they could, was now their pleasant care. In a short time, each had its cheerful fire glowing and crackling on the hearth, and reddening the pale old wall with a hale and healthy blush. Nell, busily plying her needle, repaired the tattered window-hangings, drew together the rents that time had worn in the threadbare scraps of carpet, and made them whole and decent. The schoolmaster swept and smoothed the ground before the door, trimmed the long grass, trained the ivy and creeping plants which hung their drooping heads in melancholy neglect; and gave to the outer walls a cheery air of home. The old man, sometimes by his side and sometimes with the child, lent his aid to both, went here and there on little patient services, and was happy. Neighbours too, as they came from work, proffered their help; or sent their children with such small presents or loans as the strangers needed most. It was a busy day; and night came on, and found them wondering that there was yet so much to do, and that it should be dark so soon.

They took their supper together, in the house which may be henceforth called the child's; and when they had finished their meal drew round the fire, and almost in whispers—their hearts were too quiet and glad for loud expression—discussed their future plans. Before they separated, the schoolmaster read some prayers aloud; and then, full of gratitude and happiness, they parted for the night.

At that silent hour, when her grandfather was sleeping peacefully in his bed, and every sound was hushed, the child lingered before the dying embers, and thought of her past fortunes as if they had been a dream and she only now awoke. The glare of the sinking flame, reflected in the oaken panels whose carved tops were dimly seen in the gloom of the dusky roof—the aged walls, where

strange shadows came and went with every flickering of the fire
—the solemn presence, within, of that decay which falls on sense-
less things the most enduring in their nature: and, without, and
round about on every side, of Death—filled her with deep and
thoughtful feelings, but with none of terror or alarm. A change
had been gradually stealing over her, in the time of her loneliness
and sorrow. With failing strength and heightening resolution,
there had sprung up a purified and altered mind; there had grown
in her bosom blessed thoughts and hopes, which are the portion of
few but the weak and drooping. There were none to see the frail,
perishable figure, as it glided from the fire and leaned pensively at
the open casement; none but the stars, to look into the upturned
face and read its history. The old church bell rang out the hour
with a mournful sound, as if it had grown sad from so much com-
muning with the dead and unheeded warning to the living; the
fallen leaves rustled; the grass stirred upon the graves; all else was
still and sleeping.

Some of those dreamless sleepers lay close within the shadow
of the church—touching the wall, as if they clung to it for comfort and protection. Others had chosen to lie beneath the changing
shade of trees; others by the path, that footsteps might come near
them; others among the graves of little children. Some had desired
to rest beneath the very ground they had trodden in their daily
walks; some where the setting sun might shine upon their beds;
some where its light would fall upon them when it rose. Perhaps
not one of the imprisoned souls had been able quite to separate
itself in living thought from its old companion. If any had, it had
still felt for it a love like that which captives have been known
to bear towards the cell in which they have been long confined, and even at parting hung upon its narrow bounds affec-
tionately.

It was long before the child closed the window, and ap-
proached her bed. Again something of the same sensation as be-

fore—an involuntary chill—a momentary feeling akin to fear—but vanishing directly, and leaving no alarm behind. Again, too, dreams of the little scholar; of the roof opening, and a column of bright faces, rising far away into the sky, as she had seen in some old Scriptural picture once, and looking down on her, asleep. It was a sweet and happy dream. The quiet spot, outside, seemed to remain the same, saving that there was music in the air, and a sound of angels' wings. After a time the sisters came there hand in hand, and stood among the graves. And then the dream grew dim, and faded.

With the brightness and joy of morning, came the renewal of yesterday's labours, the revival of its pleasant thoughts, the restoration of its energies, cheerfulness, and hope. They worked gaily in ordering and arranging their houses until noon, and then went to visit the clergyman.

He was a simple-hearted old gentleman, of a shrinking, subdued spirit, accustomed to retirement, and very little acquainted with the world, which he had left many years before to come and settle in that place. His wife had died in the house in which he still lived, and he had long since lost sight of any earthly cares or hopes beyond it.

He received them very kindly, and at once showed an interest in Nell; asking her name, and age, her birthplace, the circumstances which had led her there, and so forth. The schoolmaster had already told her story. They had no other friends or home to leave, he said, and had come to share his fortunes. He loved the child as though she were his own.

"Well, well," said the clergyman. "Let it be as you desire. She is very young."

"Old in adversity and trial, sir," replied the schoolmaster.

"God help her! Let her rest, and forget them," said the old gentleman. "But an old church is a dull and gloomy place for one so young as you, my child."

"Oh, no, sir," returned Nell. "I have no such thoughts, indeed."

"I would rather see her dancing on the green at nights," said the old gentleman, laying his hand upon her head, and smiling sadly, "than have her sitting in the shadow of our mouldering arches. You must look to this, and see that her heart does not grow heavy among these solemn ruins. Your request is granted, friend."

After more kind words, they withdrew, and repaired to the child's house; where they were yet in conversation on their happy fortune, when another friend appeared.

This was a little old gentleman, who lived in the parsonage-house, and had resided there (so they learnt soon afterwards) ever since the death of the clergyman's wife, which had happened fifteen years before. He had been his college friend and always his close companion; in the first shock of his grief had come to console and comfort him; and from that time they had never parted company. The little old gentleman was the active spirit of the place; the adjuster of all differences, the promoter of all merry-makings, the dispenser of his friend's bounty, and of no small charity of his own besides; the universal mediator, comforter, and friend. None of the simple villagers had cared to ask his name, or, when they knew it, to store it in their memory. Perhaps from some vague rumour of his college honours which had been whispered abroad on his first arrival, perhaps because he was an unmarried, unencumbered gentleman, he had been called the Bachelor. The name pleased him, or suited him as well as any other, and the Bachelor he had ever since remained. And the bachelor it was, it may be added, who with his own hands had laid in the stock of fuel which the wanderers had found in their new habitation.

The bachelor, then—to call him by his usual appellation—lifted the latch, showed his little round mild face for a moment at the door, and stepped into the room like one who was no stranger to it.

"You are Mr Marton, the new schoolmaster?" he said, greeting Nell's kind friend.

"I am, sir."

"You come well recommended, and I am glad to see you. I should have been in the way yesterday, expecting you, but I rode across the country to carry a message from a sick mother to her daughter in service some miles off, and have but just now returned. This is our young church-keeper? You are not the less welcome, friend, for her sake, or for this old man's; nor the worse teacher for having learnt humanity."

"She has been ill, sir, very lately," said the schoolmaster, in answer to the look with which their visitor regarded Nell when he had kissed her cheek.

"Yes, yes. I know she has," he rejoined. "There have been suffering and heartache here."

"Indeed there have, sir."

The little old gentleman glanced at the grandfather, and back again at the child, whose hand he took tenderly in his, and held.

"You will be happier here," he said; "we will try, at least, to make you so. You have made great improvements here already. Are they the work of your hands?"

"Yes, sir."

"We may make some others—not better in themselves, but with better means perhaps," said the bachelor. "Let us see now, let us see."

Nell accompanied him into the other little rooms, and over both the houses, in which he found various small comforts wanting, which he engaged to supply from a certain collection of odds and ends he had at home, and which must have been a very miscellaneous and extensive one, as it comprehended the most opposite articles imaginable. They all came, however, and came without loss of time; for the little old gentleman, disappearing for some five or ten minutes, presently returned, laden with old shelves, rugs, blankets, and other household gear, and followed by a boy bearing a similar load. These being cast on the floor in a promiscuous heap, yielded a quantity of occupation in arranging, erecting, and putting away; the superintendence of which task evidently afforded the old gentleman extreme delight, and engaged him for some time with great briskness and activity. When nothing more was left to be done, he charged the boy to run off and bring his schoolmates to be marshalled before their new master, and solemnly reviewed.

"As good a set of fellows, Marton, as you'd wish to see," he said, turning to the schoolmaster when the boy was gone; "but I don't let 'em know I think so. That wouldn't do, at all."

The messenger soon returned at the head of a long row of urchins, great and small, who, being confronted by the bachelor at the house door, fell into various convulsions of politeness; clutching their hats and caps, squeezing them into the smallest possible dimensions, and making all manner of bows and scrapes, which the little old gentleman contemplated with excessive satisfaction, and expressed his approval of by a great many nods and smiles. Indeed, his approbation of the boys was by no means so scrupulously disguised as he had led the schoolmaster to suppose, inasmuch as it broke out in sundry loud whispers and confidential remarks which were perfectly audible to them every one.

"This first boy, schoolmaster," said the bachelor, "is John Owen; a lad of good parts, sir, and frank, honest temper; but too thoughtless, too playful, too light-headed by far. That boy, my good sir, would break his neck with pleasure, and deprive his parents of their chief comfort—and between ourselves, when you come to see him at hare and hounds, taking the fence and ditch by the finger-post, and sliding down the face of the little quarry, you'll never forget it. It's beautiful!"

John Owen having been thus rebuked, and being in perfect possession of the speech aside, the bachelor singled out another boy.

"Now, look at that lad, sir," said the bachelor. "You see that fellow? Richard Evans his name is, sir. An amazing boy to learn, blessed with a good memory, and a ready understanding, and moreover with a good voice and ear for psalm-singing, in which he is the best among us. Yet, sir, that boy will come to a bad end; he'll never die in his bed; he's always falling asleep in church in sermon-time—and to tell the truth, Mr Marton, I always did the same at his age, and feel quite certain that it was natural to my constitution and I couldn't help it."

This hopeful pupil edified by the above terrible reproval, the bachelor turned to another.

"But if we talk of examples to be shunned," said he, "if we come to boys that should be a warning and a beacon to all their fellows, here's the one, and I hope you won't spare him. This is the lad, sir; this one with the blue eyes and light hair. This is a swimmer, sir, this fellow—a diver, Lord save us! This is a boy, sir, who had a fancy for plunging into eighteen feet of water, with his clothes on, and bringing up a blind man's dog, who was being drowned by the weight of his chain and collar, while his master stood wringing his hands upon the bank, bewailing the loss of his guide and friend. I sent the boy two guineas anonymously, sir," added the bachelor, in his peculiar whisper, "directly I heard of it; but never mention it on any account, for he hasn't the least idea that it came from me."

Having disposed of this culprit, the bachelor turned to another, and from him to another, and so on through the whole array, laying, for their wholesome restriction within due bounds, the same cutting emphasis on such of their propensities as were dearest to his heart and were unquestionably referable to his own precept and example. Thoroughly persuaded, in the end, that he had made them miserable by his severity, he dismissed them with a small present, and an admonition to walk quietly home, without any leapings, scufflings, or turnings out of the way; which injunction (he informed the schoolmaster in the same audible confidence) he did not think he could have obeyed when he was a boy, had his life depended on it.

Hailing these little tokens of the bachelor's disposition as so many assurances of his own welcome course from that time, the schoolmaster parted from him with a light heart and joyous spirits, and deemed himself one of the happiest men on earth. The windows of the two old houses were ruddy again that night with the reflection of the cheerful fires that burnt within; and the bachelor and his friend, pausing to look upon them as they returned from their evening walk, spoke softly together of the beautiful child, and looked round upon the churchyard with a sigh.

John Ruskin (1819–1900) is not easy to grasp. His talent and his stuffiness are equally undeniable. His social ideas influenced such diverse revolutionists as Engels and Gandhi and such diverse dreamers as William Morris and (pardon the expression) T. S. Eliot; his aesthetics influenced such diverse artists as Proust and the Pre-Raphaelites; in the nineteenth century he was variously regarded as a revolutionist, a reformer, a conservative and a reactionary, but in the twentieth he is hardly regarded at all. J. L. and Barbara Hammond, in their excellent study of social conditions in Victorian England, *The Bleak Age* (1934), don't mention Ruskin; Croce, in his *Aesthetics* (1902), dismisses him briefly: "a dogmatic tone and the appearance of theoretical form veil, in his exquisite and enthusiastic pages, a texture of dreams and fancies. The reader who recalls those pages will regard as irreverent any detailed and prosaic review of Ruskin's aesthetic thought, which must inevitably reveal its poverty and incoherence." But we must set against these negative judgments two paragraphs from Proust's *Within a Budding Grove* (1918), which (notwithstanding the implied admiration of Whistler, a painter whose virtues Ruskin was unable to see) clearly show the influence of Ruskin's thought, social as well as aesthetic:

> Then Mamma sought to distract my mind, asked me what I thought of having for dinner, drew my attention to Françoise, complimented her on a hat and cloak which she did not recognise, in spite of their having horrified her long ago when she first saw them, new, upon my great-aunt, one with an immense bird towering over it, the other decorated with a hideous pattern and jet beads. But the cloak having grown too shabby to wear, Françoise had had it turned, exposing an "inside" of plain cloth and quite a good colour. As for the bird, it had long since come to grief and been thrown away. And just as it is disturbing, sometimes, to find the effects which the most conscious artists attain only by an effort occurring in a folk-song, on the wall of some peasant's cottage where above the door, at the precisely right spot in the composition, blooms a white or yellow rose—so the velvet band, the loop of ribbon which would have delighted one in a portrait by Chardin or Whistler, Françoise had set with a simple but unerring taste upon the hat, which was now charming.
>
> To take a parallel from an earlier age, the modesty and integrity which often gave an air of nobility to the face of our old servant having spread also to the garments which, as a woman reserved but not humbled, who knew how to hold her own and to keep her place, she had put on for the journey so as to be fit to be seen in our company without at the same time seeming or wishing to make herself conspicuous,—Françoise in the cherry-coloured cloth, now faded, of her cloak, and the discreet nap of her fur collar, brought to mind one of those miniatures of Anne of Brittany painted in Books of Hours by an old master, in which everything is so exactly in the right place, the sense of the whole is so evenly distributed throughout the parts that the rich and obsolete singularity of the costume expresses the same pious gravity as the eyes, lips and hands.

We know now, if we didn't know before, that this view of a servant's mind is a master's comfortable delusion, to which the servant caters; that is a weakness in Proust's social attitude, and one of many weaknesses in Ruskin's. And even so, any thinker, however weak, who helped to inspire such beauty, however false in its presuppositions, should not be merely ignored. But how can such a writer be neatly summed up and presented? A textbook of writing is not an appropriate place to try, and I am not sufficiently enthusiastic about Ruskin to try in any case; for those who want a good brief discussion I recommend Horace M. Kallen's *Art and Freedom*, Book IV (1942). But Ruskin was an interesting stylist, and as such he is worth a few pages here.

From 1871 to 1884 he published a series of "Letters to the Workmen and Labourers of Great Britain," under the Latin title *Fors Clavigera* (Fortune the Keybearer). He addressed his readers—among whom there can have been few workmen and fewer laborers—as "my scholars" and even as "my pupils." In the excerpt that follows we have Victorian didacticism at its most fatuous, both from Ruskin himself and from Harriet Martineau (1802–1876); and we see how a man's non-literary values can sometimes throw off his literary judgment, even though they don't always throw it off.

The St. George Ruskin mentions is the patron saint of his reformist organization, the Guild of St. George. *Fors Clavigera* was its official organ.

☙

JOHN RUSKIN [1819–1900]

Excerpt from FORS CLAVIGERA, *Letter 88, 1877*

Yea, the work of our hands, establish thou it.

By my promise that, in the text of this series of *Fors*, there shall be "no syllable of complaint, or of scorn," I pray the reader to understand that I in no wise intimate any change of feeling on my own part. I never felt more difficulty in my life than I do, at this instant, in not lamenting certain things with more than common lament, and in not speaking of certain people with more than common scorn.

Nor is it possible to fulfil these rightly warning functions of *Fors* without implying *some* measure of scorn. For instance, in the matter of choice of books, it is impossible to warn my scholars against a book, without implying a certain kind of contempt for it. For I never would warn them against any writer whom I had complete respect for,—however adverse to me, or my work. There are few stronger adversaries to St. George than Voltaire. But my scholars are welcome to read as much of Voltaire as they like. His voice is mighty among the ages. Whereas they are entirely forbidden Miss Martineau,—not because she is an infidel, but because she is a vulgar and foolish one.*

Do not say, or think, I am breaking my word in asserting, once for all, with reference to example, this necessary principle. This very vow and law that I have set myself, *must* be honoured sometimes in the breach of it, so only that the transgression be visibly not wanton or incontinent. Nay, in this very instance it is because I am not speaking in *pure* contempt, but have lately been as much surprised by the beauty of a piece of Miss Martineau's writings, as I have been grieved by the deadly effect of her writings generally on the mind of one of my best pupils, who had read them without telling me, that I make her a definite example. In future, it will be ordinarily enough for me to say to my pupils privately that they are not to read such and such books; while, for general order to my *Fors* readers, they may be well content, it seems to me,

---

* I use the word vulgar, here, in its first sense of egoism, not of selfishness, but of not seeing one's own relations to the universe. Miss Martineau plans a book—afterwards popular—and goes to breakfast, "not knowing what a great thing had been done." So Mr. Buckle, dying, thinks only—he shall not finish *his* book. Not at all whether God will ever make up *His*.

with the list of the books I want them to read constantly, and with such casual recommendation as I may be able to give of current literature. For instance, there is a quite lovely little book just come out about Irish children, *Castle Blair,*—(which, let me state at once, I have strong personal, though stronger impersonal, reasons for recommending, the writer being a very dear friend; and some Irish children, for many and many a year, much more than that). But the *im*personal reasons are—first, that the book is good and lovely, and true; having the best description of a noble child in it, (Winny,) that I ever read; and nearly the best description of the next best thing—a noble dog; and reason second is that, after Miss Edgeworth's *Ormond* and *Absentee,* this little book will give more true insight into the proper way of managing Irish people than any other I know.*

Wherewith I have some more serious recommendations to give; and the first shall be of this most beautiful passage of Miss Martineau, which is quoted from *Deerbrook* in the review of her autobiography:—

> "In the house of every wise parent, may then be seen an epitome of life—a sight whose consolation is needed at times, perhaps, by all. Which of the little children of a virtuous household can conceive of his entering into his parents' pursuits, or interfering with them? How sacred are the study and the office, the apparatus of a knowledge and a power which he can only venerate! Which of these little ones dreams of disturbing the course of his parents' thought or achievement? Which of them conceives of the daily routine of the household—its going forth and coming in, its rising and its rest—having been different before its birth, or that

---

* Also, I have had it long on my mind to name the *Adventures of a Phaeton* as a very delightful and wise book of its kind; very full of pleasant play, and deep and pure feeling; much interpretation of some of the best points of German character; and, last and least, with pieces of description in it which I should be glad, selfishly, to think inferior to what the public praise in *Modern Painters,*—I can only say, they seem to *me* quite as good.

it would be altered by his absence? It is even a matter of surprise to him when it now and then occurs to him that there is anything set apart for him—that he has clothes and couch, and that his mother thinks and cares for him. If he lags behind in a walk, or finds himself alone among the trees, he does not dream of being missed; but home rises up before him as he has always seen it—his father thoughtful, his mother occupied, and the rest gay, with the one difference of *his** not being there. This he believes, and has no other trust than in his shriek of terror, for being ever remembered more. Yet, all the while, from day to day, from year to year, without one moment's intermission, is the providence of his parent around him, brooding over the workings of his infant spirit, chastening its passions, nourishing its affections —now *troubling it with salutary pain,* now *animating it with even more wholesome delight.* All the while, is the order of the household affairs regulated for the comfort and profit of these lowly little ones, though they regard it reverently, because they cannot comprehend it. They may not know of all this—how their guardian bends over their pillow nightly, and lets no word of their careless talk drop unheeded, and records every sob of infant grief, hails every brightening gleam of reason and every chirp of childish glee—they may not know this, because they could not understand it aright, and each little heart would be inflated with pride, each little mind would lose the grace and purity of its unconsciousness; but the guardianship is not the less real, constant, and tender for its being unrecognised by its objects.

This passage is of especial value to me just now, because I have presently to speak about faith, and its power; and I have never myself thought of the innocent *faithlessness* of children, but only of their faith. The idea given here by Miss Martineau is entirely new to me, and most beautiful. And had she gone on thus, expressing her own feelings modestly, she would have been a most noble person, and a verily 'great' writer. She became a vulgar per-

---

* Italics mine. [Ruskin's, that is.]

son, and a little writer, in her conceit;—of which I can say no more,
else I should break my vow unnecessarily. . . .

I take, as in the chapter on
balanced styles, from my shelves, not quite, the years having in
their passage taught me, among other things, some small degree of
circumspection, at random, and, guided by the same principle,
open, Henry James' last three completed novels. I find, then, after
making, in each case, a brief search, three brief passages which
have, each of them, even out of context, some unity, and which
represent, not unfairly, as after due consideration I more or less
believe, James' latest manner:

> "Well," said Aunt Maud, whose fine onyx eyes failed to blink,
> even though Milly's questions might have been taken as drawing
> her rather further than she had originally meant to go—"well,
> Kate is thoroughly aware of my views for her, and that I take her
> being with me, at present, in the way she *is* with me, if you know
> what I mean, as a loyal assent to them. Therefore as my views
> don't happen to provide a place, at all, for Mr. Densher, much,
> in a manner, as I like him"—therefore, therefore in short she had
> been prompted to this step, though she completed her sense, but
> sketchily, with the rattle of her large fan.
>
> THE WINGS OF THE DOVE, *1902, Chapter 14*

> He had asked Mrs. Newsome moreover not to announce him
> again; he had so distinct an opinion on attacking his job, should
> he attack it at all, in his own way. Not the least of this lady's high
> merits for him was that he could absolutely rest on her word.
> She was the only woman he had known, even at Woollett, as to
> whom his conviction was positive that to lie was beyond her art.
> Sarah Pocock, for instance, her own daughter, though with social
> ideals, as they said, in some respects different—Sarah who *was*,
> in her way, esthetic, had never refused to human commerce that
> mitigation of rigour; there were occasions when he had distinctly

seen her apply it. Since, accordingly, at all events, he had had it from Mrs. Newsome that she had, at whatever cost to her more strenuous view, conformed, in the matter of preparing Chad, wholly to his restrictions, he now looked up at the fine continuous balcony with a safe sense that if the case had been bungled the mistake was at least his property.

THE AMBASSADORS, *1903, Book Second, Chapter 2*

He would have, strangely enough, as it might seem to him, to come back home for it, and there get the impression of her rather pointedly, or at least all impatiently and independently, awaiting him.

THE GOLDEN BOWL, *1904, Chapter 25*

These passages, however, as will be, from their dates, apparent, are all, strictly speaking (and we must, if we are to be, in this chapter, at all consistent, speak strictly), post-Victorian. Moreover, they are, as I have admitted, isolated, torn bleeding, as it were, though not, I hope, fatally, from their contexts. Let us therefore read a more extended passage, two facing pages, chosen, again, according to my rule in these matters, not quite at random, from a novel of James' late Victorian stage.

ॐ

HENRY JAMES [1843–1916]

Excerpt from THE TURN OF THE SCREW, *1898, Chapter 11*

At the hour I now speak of she had joined me, under pressure, on the terrace, where, with the lapse of the season, the afternoon sun was now agreeable; and we sat there together while, before us, at a distance, but within call if we wished, the children strolled to and fro in one of their most manageable moods. They moved slowly, in unison, below us, over the lawn, the boy, as they went, reading aloud from a story-book and passing his arm round his sister to keep her quite in touch. Mrs. Grose watched them with positive placidity; then I caught the suppressed intellectual creak with which she conscientiously turned to take from me a view of the back of the tapestry. I had made her a receptacle of lurid things, but there was an odd recognition of my superiority—my accomplishments and my function—in her patience under my pain. She offered her mind to my disclosures as, had I wished to mix a witch's broth and proposed it with assurance, she would have held out a large clean saucepan. This had become thoroughly her attitude by the time that, in my recital of the events of the night, I reached the point of what Miles had said to me when, after seeing him, at such a monstrous hour, almost on the very spot where he happened now to be, I had gone down to bring him in; choosing then, at the window, with a concentrated need of not alarming the house, rather that method than a signal more resonant. I had left her meanwhile in little doubt of my small hope of representing with success even to her actual sympathy my sense of the real splendour of the little inspiration with which, after I had got him into the house, the boy met my final articulate challenge. As soon as I appeared in the moonlight on the terrace, he had come to me as straight as possible; on which I had taken his hand without a word and led him, through the dark spaces, up the staircase where Quint had so hungrily hovered for him, along the lobby where I had listened and trembled, and so to his forsaken room.

Not a sound, on the way, had passed between us, and I had wondered—oh, *how* I had wondered!—if he were groping about in his little mind for something plausible and not too grotesque. It would tax his invention, certainly, and I felt, this time, over his real embarrassment, a curious thrill of triumph. It was a sharp trap for the inscrutable! He couldn't play any longer at innocence; so how the deuce would he get out of it? There beat in me indeed, with the passionate throb of this question, an equal dumb appeal as to how the deuce *I* should. I was confronted at last, as never yet, with all the risk attached even now to sounding my own horrid note. I remember in fact that as we pushed into his little chamber, where the bed had not been slept in at all and the window, uncovered to the moonlight, made the place so clear that there was no need of striking a match—I remember how I suddenly dropped, sank upon the edge of the bed from the force of the idea that he must know how he really, as they say, "had" me. He could do what he liked, with all his cleverness to help him, so long as I should continue to defer to the old tradition of the criminality of those caretakers of the young who minister to superstitions and fears. He "had" me indeed, and in a cleft stick; for who would ever absolve me, who would consent that I should go unhung, if, by the faintest tremor of an overture, I were the first to introduce into our perfect intercourse an element so dire? No, no: it was useless to attempt to convey to Mrs. Grose, just as it is scarcely less so to attempt to suggest here, how, in our short, stiff brush in the dark, he fairly shook me with admiration. I was of course thoroughly kind and merciful; never, never yet had I placed on his little shoulders hands of such tenderness as those with which, while I rested against the bed, I held him there well under fire. I had no alternative but, in form at least, to put it to him.

  "You must tell me now—and all the truth. What did you go out for? What were you doing there?"

          In my parodies of James, as you no doubt will have observed, I have grossly, nay, crudely, exaggerated. James is not so hard to read as I have suggested. If he were, he would hardly be read. He is in fact read with intense pleasure by many people, and with mild pleasure even by me. My wife, who is more enthusiastic, says James' prose is like highly decorated British china: some is monstrous, but some is beautiful. The best brief exposition of James' virtues that I know of is a pamphlet entitled simply *Henry James*, by his great biographer, Leon Edel. It is No. 4 of the University of Minnesota Pamphlets on American writers.

Exercises

1. If there is a social reform you favor, write two pages opposing it, in the manner of Carlyle.

2. If there is a state or federal policy you oppose, write two pages supporting it, in the manner of Carlyle.

3. Write two pages about your worst enemy, or about a public figure you despise, in the manner of Dickens writing about the old Bachelor.

4. Write two pages condemning this book, in the manner of *Fors Clavigera,* because it pays too much attention to literary technique and too little to moral uplift and the noble dog.

5. You are the good friend and confidant of a married couple. The man tells you that he is having an adulterous affair with another woman. Of course you won't violate his confidence, but you feel that by not telling the wife you have become a party to his betrayal of her. Stated thus flatly, this dilemma sounds like material for a soap opera or a confession-magazine story: the kind of thing that happens only in real life and cheap fiction. But good writers also deal with dilemmas of this kind—not by stating them flatly or merely revealing them, not by adapting them to the taste of those readers who at once lasciviously enjoy and virtuously disapprove, but by using them to explore the changes that take place in the way people feel about each other. In this case, explore the changes that take place in your attitude toward the wife, toward the husband, and toward yourself. You will find the style of Henry James quite appropriate, not only for conveying subtleties but even for discovering them.

SOME TWENTIETH-CENTURY STYLES

There was a time when people recognised things quite easily in pictures when it was Fromentin who had painted them, and could not recognise them at all when it was Renoir.

PROUST
The Guermantes Way

Art doesn't reproduce the visible; it makes visible.

PAUL KLEE
Theory of Modern Art

PERHAPS MORE THAN ANY other, the twentieth century is an age of variety: variety of knowledge, variety of thought, variety of technique. We have the whole European and American past to draw on, and the whole contemporary planet; André Malraux has observed that in painting, sculpture and architecture we have a planetary past; and with our gradually increasing knowledge of non-European cultures we are beginning to have a planetary past in literature. This expanded awareness on the part of writers and readers has resulted in an unprecedented openness to ideas and techniques; we prize originality as it was never prized before.

There are therefore many highly individual styles in twentieth-century prose. The examples that follow are from only a few of the best and most influential writers. Not only is each writer different in principle from each, but some of them differ from themselves. At this point an analogy from another art may help. Bach (1685–1750) and Handel (1685–1759) both composed music in the same general style, but with a little experience of listening we can learn to distinguish one from the other: hearing a piece of music we have never heard before, we can tell, by differences of personal style within the general classic style, whether it is by Bach or by Handel or by someone else. Likewise, we can distinguish Dr. Johnson's style from Gibbon's, and Gibbon's from Burke's. There is an unmistakable Johnson style; there is an unmistakable Gibbon style; there is an unmistakable Burke style.

But in the twentieth century things are more complicated; for, though we can easily distinguish Joyce from Gertrude Stein and from Faulkner, we cannot speak of "the style of Joyce" or "the style of Gertrude Stein" or "the style of Faulkner."

What is the style of Joyce? He wrote all but the last of the fifteen stories of *Dubliners* (1914), as he said, "in a style of scrupulous meanness": flatness, ordinariness, drabness. The successive styles of *A Portrait of the Artist as a Young Man* (1915) follow the hero's growth, beginning with babytalk and ending with the high-flying bombast of an adolescent poet's diary. The eighteen chapters of *Ulysses* (1922) are written according to eighteen different "techniques," which Joyce named:

narrative (young)
catechism (personal)
monologue (male)
narrative (mature)
narcissism
incubism
enthymemic
peristaltic
dialectic
labyrinth
fuga per canonem
gigantism
tumescence, detumescence
embryonic development
hallucination
narrative (old)
catechism (impersonal)
monologue (female)

But there are many more than eighteen styles in *Ulysses*, for each "technique" accommodates at least two. In the chapter of "gigantism," for example, the rough speech of some rather crude characters in a Dublin saloon is paralleled by some very turgid phony poetic prose about their heroic forerunners in ancient Irish myth; the "labyrinth" chapter, which gives us brief glimpses of nineteen ordinary human encounters occurring simultaneously in different parts of Dublin at 3 P.M., presents them through at least thirty-eight distinct personal styles; and the "embryonic development" chapter traces the evolution of English prose in brilliant parodies of twenty-three literary styles, the slang of 1904, and the rhetoric of a revivalist preacher. As for the stylistic variety of *Finnegans Wake* (1939), the least that can be said is that it is even richer than that of *Ulysses*.

The first excerpt from *Ulysses* given here is one in the style of Leopold Bloom, the chief character. We follow his stream of consciousness—his silent thoughts and half-thoughts—as well as his outward action and conversation. He is having a clandestine affair—so far by correspondence only—with a woman. He has rented a post office box to receive her letters, so his wife won't see them. He goes to the post office, picks up a letter (his nervous haste being indicated by the omission of the words "her" and "the"), looks at a British army recruiting poster, meets an acquaintance named McCoy, and while talking to him waits for a woman across the street to step up into a horsedrawn cab, of the kind known as outsiders because the passengers sit sideways back to back, with their feet on running boards outside. When she steps up she will lift her skirt and Bloom will see the calf of her leg, or so he hopes. (That was in 1904. We modern men's minds are on higher things.)

The difficulty is in following Bloom's silent thoughts and half-thoughts. The sentences "Talk: as if that would mend matters," and "Women will pay a lot of heed, I don't think," refer back to Maud Gonne's letter to the newspaper and Griffith's editorial, which have been brought to Bloom's mind by the sight of the recruiting poster. The "baton" with which he "reviews" the soldiers in the poster is a rolled-up newspaper. "A photo it isn't. A badge maybe" refers back to "Something pinned on: photo perhaps."

The conversation with McCoy is more complicated. Bloom is dressed in black because at 11 A.M. he is going to the funeral of one Paddy Dignam; McCoy tells him he has learned of Dignam's death only last night, in Conway's pub, from one Hoppy Holohan. McCoy's speech, with Bloom's stream of consciousness left out, goes as follows:

> I was with Bob Doran, he's on one of his periodical bends, and what do you call him Bantam Lyons. Just down there in Conway's we were. In came Hoppy. And he said: *Sad thing about our poor friend Paddy! What Paddy?* I said. *Poor little Paddy Dignam,* he said. *Why?* I said. *What's wrong with him?* I said. *What's wrong with him?* he said. *He's dead,* he said. And, faith, he filled up. I couldn't believe it when I heard it. I was with him on Friday last or Thursday was it in the Arch. *Yes,* he said. *He's gone. He died on Monday, poor fellow.*

Bloom is so much taken up with the woman across the street that the only word he speaks during this monologue—"Yes"—is irrelevant. Later he is reminded of the title of a Gilbert-and-Sullivan operetta, *Iolanthe; or The Peer and the Peri,* but for a Freudian reason gets it wrong: his guilt blocks the word "peer" from his mind.

Joyce did not invent the stream-of-consciousness method, but he developed it to its highest point, and here we see it at its best. His name is often linked with that of Gertrude Stein, but never by anyone who relishes the work of either; for these two writers were not doing at all the same thing or even the same kind of thing. Gertrude Stein was not interested in the stream of consciousness, though the term had been coined by her teacher William James; she was interested in constructing sentences that would express her sense of the present moment—the impact of objects, people, events, and situations—not in the conventional terms that tend to reduce things to the features or elements they have in common, but in terms that present each thing as it strikes her sensibility at the moment: "An eye glass, what is an eye glass, it is water," and "A sudden slice changes a whole plate, it does so suddenly." These two sentences from *Tender Buttons* (1914), which attempt to do in language what the cubists were doing in painting, seem to me quite successful. "Dirt and Not Copper" seems to suggest, without flatly saying so, that daily use makes things more comfortable to live with and thus makes life pleasanter; "Mildred's Umbrella" seems to suggest the earnestness and gracelessness of a fanatic working for a cause (one of Gertrude Stein's friends tried in vain to get her to work for women's suffrage, and it seems to me extremely graceless of Gertrude to sneer at her); and "A Method of a Cloak" suggests an elegant portrait in black and silver. But most of her radical experiments—as in *The Making of Americans* (1925), *As a Wife Has a Cow* (1926), and *Tender Buttons* as a rule—are not successful; her long novel, *The Making of Americans*, which uses cinematic techniques, has flashes of brilliance and would probably be as intelligible as the brilliant "Picasso" (1912) to anyone who had the patience to read it, but I haven't and I don't know of anyone who has; *Tender Buttons* and *As a Wife* . . . baffle me: I can seldom see the analogy with cubism: most of the time I have no idea what they mean or what they are supposed to do, and I can't care enough to wonder. But in *The Autobiography of Alice B. Toklas* (1933) she took the advice she had given Ernest Hemingway back in 1920 (see pages 220–229), and the result is very fine indeed: conversational, gossipy, natural and delightful; in "The Winner Loses" (1940) and *Wars I Have Seen* (1944) we see the reciprocal influence of Hemingway on Gertrude Stein. The Stein-Hemingway style is a literary manifestation of the philosophy of pragmatism. For a discussion of how this came about, see my paper, "The Influence of American Pragmatism on the French 'New Novel,'" *Proceedings* of the Fourth Congress of the International Comparative Literature Association, 1964 (Fribourg, 1966), pages 1025–1030.

As Hemingway was a disciple of Gertrude Stein, so Faulkner was a disciple of Joyce. In the first selection here, from *The Old Man* (1939), a Mississippi prisoner is telling his cell-mates of his adventures and misfortunes during a flood. Guards at the state prison farm had ordered him to go out in a rowboat and rescue a pregnant woman who had climbed a tree. Faulkner puts the prisoner's story in indirect discourse, interrupted from time to time by direct questions and answers. If you follow the dashes that surround these interruptions you will have no difficulty. If we omit the interruptions, the passages that are interrupted read as follows: "He could have put her back into another tree at any time, but he had not done that." "He told how the skiff fled on while he tried merely to keep it afloat, until the darkness thinned and lifted and revealed the skiff to be moving still rapidly. . . ."

In the second selection, from *Absalom, Absalom!* (1936), the only difficulty is in the italicized passage indicating a silent dialogue that takes place in Quentin's mind. The second Quentin interrupts the first from time to time, with a correction or an amendment or a comment, in parentheses; the second repeats these interjections, to show his agreement. Perhaps the best way to clarify this dialogue is for two people to read it aloud as if they were rehearsing a play, one reading only the passages in parentheses, the other reading everything else.

John Dos Passos was another disciple of Joyce who developed a style of his own. He was one of the first novelists to use cinematic techniques, and is thus one of the fathers of the contemporary novel. He also uses montage, collage and other techniques developed by the cubist painters: the juxtaposition of disparate elements in order to convey the sense of a scene—or a culture—made up of disparate elements.

Samuel Beckett has many styles. The examples given here, from *Watt* (1953) and *Molloy* (French 1951, English 1955), all show the influence of classicism; the one from *Molloy* shows also Beckett's fine simplicity of language and his delight in what he called in his study *Proust* "the comedy of exhaustive enumeration"; the longer of the two passages from *Watt* illustrates his use of rare words for precision, and its pedantically careful punctuation tells us something about Watt's personality.

Absolute precision in the use of words is also one of the marks of Nabokov's style:

> A kerosene lamp is steered into the gloaming. Gently it floats and comes down; the hand of memory, now in a footman's white cotton glove, places it in the centre of a round table.

Observe that he doesn't say, "Gently it floats down"; his observation is clearer. An ordinary writer might have said, "In my childhood we used kerosene lamps. As I look back in memory I seem to see a footman wearing white cotton gloves putting such a lamp in the middle of a circular table." "Places," "centre" (British spelling and all) and "round" are the right words; "putting," "middle" and "circular" are wrong. This is not a matter of taste or opinion, it is a matter of fact; look up the words in an unabridged dictionary. Moreover, the words Nabokov chose are right in terms of euphony as well as meaning. And as for showing only the hand instead of the whole footman, that is a matter of art: of selection and concentration, omitting everything that is not essential. It also induces the reader's imagination to—not to supply the rest of the footman, that would undo Nabokov's art, but to concentrate on what is essential and thus participate in Nabokov's art.

The quite different prose of Thorstein Veblen, as I said on page 85, is also the prose of a man for whom English was a second language. Whenever I read it I see in my mind's eye a huge wrought-iron gate: heavy, massive, ponderous, but beautiful and full of grace and seeming lightness, its leaves and flowers and flourishing grapevines charming us by the spaces they define. Like Dr. Johnson addressing Lord Chesterfield, Veblen the carpenter's son addresses the leisure class in prose that is superior to that of its own best manner: Latinate, complex, formal, ceremonious, dry, unsmiling, outrageous. He is a supreme ironist. *The Theory of the Leisure Class* is full of the most beautiful wrought irony in the language.

JAMES JOYCE [1882–1941]

Excerpt from ULYSSES, *1922, Chapter 5*

He handed the card through the brass grill.

—Are there any letters for me? he asked.

While the postmistress searched a pigeonhole he gazed at the recruiting poster with soldiers of all arms on parade: and held the top of his baton [a rolled-up newspaper] against his nostrils, smelling freshprinted rag paper. No answer probably. Went too far last time.

The postmistress handed him back through the grill his card with a letter. He thanked and glanced rapidly at the typed envelope.

Henry Fowler, Esq.
c/o P.O. Westland Row,
City.

Answered anyhow. He slipped card and letter into his side-pocket, reviewing again the soldiers on parade. Where's old Tweedy's regiment? Castoff soldier. There: bearskin cap and hackle plume. No, he's a grenadier. Pointed cuffs. There he is: royal Dublin fusiliers. Redcoats. Too showy. That must be why the women go after them. Uniform. Easier to enlist and drill. Maud Gonne's letter about taking them off O'Connell street at night: disgrace to our Irish capital. Griffith's paper is on the same tack now: an army rotten with venereal disease: overseas or half-seasover empire. Half baked they look: hypnotised like. Eyes front. Mark time. Table: able. Bed: ed. The King's own. Never see him dressed up as a fireman or a bobby. A mason, yes.

He strolled out of the postoffice and turned to the right. Talk: as if that would mend matters. His hand went into his pocket and a forefinger felt its way under the flap of the envelope, ripping it open in jerks. Women will pay a lot of heed, I don't think. His fingers drew forth the letter and crumpled the envelope in his pocket. Something pinned on: photo perhaps. Hair? No.

M'Coy. Get rid of him quickly. Take me out of my way. Hate company when you.

—Hello, Bloom. Where are you off to?

—Hello, M'Coy. Nowhere in particular.

—How's the body?

—Fine. How are you?

—Just keeping alive, M'Coy said.

His eyes on the black tie and clothes he asked with low respect:

—Is there any . . . no trouble I hope? I see you're . . .

—O no, Mr. Bloom said. Poor Dignam, you know. The funeral is today.

—To be sure, poor fellow. So it is. What time?

A photo it isn't. A badge maybe.

—E . . . eleven, Mr. Bloom answered.

—I must try to get out there, M'Coy said. Eleven, is it? I only heard it last night. Who was telling me? Holohan. You know Hoppy?

—I know.

Mr Bloom gazed across the road at the outsider drawn up before the door of the Grosvenor. The porter hoisted the valise up on the well. She stood still, waiting, while the man, husband, brother, like her, searched his pockets for change. Stylish kind of coat with that roll collar, warm for a day like this, looks like blanketcloth. Careless stand of her with her hands in those patch pockets. Like that haughty creature at the polo match. Women all for caste till you touch the spot. Handsome is and handsome does. Reserved about to yield. The honourable Mrs and Brutus is an honourable man. Possess her once take the starch out of her.

—I was with Bob Doran, he's on one of his periodical bends, and what do you call him Bantam Lyons. Just down there in Conway's we were.

Doran, Lyons in Conway's. She raised a gloved hand to her hair. In came Hoppy. Having a wet. Drawing back his head and gazing from beneath his veiled eyelids he saw the bright fawn skin shine in the glare, the braided drums. Clearly I can see today. Moisture about gives long sight perhaps. Talking of one thing or another. Lady's hand. Which side will she get up?

—And he said: *Sad thing about our poor friend Paddy! What Paddy?* I said. *Poor little Paddy Dignam*, he said.

Off to the country: Broadstone probably. High brown boots with laces dangling. Wellturned foot. What is he fostering over that change for? Sees me looking. Eye out for other fellow always. Good fallback. Two strings to her bow.

—*Why?* I said. *What's wrong with him?* I said.

Proud: rich: silk stockings.

—Yes, Mr Bloom said.

He moved a little to the side of M'Coy's talking head. Getting up in a minute.

—*What's wrong with him?* he said. *He's dead*, he said. And, faith, he filled up. *Is it Paddy Dignam?* I said. I couldn't believe it when I heard it. I was with him no later than Friday last or Thursday was it in the Arch. *Yes*, he said. *He's gone. He died on Monday, poor fellow.*

Watch! Watch! Silk flash rich stockings white. Watch!

A heavy tramcar honking its gong slewed between.

Lost it. Curse your noisy pugnose. Feels locked out of it. Paradise and the peri. Always happening like that. The very moment. Girl in Eustace street hallway Monday was it settling her garter. Her friend covering the display of. *Esprit de corps*. Well, what are you gaping at?

—Yes, yes, Mr Bloom said after a dull sigh. Another gone.

—One of the best, M'Coy said.

Excerpt from ULYSSES, *Chapter 14*

[In my chapter on Victorian styles I said that Carlyle was brilliantly parodied by Joyce in *Ulysses*. Here is the passage I was referring to. Chapter 14, "The Oxen of the Sun," represents the conception, gestation and birth of a child in terms of the evolution of English prose style from the beginning to the present—from the mating of Anglo-Saxon words with Church Latin syntax to the slang of June 16, 1904, the day on which the events of *Ulysses* take place. Throughout the day the principal characters in the novel have been wondering whether it will rain or not (rain being a well-established literary symbol suggesting fertility) and whether Mrs. Theodore Purefoy, whose name means Godgiven Purefaith and who is in her third day of labor, will or will not succeed in giving birth. Finally, about 10:30 p.m., there is a terrific

crash of thunder, rain comes pouring down like a waterfall, and Mrs.
Purefoy gives birth to a boy. Joyce congratulates her in the style of
Dickens at his most sentimental, and her husband in the style of Carlyle
at his most eructant. Here is the passage congratulating the husband.]

The air without is impregnated with raindew moisture, life-essence
celestial, glistering on Dublin stone there under starshiny *coelum*
[Heaven]. God's air, the Allfather's air, scintillant circumambient
cessile air. Breathe it deep into thee. By heaven, Theodore Purefoy,
thou hast done a doughty deed and no botch! Thou art, I vow, the
remarkablest progenitor barring none in this chaffering allincluding
most farraginous chronicle. Astounding! In her lay a Godframed
Godgiven preformed possibility which thou hast fructified with
thy modicum of man's work. Cleave to her! Serve! Toil on, labour
like a very bandog and let scholarment and all Malthusiasts go hang.
Thou art all their daddies, Theodore. Art drooping under thy load,
bemoiled with butcher's bills at home and ingots (not thine!) in
the countinghouse? Head up! For every newbegotten thou shalt
gather thy homer of ripe wheat. See, thy fleece is drenched. Dost
envy Darby Dullman there with his Joan? A canting jay and a
rheumeyed curdog is all their progeny. Pshaw, I tell thee! He is
a mule, a dead gasteropod, without vim or stamina, not worth a
cracked kreutzer. Copulation without population! No, say I!
Herod's slaughter of the innocents were the truer name. Vegetables,
forsooth, and sterile cohabitation! Give her beefsteaks, red, raw,
bleeding! She is a hoary pandemonium of ills, enlarged glands,
mumps, quinsy, bunions, hayfever, bedsores, ringworm, floating
kidney, Derbyshire neck, warts, bilious attacks, gallstones, cold
feet, varicose veins. A truce to threnes and trentals and jeremies and
all such congenital defunctive music. Twenty years of it, regret
them not. With thee it was not as with many that will and would
and wait and never do. Thou sawest thy America, thy lifetask, and
didst charge to cover like the transpontine bison. How saith Zara-

thustra? *Deine Kuh Trübsal melkest Du. Nun trinkst Du die süsse Milch des Euters.* [Thou milkest thy cow Affliction. Now drinkest thou the sweet milk of her udder.] See! It displodes for thee in abundance. Drink, man, an udderful! Mother's milk, Purefoy, the milk of human kin, milk too of those burgeoning stars overhead, radiant in thin rainvapour, punch milk, such as those rioters will quaff in their guzzlingden, milk of madness, the honeymilk of Canaan's land. Thy cow's dug was tough, what? Ay, but her milk is hot and sweet and fattening. No dollop this but thick rich bonny-clabber. To her, old patriarch! Pap! *Per Deam Partulam et Pertundam nunc est bibendum!* [This is a kind of dog-Latin with naughty overtones; it means, very roughly, "By the Goddess of Bearing and Sharing and Bursting Through, now is the time to have a drink!"]

The word "cessile" anticipates the etymological games Joyce will play in *Finnegans Wake* (1939). There is no such word in any English dictionary. But it seems to combine *sessile*, stationary, with the Latin *caecilius*, blind, dim-sighted, misty, dark; since the air is "impregnated with raindew moisture," Joyce's Carlyle is telling his poor bank clerk to fill his lungs and his mind with unmoving fog. And, as an etymologically possible adjective related to the noun *cession*, from the French verb *cesser*, "cessile" would mean yielding to or making way for a conqueror, and free of charge. Such multiplicities of meaning within a single word, which make *Finnegans Wake* difficult (see Appendix I), occur only rarely in *Ulysses*. But readers of Joyce know from experience that all kinds of things are going on beneath even his most innocent-seeming surfaces. Thus, the word "Pap!" may very well be Joyce's personal comment on Carlyle's advice to labor. Earlier, the word "Pshaw" may very well signify Bernard Shaw (as it unmistakably does in *Finnegans Wake*), especially since here it refers to vegetarianism and childlessness—and since Joyce was jealous of Shaw's popular success. Theodore Purefoy is surely Joyce himself, who had worked in a bank, and his child is *Ulysses*. Of this, for a number of reasons, there is no possible doubt whatever. Joyce was not modest. But we must watch our step. It would not do to think of the "Joan" in this passage as Shaw's Saint Joan, since his play about her did not appear until two years after *Ulysses* was published. She seems rather to be Ireland, and a sterile Muse. Among Joyce's Irish contemporaries, the poet AE (George William Russell) was recommending vegetarianism as a contribution to the solution of Ireland's troubles, and the novelist George Moore was recommending half-seriously that the Irish should exterminate themselves by practicing birth control, a thing Joyce disapproved of. (Look up H. W. Fowler's article on the prepositional ending in *A Dictionary of Modern English Usage.*) Thus, Joyce is simultaneously, in the same words, mocking Carlyle's empty abstractions, congratulating himself as the greatest prose writer in all Engish literature, and sneering at his contemporaries. The term literary critics use for this sort of thing is "ambiguity." Thus, the sentence "Thou art, I vow, the remarkablest progenitor barring none in this chaffering all-including most farraginous chronicle," makes Theodore Purefoy the remarkablest progenitor in *Ulysses* and Joyce the remarkablest progenitor in Chapter 14 of *Ulysses*—i.e., in the whole chronicle of English prose.

◈

GERTRUDE STEIN [1874–1946]

Excerpt from THE MAKING OF AMERICANS, *written 1906–1908, published 1925*

I am writing for myself and strangers. This is the only way that I can do it. Everybody is a real one to me, everybody is like some one else too to me. No one of them that I know can want to know it and so I write for myself and strangers.

Every one is always busy with it, no one of them then ever want to know it that every one looks like some one else and they see it. Mostly every one dislikes to hear it. It is very important to me to always know it, to always see it which one looks like others and to tell it. I write for myself and strangers. I do this for my own sake and for the sake of those who know I know it that they look like other ones, that they are separate and yet always repeated. There are some who like it that I know they are like many others and repeat it, there are many who never can really like it.

There are many that I know and they know it. They are all of them repeating and I hear it. I love it and I tell it, I love it and now I will write it. This is now the history of the way some of them are it.

I write for myself and strangers. No one who knows me can like it. At least they mostly do not like it that every one is of a kind of men and women and I see it. I love it and I write it.

I want readers so strangers must do it. Mostly no one knowing me can like it that I love it that every one is a kind of men and women, that always I am looking and comparing and classifying of them, always I am seeing their repeating. Always more and more I love repeating, it may be irritating to hear from them but always more and more I love it of them. More and more I love it of them, the being in them, the mixing in them, the repeating in them, the deciding the kind of them every one is who has human being.

This is now a little of what I love and how I write it. Later there will be much more of it.

There are many ways of making kinds of men and women. Now there will be descriptions of every kind of way every one can be a kind of men and women.

This is now a history of Martha Hersland. This is now a history of Martha and of every one who came to be of her living.

There will then be soon much description of every way one can think of men and women, in their beginning, in their middle living, and their ending.

Every one then is an individual being. Every one then is like many others always living, there are many ways of thinking of every one, this is now a description of all of them. There must then be a whole history of each one of them. There must then now be a description of all repeating. Now I will tell all the meaning to me in repeating, the loving there is in me for repeating.

Every one is one inside them, every one reminds some one of some other one who is or was or will be living. Every one has it to say of each one he is like such a one I see it in him, every one has it to say of each one she is like some one else I can tell by remembering. So it goes on always in living, every one is always remembering some one who is resembling to the one at whom they are then looking. So they go on repeating, every one is themselves inside them and every one is resembling to others, and that is always interesting. There are many ways of making kinds of men and women. In each way of making kinds of them there is a different system of finding them resembling. Sometime there will be here every way there can be of seeing kinds of men and women. Sometime there will be then a complete history of each one. Every one always is repeating the whole of them and so sometime some one who sees them will have a complete history of every one. Sometime some one will know all the ways there are for people to be resembling, some one sometime then will have a completed history of every one.

Soon now there will be a history of the way repeating comes out of them comes out of men and women when they are young, when they are children, they have then their own system of being resembling; this will soon be a description of the men and women in beginning, the being young in them, the being children.

There is then now and here the loving repetition, this is then, now and here, a description of the loving of repetition and then there will be a description of all the kinds of ways there can be seen to be kinds of men and women. Then there will be realised the complete history of every one, the fundamental character of every one, the bottom nature in them, the mixtures in them, the strength and weakness of everything they have inside them, the flavor of them, the meaning in them, the being in them, and then you have a whole history then of each one. Everything then they do in living is clear to the completed understanding, their living, loving, eating, pleasing, smoking, thinking, scolding, drinking, working, dancing, walking, talking, laughing, sleeping, everything in them. There are whole beings then, they are themselves inside them, repeating coming out of them makes a history of each one of them.

Always from the beginning there was to me all living as repeating. This is now a description of my feeling. As I was saying listening to repeating is often irritating, always repeating is all of living, everything in a being is always repeating, more and more listening to repeating gives to me completed understanding. Each one slowly comes to be a whole one to me. Each one slowly comes to be a whole one in me. Soon then it commences to sound through my ears and eyes and feelings the repeating that is always coming out from each one, that is them, that makes then slowly of each one of them a whole one. Repeating then comes slowly then to be to one who has it to have loving repeating as natural being comes to be a full sound telling all the being in each one such a one is ever knowing. Sometimes it takes many years of knowing some one before the repeating that is that one gets to be a steady sounding to the hearing of one who has it as a natural being to love repeating that slowly comes out from every one. Sometimes it takes many years of knowing some one before the repeating in that one comes to be a clear history of such a one. Natures sometimes are so mixed up in some one that steady repeating in them is mixed up with changing. Soon then there will be a completed history of each one. Sometimes it is difficult to know it in some, for what these are saying is repeating in them is not the real repeating of them, is not the complete repeating for them. Sometimes many years of knowing some one pass before repeating of all being in them comes out clearly from them. As I was saying it is often irritating to listen to the repeating they are doing, always then that one that has it as being to love repeating that is the whole history of each one, such a one has it then that this irritation passes over into patient completed understanding. Loving repeating is one way of being. This is now a description of such feeling.

There are many that I know and they know it. They are all of them repeating and I hear it. I love it and I tell it. I love it and now I will write it. This is now a history of my love of it. I hear it and I love it and I write it. They repeat it. They live it and I see it and I hear it. They live it and I hear it and I see it and I love it and now and always I will write it. There are many kinds of men and women and I know it. They repeat it and I hear it and I love it. This is now a history of the way they do it. This is now a history of the way I love it.

Now I will tell of the meaning to me in repeating, of the loving there is in me for repeating.

Sometime every one becomes a whole one to me. Sometime every one has a completed history for me. Slowly each one is a whole one to me, with some, all their living is passing before they are a whole one to me. There is a completed history of them to me then when there is of them a completed understanding of the bottom nature in them of the nature or natures mixed up in them with the bottom nature of them or separated in them. There is then a history of the things they say and do and feel, and happen to them. There is then a history of the living in them. Repeating is always in all of them. Repeating in them comes out of them, slowly making clear to any one that looks closely at them the nature and the natures mixed up in them. This sometimes comes to be clear in every one.

Often as I was saying repeating is very irritating to listen to from them and then slowly it settles into a completed history of them. Repeating is a wonderful thing in living being. Sometime then the nature of every one comes to be clear to some one listening to the repeating coming out of each one.

This is then now to be a little description of the loving feeling for understanding of the completed history of each one that comes to one who listens always steadily to all repeating. This is the history then of the loving feeling in me of repeating, the loving feeling in me for completed understanding of the completed history of every one as it slowly comes out in every one as patiently and steadily I hear it and see it as repeating in them. This is now a little a description of this loving feeling. This is now a little a history of it from the beginning.

"Picasso," from THREE PORTRAITS OF PAINTERS, *1912*

[Observe the various interweavings of "certainly," "following," "completely" and "charming" in the first paragraph, and the weaving in of additional elements in succeeding paragraphs.]

One whom some were certainly following was one who was completely charming. One whom some were certainly following was one who was charming. One whom some were following was one who was completely charming. One whom some were following was one who was certainly completely charming.

Some were certainly following and were certain that the one they were then following was one working and was one bringing out of himself then something. Some were certainly following and were certain that the one they were then following was one bringing out of himself then something that was coming to be a heavy thing, a solid thing and a complete thing.

One whom some were certainly following was one working and certainly was one bringing something out of himself then and was one who had been all his living had been one having something coming out of him.

Something had been coming out of him, certainly it had been coming out of him, certainly it was something, certainly it had been coming out of him and it had meaning, a charming meaning, a solid meaning, a struggling meaning, a clear meaning.

One whom some were certainly following and some were certainly following him, one whom some were certainly following was one certainly working.

One whom some were certainly following was one having something coming out of him something having meaning and this one was certainly working then.

This one was working and something was coming then, something was coming out of this one then. This one was one and always there was something coming out of this one and always there had been something coming out of this one. This one had never been one not having something coming out of this one. This one was one having something coming out of this one. This one had been one whom some were following. This one was one whom some were following. This one was being one whom some were following. This one was one who was working.

This one was one who was working. This one was one being one having something being coming out of him. This one was one going on having something come out of him. This one was one going on working. This one was one whom some were following. This one was one who was working.

This one always had something being coming out of this one. This one was working. This one always had been working. This one was always having something that was coming out of this one that was a solid thing, a charming thing, a lovely thing, a perplexing thing, a disconcerting thing, a simple thing, a clear thing, a complicated thing, an interesting thing, a disturbing thing, a repellant thing, a very pretty thing. This one was one certainly being one having something coming out of him. This one was one whom some were following. This one was one who was working.

This one was one who was working and certainly this one was needing to be working so as to be one being working. This one was one having something coming out of him. This one would be one all his living having something coming out of him. This one was working and then this one was working and this one was needing to be working, not to be one having something coming out of him something having meaning, but was needing to be working so as to be one working.

This one was certainly working and working was something this one was certain this one would be doing and this one was doing that thing, this one was working. This one was not one completely working. This one certainly was not completely working.

This one was one having always something being coming out of him, something having completely a real meaning. This one was one whom some were following. This one was one who was working. This one was one who was working and he was one needing this thing needing to be working so as to be one having some way of being one having some way of working. This one was one who was working. This one was one having something come out of him something having meaning. This one was one always having something come out of him and this thing the thing coming out of him always had real meaning. This one was one who was working. This one was one who was almost always working. This one was not one completely working. This one was one not ever completely working. This one was not one working to have anything come out of him. He always did have something having meaning that did come out of him. He always did have something come out of him. He was working, he was not ever completely working. He did have some following. They were always following him. Some were certainly following him. He was one who was working. He was one having something coming out of him something having meaning. He was not ever completely working.

Excerpts from TENDER BUTTONS, 1914

DIRT AND NOT COPPER

Dirt and not copper makes a color darker. It makes the shape so heavy and makes no melody harder.

It makes mercy and relaxation and even a strength to spread a table fuller. There are more places not empty. They see cover.

NOTHING ELEGANT

A charm a single charm is doubtful. If the red is rose and there is a gate surrounding it, if inside is let in and there places change then certainly something is upright. It is earnest.

MILDRED'S UMBRELLA

A cause and no curve, a cause and loud enough, a cause and extra a loud clash and an extra wagon, a sign of extra, a sac a small sac and an established color and cunning, a slender grey and no ribbon, this means a loss a great loss a restitution.

A METHOD OF A CLOAK

A single climb to a line, a straight exchange to a cane, a desperate adventure and courage and a clock, all this which is a system, which has feeling, which has resignation and success, all makes an attractive black silver.

A RED STAMP

If lilies are lily white if they exhaust noise and distance and even dust, if they dusty will dirt a surface that has no extreme grace, if they do this and it is not necessary it is not at all necessary if they do this they need a catalogue.

A BOX

A large box is handily made of what is necessary to replace any substance. Suppose an example is necessary, the plainer it is made the more reason there is for some outward recognition that there is a result.

A box is made sometimes and them to see to see to it neatly and to have the holes stopped up makes it necessary to use paper.

A custom which is necessary when a box is used and taken is that a large part of the time there are three which have different connections. The one is on the table. The two are on the table. The three are on the table. The one, one is the same length as is shown by the cover being longer. The other is different there is more cover that shows it. The other is different and that makes the corners have the same shade the eight are in singular arrangement to make four necessary.

Lax, to have corners, to be lighter than some weight, to indicate a wedding journey, to last brown and not curious, to be wealthy, cigarettes are established by length and by doubling.

Left open, to be left pounded, to be left closed, to be circulating in summer and winter, and sick color that is grey that is not dusty and red shows, to be sure cigarettes do measure an empty length sooner than a choice in color.

Winged, to be winged means that white is yellow and pieces pieces that are brown are dust color if dust is washed off, then it is choice that is to say it is fitting cigarettes sooner than paper.

An increase why is an increase idle, why is silver cloister, why is the spark brighter, if it is brighter is there any result, hardly more than ever.

A PLATE

An occasion for a plate, an occasional resource is in buying and how soon does washing enable a selection of the same thing neater. If the party is small a clever song is in order.

Plates and a dinner set of colored china. Pack together a string and enough with it to protect the centre, cause a considerable haste and gather more as it is cooling, collect more trembling and not any even trembling, cause a whole thing to be a church.

A sad size a size that is not sad is blue as every bit of blue is precocious. A kind of green a game in green and nothing flat nothing quite flat and more round, nothing a particular color strangely, nothing breaking the losing of no little piece.

A splendid address a really splendid address is not shown by giving a flower freely, it is not shown by a mark or by wetting.

Cut cut in white, cut in white so lately. Cut more than any other and show it. Show it in the stem and in starting and in evening coming complication.

A lamp is not the only sign of glass. The lamp and the cake are not the only sign of stone. The lamp and the cake and the cover are not the only necessity altogether.

A plan a hearty plan, a compressed disease and no coffee, not even a card or a change to incline each way, a plan that has that excess and that break is the one that shows filling.

A SELTZER BOTTLE

Any neglect of many particles to a cracking, any neglect of this makes around it what is lead in color and certainly discolor in silver. The use of this is manifold. Supposing a certain time selected is assured, suppose it is even necessary, suppose no other extract is permitted and no more handling is needed, suppose the rest of the message is mixed with a very long slender needle and even if it could be any black border, supposing all this altogether made a dress and suppose it was actual, suppose the mean way to state it was occasional, if you suppose this in August and even more melodiously, if you suppose this even in the necessary incident of there certainly being no middle in summer and winter, suppose this and an elegant settlement a very elegant settlement is more than of consequence, it is not final and sufficient and substituted. This which was so kindly a present was constant.

A LONG DRESS

What is the current that makes machinery, that makes it crackle, what is the current that presents a long line and a necessary waist. What is this current.

What is the wind, what is it.

Where is the serene length, it is there and a dark place is not a dark place, only a white and red are black, only a yellow and green are blue, a pink is scarlet, a bow is every color. A line distinguishes it. A line just distinguishes it.

A RED HAT

A dark grey, a very dark gray, a quite dark gray is monstrous ordinarily, it is so monstrous because there is no red in it. If red is in everything it is not necessary. Is that not an argument for any use of it and even so is there any place that is better, is there any place that has so much stretched out.

A BLUE COAT

A blue coat is guided guided away, guided and guided away, that is the particular color that is used for that length and not any width not even more than a shadow.

A PIANO

If the speed is open, if the color is careless, if the selection of a strong scent is not awkward, if the button holder is held by all the waving color and there is no color, not any color. If there is no dirt in a pin and there can be none scarcely, if there is not then the place is the same as up standing.

This is no dark custom and it even is not acted in any such a way that a restraint is not spread. That is spread, it shuts and it lifts and awkwardly not awkwardly the centre is in standing.

A CHAIR

A widow in a wise veil and more garments shows that shadows are even. It addresses no more, it shadows the stage and learning. A regular arrangement, the severest and the most preserved is that which has the arrangement not more than always authorised.

A suitable establishment, well housed, practical, patient and staring, a suitable bedding, very suitable and not more particularly than complaining, anything suitable is so necessary.

A fact is that when the direction is just like that, no more, longer, sudden and at the same time not any sofa, the main action is that without a blaming there is no custody.

Practice measurement, practice the sign that means that really means a necessary betrayal, in showing that there is wearing.

Hope, what is a spectacle, a spectacle is the resemblance between the circular side place and nothing else, nothing else.

To choose it is ended, it is actual and more and more than that it has it certainly has the same treat, and a seat all that is practiced and more easily much more easily ordinarily.

Pick a barn, a whole barn, and bend more slender accents than have ever been necessary, shine in the darkness necessarily.

Actually not aching, actually not aching, a stubborn bloom is so artificial and even more than that, it is a spectacle, it is a binding accident, it is animosity and accentuation.

If the chance to dirty diminishing is necessary, if it is why is there no complexion, why is there no rubbing, why is there no special protection.

A FRIGHTFUL RELEASE
A bag which was left and not only taken but turned away was not found. The place was shown to be very like the last time. A piece was not exchanged, not a bit of it, a piece was left over. The rest was mismanaged.

A PURSE
A purse was not green, it was not straw color, it was hardly seen and it had a use a long use and the chain, the chain was never missing, it was not misplaced, it showed that it was open, that is all that it showed.

A MOUNTED UMBRELLA
What was the use of not leaving it there where it would hang what was the use if there was no chance of ever seeing it come there and show that it was handsome and right in the way it showed it. The lesson is to learn that it does show it, that it shows it and that nothing, that there is nothing, that there is no more to do about it and just so much more is there plenty of reason for making an exchange.

A CLOTH
Enough cloth is plenty and more, more is almost enough for that and besides if there is no more spreading is there plenty of room for it. Any occasion shows the best way.

MORE
An elegant use of foliage and grace and a little piece of white cloth and oil.

Wondering so winningly in several kinds of oceans is the reason that makes red so regular and enthusiastic. The reason that there is more snips are the same shining very colored rid of no round color.

AS A WIFE HAS A COW, A LOVE STORY, *1926*

Nearly all of it to be as a wife has a cow, a love story. All of it to be as a wife has a cow, all of it to be as a wife has a cow, a love story.

As to be all of it as to be a wife as a wife has a cow, a love story, all of it as to be all of it as a wife all of it as to be as a wife has a cow a love story, all of it as a wife has a cow as a wife has a cow a love story.

Has made, as it has made as it has made, has made has to be as a wife has a cow, a love story. Has made as to be as a wife has a cow a love story. As a wife has a cow, as a wife has a cow, a love story. Has to be as a wife has a cow a love story. Has made as to be as a wife has a cow a love story.

When he can, and for that when he can, for that. When he can and for that when he can. For that. When he can. For that when he can. For that. And when he can and for that. For that, and when he can. For that and when he can.

And to in six and another. And to and in and six and another. And to and in and six and another. And to in six and and to and in and six and another. And to and in and six and another. And to and six and in and another and and to and six and another and and to and in and six and and to and six and in and another.

In came in there, came in there come out of there. In came in come out of there. Come out there in came in there. Come out of there and in and come out of there. Came in there, come out of there.

Feeling or for it, as feeling or for it, came in or come in, or come out of there or feeling as feeling or feeling as for it.

As a wife has a cow.

Came in and come out.

As a wife has a cow a love story.

As a love story, as a wife has a cow, a love story.

Not and now, now and not, not and now, by and by not and now, as not, as soon as not not and now, now as soon now now as soon, now as soon as soon as now. Just as soon just now just now just as soon just as soon as now. Just as soon as now.

And in that, as and in that, in that and and in that, so that, so that and in that, and in that and so that and as for that and as for that and that. In that. In that and and for that as for that and in that. Just as soon and in that. In that as that and just as soon. Just as soon as that.

Even now, now and even now and now and even now. Not as even now, therefor, even now and therefor, therefor and even now and even now and therefor even now. So not to and moreover and even now and therefor and moreover and even now and so and even now and therefor even now.

Do they as they do so. And do they do so.

We feel we feel. We feel or if we feel if we feel or if we feel. We feel or if we feel. As it is made made a day made a day or two made a day, as it is made a day or two, as it is made a day. Made a day. Made a day. Not away a day. By day. As it is made a day.

On the fifteenth of October as they say, said anyway, what is it as they expect, as they expect it or as they expected it, as they expect it and as they expected it, expect it or for it, expected it and it is expected of it. As they say said anyway. What is it as they expect for it, what is it and it is as they expect of it. What is it. What is it the fifteenth of October as they say as they expect or as they expected as they expect for it. What is it as they say the fifteenth of October as they say and as expected of it, the fifteenth of October as they say, what is it as expected of it. What is it and the fifteenth of October as they say and expected of it.

And prepare and prepare so prepare to prepare and prepare to prepare and prepare so as to prepare, so to prepare and prepare to prepare to prepare for and to prepare for it to prepare, to prepare for it, in preparation, as preparation in preparation by preparation. They will be too busy afterwards to prepare. As preparation prepare, to prepare, as to preparation and to prepare. Out there.

Have it as having having it as happening, happening to have it as having, having to have it as happening. Happening and have it as happening and having it happen as happening and having to have it happen as happening, and my wife has a cow as now, my wife having a cow as now, my wife having a cow as now and having a cow as now and having a cow and having a cow now, my wife has a cow and now. My wife has a cow.

Excerpt from THE AUTOBIOGRAPHY OF ALICE B. TOKLAS, *1933*

The first thing that happened when we were back in Paris was Hemingway with a letter of introduction from Sherwood Anderson.

I remember very well the impression I had of Hemingway that first afternoon. He was an extraordinarily good-looking young man, twenty-three years old. It was not long after that that everybody was twenty-six. It became the period of being twenty-six. During the next two or three years all the young men were twenty-six years old. It was the right age apparently for that time and place. There were one or two under twenty, for example George Lynes but they did not count as Gertrude Stein carefully explained to them. If they were young men they were twenty-six.

Later on, much later on they were twenty-one and twenty-two.

So Hemingway was twenty-three, rather foreign looking, with passionately interested, rather than interesting eyes. He sat in front of Gertrude Stein and listened and looked.

They talked then, and more and more, a great deal together. He asked her to come and spend an evening in their apartment and look at his work. Hemingway had then and has always a very good instinct for finding apartments in strange but pleasing localities and good femmes de ménage and good food. This his first apartment was just off the place du Tertre. We spent the evening there and he and Gertrude Stein went over all the writing he had done up to that time. He had begun the novel that it was inevitable he would begin and there were the little poems afterwards printed by McAlmon in the Contact Edition. Gertrude Stein rather liked the poems, they were direct, Kiplingesque, but the novel she found wanting. There is a great deal of description in this, she said, and not particularly good description. Begin over again and concentrate, she said.

Hemingway was at this time Paris correspondent for a canadian newspaper. He was obliged there to express what he called the canadian viewpoint.

He and Gertrude Stein used to walk together and talk together a great deal. One day she said to him, look here, you say you and your wife have a little money between you. Is it enough to live on if you live quietly. Yes, he said. Well, she said, then do it. If you keep on doing newspaper work you will never see things, you will only see words and that will not do, that is of course if you intend to be a writer. Hemingway said he undoubtedly intended to be a writer. He and his wife went away on a trip and shortly after Hemingway turned up alone. He came to the house about ten o'clock in the morning and he stayed, he stayed for lunch, he stayed all afternoon, he stayed for dinner and he stayed until about ten o'clock at night and then all of a sudden

he announced that his wife was enceinte and then with great bit-
terness, and I, I am too young to be a father. We consoled him as
best we could and sent him on his way.

When they came back Hemingway said that he had made
up his mind. They would go back to America and he would work
hard for a year and with what he would earn and what they had
they would settle down and he would give up newspaper work
and make himself a writer. They went away and well within the
prescribed year they came back with a new born baby. Newspaper work was over.

The first thing to do when they came back was as they
thought to get the baby baptised. They wanted Gertrude Stein
and myself to be god-mothers and an english war comrade of
Hemingway was to be god-father. We were all born of different
religions and most of us were not practising any, so it was rather
difficult to know in what church the baby could be baptised.
We spent a great deal of time that winter, all of us, discussing
the matter. Finally it was decided that it should be baptised episcopalian and episcopalian it was. Just how it was managed with
the assortment of god-parents I am sure I do not know, but it was
baptised in the episcopalian chapel.

Writer or painter god-parents are notoriously unreliable.
That is, there is certain before long to be a cooling of friendship.
I know several cases of this, poor Paulot Picasso's god-parents
have wandered out of sight and just as naturally it is a long time
since any of us have seen or heard of our Hemingway god-child.

However in the beginning we were active god-parents, I
particularly. I embroidered a little chair and I knitted a gay coloured garment for the god-child. In the meantime the god-child's
father was very earnestly at work making himself a writer.

Gertrude Stein never corrects any detail of anybody's writing, she sticks strictly to general principles, the way of seeing what
the writer chooses to see, and the relation between that vision and

the way it gets down. When the vision is not complete the words are flat, it is very simple, there can be no mistake about it, so she insists. It was at this time that Hemingway began the short things that afterwards were printed in a volume called In Our Time.

One day Hemingway came in very excited about Ford Madox Ford and the Transatlantic. Ford Madox Ford had started the Transatlantic some months before. A good many years before, indeed before the war, we had met Ford Madox Ford who was at that time Ford Madox Hueffer. He was married to Violet Hunt and Violet Hunt and Gertrude Stein were next to each other at the tea table and talked a great deal together. I was next to Ford Madox Hueffer and I liked him very much and I like his stories of Mistral and Tarascon and I liked his having been followed about in that land of the french royalist, on account of his resemblance to the Bourbon claimant. I had never seen the Bourbon claimant but Ford at that time undoubtedly might have been a Bourbon.

We had heard that Ford was in Paris, but we had not happened to meet. Gertrude Stein had however seen copies of the Transatlantic and found it interesting but had thought nothing further about it.

Hemingway came in then very excited and said that Ford wanted something of Gertrude Stein's for the next number and he, Hemingway, wanted The Making of Americans to be run in it as a serial and he had to have the first fifty pages at once. Gertrude Stein was of course quite overcome with her excitement at this idea, but there was no copy of the manuscript except the one that we had had bound. That makes no difference, said Hemingway, I will copy it. And he and I between us did copy it and it was printed in the next number of the Transatlantic. So for the first time a piece of the monumental work which was the beginning, really the beginning of modern writing, was printed, and we were very happy. Later on when things were difficult between

Gertrude Stein and Hemingway, she always remembered with gratitude that after all it was Hemingway who first caused to be printed a piece of The Making of Americans. She always says, yes sure I have a weakness for Hemingway. After all he was the first of the young men to knock at my door and he did make Ford print the first piece of The Making of Americans.

I myself have not so much confidence that Hemingway did do this. I have never known what the story is but I have always been certain that there was some other story behind it all. That is the way I feel about it.

Gertrude Stein and Sherwood Anderson are very funny on the subject of Hemingway. The last time that Sherwood was in Paris they often talked about him. Hemingway had been formed by the two of them and they were both a little proud and a little ashamed of the work of their minds. Hemingway had at one moment, when he had repudiated Sherwood Anderson and all his works, written him a letter in the name of american literature which he, Hemingway, in company with his contemporaries was about to save, telling Sherwood just what he, Hemingway thought about Sherwood's work, and, that thinking, was in no sense complimentary. When Sherwood came to Paris Hemingway naturally was afraid. Sherwood as naturally was not.

As I say he and Gertrude Stein were endlessly amusing on the subject. They admitted that Hemingway was yellow, he is, Gertrude Stein insisted, just like the flat-boat men on the Mississippi river as described by Mark Twain. But what a book, they both agreed, would be the real story of Hemingway, not those he writes but the confessions of the real Ernest Hemingway. It would be for another audience than the audience Hemingway now has but it would be very wonderful. And then they both agreed that they have a weakness for Hemingway because he is such a good pupil. He is a rotten pupil, I protested. You don't understand, they both said, it is so flattering to have a pupil who does it without understanding it, in other words he takes training and anybody who takes training is a favourite pupil. They both admit it to be a weakness. Gertrude Stein added further, you see he is like Derain. You remember Monsieur de Tuille said, when I did not understand why Derain was having the success he was having that it was because he looks like a modern and he smells of the museums. And that is Hemingway, he looks like a modern and he smells of the museums. But what a story that of the real Hem, and one he should tell himself but alas he never will. After all, as he himself once murmured, there is the career, the career.

But to come back to the events that were happening.

Hemingway did it all. He copied the manuscript and corrected the proofs. Correcting proofs is, as I said before, like dusting, you learn the values of the thing as no reading suffices to teach it to you. In correcting these proofs Hemingway learned a great deal and he admired all that he learned. It was at this time that he wrote to Gertrude Stein saying that it was she who had done the work in writing The Making of Americans and he and all his had but to devote their lives to seeing that it was published.

He had hopes of being able to accomplish this. Some one, I think by the name of Sterne, said that he could place it with a publisher. Gertrude Stein and Hemingway believed that he could, but soon Hemingway reported that Sterne had entered into his period of unreliability. That was the end of that.

In the meantime and sometime before this Mina Loy had brought McAlmon to the house and he came from time to time and he brought his wife and brought William Carlos Williams. And finally he wanted to print The Making of Americans in the Contact Edition and finally he did. I will come to that.

In the meantime McAlmon had printed the three poems and ten stories of Hemingway and William Bird had printed In Our Time and Hemingway was getting to be known. He was coming to know Dos Passos and Fitzgerald and Bromfield and George

Antheil and everybody else and Harold Loeb was once more in Paris. Hemingway had become a writer. He was also a shadow-boxer, thanks to Sherwood, and he heard about bull-fighting from me. I have always loved spanish dancing and spanish bull-fighting and I loved to show the photographs of bull-fighters and bull-fighting. I also loved to show the photograph where Gertrude Stein and I were in the front row and had our picture taken there accidentally. In these days Hemingway was teaching some young chap how to box. The boy did not know how, but by accident he knocked Hemingway out. I believe this sometimes happens. At any rate in these days Hemingway although a sportsman was easily tired. He used to get quite worn out walking from his house to ours. But then he had been worn by the war. Even now he is, as Hélène says all men are, fragile. Recently a robust friend of his said to Gertrude Stein, Ernest is very fragile, whenever he does anything sporting something breaks, his arm, his leg, or his head.

In those early days Hemingway liked all his contemporaries except Cummings. He accused Cummings of having copied everything, not from anybody but from somebody. Gertrude Stein who had been much impressed by The Enormous Room said that Cummings did not copy, he was the natural heir of the New England tradition with its aridity and its sterility, but also with its individuality. They disagreed about this. They also disagreed about Sherwood Anderson. Gertrude Stein contended that Sherwood Anderson had a genius for using a sentence to convey a direct emotion, this was in the great american tradition, and that really except Sherwood there was no one in America who could write a clear and passionate sentence. Hemingway did not believe this, he did not like Sherwood's taste. Taste has nothing to do with sentences, contended Gertrude Stein. She also added that Fitzgerald was the only one of the younger writers who wrote naturally in sentences.

Gertrude Stein and Fitzgerald are very peculiar in their relation to each other. Gertrude Stein had been very much impressed
by This Side of Paradise. She read it when it came out and
before she knew any of the young american writers. She said of it
that it was this book that really created for the public the new
generation. She has never changed her opinion about this. She
thinks this equally true of The Great Gatsby. She thinks Fitzgerald will be read when many of his well known contemporaries
are forgotten. Fitzgerald always says that he thinks Gertrude
Stein says these things just to annoy him by making him think that
she means them, and he adds in his favourite way, and her doing
it is the cruellest thing I ever heard. They always however have a
very good time when they meet. And the last time they met they
had a good time with themselves and Hemingway.

Then there was McAlmon. McAlmon had one quality that
appealed to Gertrude Stein, abundance, he could go on writing,
but she complained that it was dull.

There was also Glenway Wescott but Glenway Wescott at
no time interested Gertrude Stein. He has a certain syrup but it
does not pour.

So then Hemingway's career was begun. For a little while
we saw less of him and then he began to come again. He used to
recount to Gertrude Stein the conversations that he afterwards
used in The Sun Also Rises and they talked endlessly about the
character of Harold Loeb. At this time Hemingway was preparing
his volume of short stories to submit to publishers in America. One
evening after we had not seen him for a while he turned up with
Shipman. Shipman was an amusing boy who was to inherit a
few thousand dollars when he came of age. He was not of age.
He was to buy the Transatlantic Review when he came of age,
so Hemingway said. He was to support a surrealist review when
he came of age, André Masson said. He was to buy a house in the

country when he came of age, Josette Gris said. As a matter of fact when he came of age nobody who had known him then seemed to know what he did do with his inheritance. Hemingway brought him with him to the house to talk about buying the Transatlantic and incidentally he brought the manuscript he intended sending to America. He handed it to Gertrude Stein. He had added to his stories a little story of meditations and in these he said that The Enormous Room was the greatest book he had ever read. It was then that Gertrude Stein said, Hemingway, remarks are not literature.

After this we did not see Hemingway for quite a while and then we went to see some one, just after The Making of Americans was printed, and Hemingway who was there came up to Gertrude Stein and began to explain why he would not be able to write a review of the book. Just then a heavy hand fell on his shoulder and Ford Madox Ford said, young man it is I who wish to speak to Gertrude Stein. Ford then said to her, I wish to ask your permission to dedicate my new book to you. May I. Gertrude Stein and I were both awfully pleased and touched.

For some years after this Gertrude Stein and Hemingway did not meet. And then we heard that he was back in Paris and telling a number of people how much he wanted to see her. Don't you come home with Hemingway on your arm, I used to say when she went out for a walk. Sure enough one day she did come back bringing him with her.

They sat and talked a long time. Finally I heard her say, Hemingway, after all you are ninety percent Rotarian. Can't you, he said, make it eighty percent. No, said she regretfully, I can't. After all, as she always says, he did, and I may say, he does have moments of disinterestedness.

After that they met quite often. Gertrude Stein always says she likes to see him, he is so wonderful. And if he could only tell his own story. In their last conversation she accused him of having killed a great many of his rivals and put them under the sod. I never, said Hemingway, seriously killed anybody but one man and he was a bad man and he deserved it, but if I killed anybody else I did it unknowingly, and so I am not responsible.

It was Ford who once said of Hemingway, he comes and sits at my feet and praises me. It makes me nervous. Hemingway also said once, I turn my flame which is a small one down and down and then suddenly there is a big explosion. If there were nothing but explosions my work would be so exciting nobody could bear it.

However, whatever I say, Gertrude Stein always says, yes I know but I have a weakness for Hemingway.

Excerpt from "The Winner Loses: A Picture of Occupied France," 1940

We went to Belley to buy food and the rest of the time I cut box hedges and Alice Toklas went on making raspberry jam; we had lots of raspberries; and as I did not listen to any news any more it was heavy but peaceful.

Then came the next Sunday.

I went out for a walk in the morning and stopped to talk with one of the farmers, Monsieur Tavel. 'Well,' said he, 'the battle of Lyon has commenced.' 'What?' said I. 'Are they at Lyon?' From then on they were always spoken of as 'they'; they did not have any other name. 'Yes,' he said, 'but it is all right; there are lots of soldiers there and it is all right.' 'But why is it all right?' I said. 'Well,' he said, 'because there is an old prophecy which says that the day will come when France will be betrayed by a Catholic king, not her own king but another king—that another king will be crazy, and that all the Paris region will be occupied by the enemy and, in front of Lyon, France will be saved by a very old man on a white horse.

'Well,' he said, 'the king of the Belgians was a Catholic king and he betrayed us, the king of Italy has gone mad, and the Maréchal Pétain is a very old man and he always rides a white horse. So it is all right,' said Monsieur Tavel.

Well, Lyon was awfully near and if there was going to be a great battle—well, anyway it was a bright sunny day, and I came back and I was tired and so I took out my deck chair and sat in the sun on the terrace and I went sound asleep. Then there was a half-past-twelve communiqué and I woke up just to hear that the Maréchal Pétain had asked for an armistice.

Well, then he had saved France and everything was over. But it wasn't, not at all—it was just beginning for us.

The village did not know what to say and nobody said anything; they just sighed; it was all very quiet.

We thought we could keep the shutters open and light the light, but they said no, not yet, the armistice was not signed and they, the Germans, might be anywhere.

The boys between sixteen and twenty—we have five of them in the village—were frightened lest they should be taken into the German army; they went to Belley to try to enlist in the French army, but naturally that could not be done. They came back with tears in their eyes and nervous. The peasants could not work—nobody did anything for a day or two. And then news commenced again; the man who bought the milk of Bilignin had met somebody who had seen the Germans and they had been quite kind—had given them gasoline for their car. They had been stuck somewhere without gasoline because, as the Germans advanced, the order had come that the gasoline should be poured away. Some did it and some did not. Belley is very law-abiding and so all the people who sold gasoline did.

The man who had the milk route which included Bilignin told them he would not come for the milk any more, nor would he pay them, but they could have three of his pigs. They had no way of getting them, so they asked me and I supplied the means of locomotion, and we brought back three pigs and somebody from Belley came out and butchered them and they gave us a beautiful big roast of pork, and with that and a ham we had bought and what there was to eat in the village we were very well fixed.

Everybody was getting more and more nervous and on Tuesday we went in to Belley; there was no armistice yet, but we thought we might get some soap and other things we needed.

We were in the biggest store in Belley, a sort of a bazaar, when all of a sudden the proprietor called out, 'Go to the back of the shop!' Well, naturally we didn't, and we heard a rumbling noise and there two enemy machine-gun tanks came rushing through the street, with the German cross painted on them.

Oh my, it did make us feel most uncommonly queer. 'Let's go home,' we said, and we did not do any more shopping; we went back to Bilignin.

And there we waited.

The boys between seventeen and twenty went up into the hills; they were badly frightened and excited. Their parents did not say anything. They had each taken with them their bicycles and a large loaf of bread. Naturally that did not last long and in two days they were back again. One of them, a boy named Roger, who was working for a farmer, was so frightened he ate nothing for three days and turned green with fright. He had two brothers in the French army—that was all right, but to be a German soldier! We all tried to cheer him up, but he sat in the corner and couldn't move.

The only news we had about Belley or about anything, because the electricity and the post office were cut off, was by way of the policeman of Belley, who lives in Bilignin. He had to go back to sleep in Belley, but he always managed to get out once during the day to see his mother and give us the news—yes, the Germans were there in Belley; yes, so far they had behaved very correctly; no, nobody knew anything about the armistice.

I remember the last newspaper the postman brought to us. I went out and said, 'It is nice to see you.' 'I wish,' said he, 'that I could bring you better news, and I do not think I will come again,' and he did not, not for more than three weeks.

Basket [Gertrude Stein's French poodle] and I had begun to walk again, the cows and the children began to go out again, and then we began to hear cannon.

Every day we heard the cannon; it seemed to be all around us, which, as it turned out, it was and in some strange way we all cheered up at the sound of the cannonade.

We all began to talk about hearing the cannon, we all began to try to locate the direction of the cannon; some of the *anciens combattants* thought it came from the Alps, others thought it came from right near by, and then one evening I smelt the brimstone, and the color of the earth in the setting sun was a very strange yellow green and there were clouds, strange clouds, the kind of clouds I had never seen before, thick yellow-green clouds rolling past the hills, and it reminded me of pictures of the Civil War, the battle of Lookout Mountain and that kind of thing—it looked like it and it smelled like it, and in a strange way it was comforting.

The policeman in his daily visit home told us that it was cannon and that it was all around us; the French had blown up the bridges of the Rhone all around us, some only about four kilometres away, and in all the places we knew so well there were machine guns and cannon and fighting and quantities of Germans; armored cars were going through Belley, and in all the villages around there were Germans and some motorcycle Germans came through our village.

And then came another bad Sunday; some of the children went in to Mass and came back with an exciting story that everybody that had any gasoline in their possession was going to be shot. Well, I had some extra gasoline besides what was in my car and I did not want to be shot. So, very nervous, I rushed off to the farmer, our neighbor, who is one of the municipal councilors of Belley, and asked what I should do. 'Do nothing,' he said; 'unless they put up a notice here in Bilignin you do not need to do anything. Besides,' said he, 'I am going to Belley to find out all about it.' And he came back and told us that what had happened was that Belley had gotten rid of all its gasoline and a German company had come along and they had had an accident and lost their gasoline tank, and they had asked at a garage for gasoline. Monsieur Barlet, our very gentle garage keeper, had said that he had none, and the Germans had not believed him and said they would shoot him if he did not produce it, and the mayor, who is also a gentle soul, but efficient, said he would put up a notice and have the town crier announce what was happening, and everybody who had gasoline would bring it, and everybody in Belley did, and very soon the Germans had more than they needed and everybody went home with their gasoline and Monsieur Barlet was not shot. But he was and is our local hero, and he was quite pale for some days after and we all thanked him for not being shot, and he always carries around in his pocketbook the order that was posted that saved him from being shot.

Excerpt from WARS I HAVE SEEN, *1944*

One village to another is full of rumors. In Belley they think we have guns all around us, here we were told that all sorts of things have happened in Belley, but so far it is all rumor, the latest rumor is that the maquis the mountain boys have caught a colonel a captain and two ladies with whom they were out walking, and that is the reason they have made the curfew at six o'clock. The hide of a German comes high, said our cook why don't they send them back, they are no use to anybody and then we could go and take the potato bugs off our potato plants. Well life in an occupied country is like that.

I am going on cleaning the weeds off the terrace so when the American army gets here it can sit comfortably on it, Alice Toklas thinks the weeds may get a chance to grow again but I hope not, anyway I am making it nice and neat, and as the terrace is not on the road side of the house, I can go on working at it after we have to stay indoors, that is to say that we cannot go out of doors on the roads.

In all these years I never had a wrist watch, watches to wear never particularly interested me, I like clocks and I am always buying them any kind of clock any kind of fountain pen, but watches seemed kind of dull, I like to know what time it is in the house but out of doors it is less interesting to know about the passage of time and in a city particularly in France you see so many clocks you hear so many clocks to be sure they do not tell the same time but no matter they do tell some time and when you are going to an appointment sometimes you go quickly because you are late by one clock and then you go slowly because you are early by another clock, but now that the curfew is at six o'clock, and I am sure to be out on the road somewhere and they do shoot you if you are out I thought it best to have a wrist watch and so out I went in our little village and asked the local jeweler lady whether she had a wrist watch, yes and a Swiss one and brand new and made for sport for women and men and I thought it perfectly lovely and I came home proudly and now I wear it with immense pride and joy and it seems to keep time and I get home in time and do not get shot by the Germans.

The maquis are beginning to fight again, there was a lull for a bit and now it has commenced again and the Germans are taking all the gazogene automobiles and they are threatening to take away some of the radios from some of the people not to prevent the people listening they do not seem to care very much about that but presumably to get ready to get their orders that may come by radio when all the telephone and telegraph lines are cut which they certainly will be soon. Everything does seem as if something is going to happen that is what everybody keeps on saying. In the meantime our mayor has most efficiently gotten meat and bread and wine and corn meal and butter and everybody is very cheerful because they stand in line for hours but they finally get something and that is a pleasure. How they love a piece of bread. They certainly do. And I am going on scraping weeds off the terrace so as to be all ready for the American army when it comes, one boy who came to-day and brought us fish said that he had seen an English soldier with his own eyes we none of us believed him naturally but it was a pleasure to hear and he did believe it.

The Germans are very uncertain in their minds now, they decided to-day to give us the curfew at ten instead of six in the evening, it was posted up at the mairie and everybody was happy and then at half past five they sent the local policeman around to announce that they had changed their minds and it was back to six o'clock again, then a half hour afterwards they sent him around again to announce that it was changed back to ten and that is where it is now, or so we hope. But that is the way they are about everything, they come and go and they are afraid of their shadow, it is very hard to believe but it is true, and now everybody knows it, guerrilla warfare gets on their nerves it is so darn individual and being individual is what they do not like that is to say what they can not do.

It is exciting to me to hear over the radio about Lake Trasimena, when my brother and I were still at college we spent one summer some weeks in Perugia at a pension and there were lots of us there and one day some of us went off to see Lake Trasimena because there was supposed to be a whole army at the bottom well an army of ancient days naturally with gold chariots, and we thought we would like a swim in the lake, and the young men took the boatmen with them at one end of a little island in the middle of the lake and we girls went to the other end to swim, and we swam without clothes in the sunset in Lake Trasimena, and I have swum in lots of lakes and oceans but there was something special about that and now well it is being mentioned every day. And Cherbourg, when my eldest brother was coming to Paris with his family, my brother and I had been living there some years already, my eldest brother was a little nervous about the trip and he had not much confidence in the ability of my brother and myself getting to the station in time to meet his train from Cherbourg, and so for several months my eldest brother wrote letters and each one of them ended up with a post-script it is six and a half hours from Cherbourg to Paris, six hours and a half. We used to laugh about it, it was a family joke six hours and a half from Cherbourg to Paris. Well perhaps, anyway it is Cherbourg, yes it is.

Everybody is excited so very excited and all around us there are explosions, we do not know what they are whether they are cannon or bridges blowing up or avions or just thunder but there is a lot of it and everybody hears and tells of a different lot, the Germans in French local trucks, not having any of their own, rush forward and back, and nobody seems to know just why or where. When I was out yesterday, I met five Germans with guns on bicycles and they were followed by a truck from Grenoble with soldiers having mitraillettes pointing in every direction and then followed by a local taxi-cab containing two officers of a higher rank than we are accustomed to see around here, and where they were going nobody knows, do they, and then there was a private car that went to Aix, and in this was an officer who had been here and was not popular and he was in a car with two soldiers each carrying a gun and the officer was driving and the car swerved and one of the soldiers dropped his gun which went off and killed the officer. And then there was his funeral with all the officers present. Then I have been seeing a German soldier working lately in the local carpenter shop, and I asked the carpenter why, well he said he told me in his own country he was owner of a carpenter shop and had six men working under him and he said as he has nothing to do he would like to handle tools and as I am short handed I let him, he says the war has settled his hash all right, when and if he gets back to his home he certainly will find nothing there for him.

It's a funny life all right, so far we ourselves have not seen any maquis, I went on a long walk yesterday and went over a road that had been barricaded, just trees pulled to the side of the road, all the telegraph and telephone wires down, they had not fought there but it was certainly like a battle field, it is hard to tell who is maquis and who isn't, they have an arm-band but naturally when they come home to see their people and they all do they keep it in their pocket and then there are still some firm reactionaries who are convinced that all maquis are terrorists, we have some charming neighbors who are like that and it worries me because after all people get angry and things might happen to them and we are very fond of them, it kind of reminds me of the description of the marauding bands in Cooper's Spy, but that of course is the extraordinary thing about this war it is so historical not recent history but fairly ancient history, not I suppose where the armies are actually fighting but here where we are. The mayor keeps us pretty well fed, there are no more tickets because there is no contact with the authorities, there is only the mayor, there are no police but we are all peaceable and we are very well fed, we seem to have everything but sugar. We even had a lemon and an orange which should have gotten to Switzerland but did not, the bridges keep being blown up and nobody wants to go out to repair them it is too dangerous, the Germans tried to pass an armored train through the other day, but did it get there, nobody seems to know.

They just blew up the electric line between here and Chambery and now everybody is walking, they walk to Grenoble they walk to Lyon, even children of three and five walk along with their elders, and sometimes somebody lends them a bicycle and sometimes the children fall off but not often they stick on holding on to anything in front of them, and so they still move around, everybody has to go somewhere and French people always find a way, they are wonders at always finding a way. The death of Henriot killed by the militia or somebody in their uniform has been an immense excitement, it is hard to make any one who has not lived with them realise how really tormented the population has been in its opinions and Henriot did perhaps more than anybody to turn Frenchmen against Frenchmen, he was a very able propagandist, he used the method not of a politician but of a churchman, he had that education, and he knew how to appeal like a revivalist sermon, and he did do it awfully well, and he held the middle classes they could not get away from him, what said I to one friend whose mother always listened to him, what will your mother do now, oh she mourns but at least for a week she will be busy with all the funeral orations, but after that, good gracious after that what will she do. A great many of the middle classes feel like that, of course the immense majority of French people are delighted at his putting off, they breathe more freely, there was no one else in the government who had the power he had, no one else. I do not think outside of France this was realised, I do not think so.

And now he is dead and except a few of the die hards everybody is happy and relieved and everybody can now get ready for the end of the war that is to say for the evacuation of France by the Germans.

One of our friends wants to be taught to say to a parachutist who comes to her door, and upon whom she has closed the door, she wants to say to him in English through the keyhole please break down the door and come in by force and take everything you want by force in that way you will have what you need and the Germans and the government cannot blame me and now said she just how can I say that to the parachutist through the keyhole. The rest of the population just wants to be taught to say we are glad to see you, and some of them are learning to say it very nicely, every one is certain that a large party of Canadians have been para-chuted somewhere in our neighborhood and that they are only waiting the arrival of an English general expected any day this is the first of July for the advance to begin. As a matter of fact the forty-odd Germans who are here and who no longer get their pay are getting more and more peaceful, they ask for work they wander around unarmed and they used never to stir without a gun on their back and never less than three together, now they wander all about the country alone and unarmed. It certainly is a change this conquering army this occupying army now wandering around hoping some one will speak to them and that some one will give them a job. It certainly does look like the beginning of the end. The breathlessness of the situation is a bit on everybody's nerves but the most selfish of all the women here did to-day in a great burst announced that it was all right there must be no bread, no money no anything and then the Germans would leave, that is the way it was going to be. There are no more trains here any more, and this Culoz where we are was a very important railroad junction for Italy, Switzerland the Savoys and Lyon, but not a train not one single or solitary train not one. No wonder the Germans are meek, here they are and here they must stay until the maquis come and take them away.

They are getting away from here, the last lot that were in Artemarre are leaving and they are trying to sell the wagons that they had attached to their horses and all that is left in the region are right here in Culoz, we still have forty odd and when will they leave very soon we are hoping, they do not do anything very disagreeable here but oh dear what a relief it will be when they are gone, as everybody says even when they are not doing anything they are an oppressive burden, they are.

The Germans still eat sausages, just like the old jokes, the Hitler regime has not changed that, they borrow a sausage machine from an old woman here who is called the old Maria, and they tell her all their troubles and how they are all going home very soon now, and the soldier who accidentally killed his adjutant and who has been crying ever since locked up in a room and he wanted to commit suicide but the officers decided instead of shooting him he would be sent to the Russian front and we all laughed and said by the time he gets there there wont be any Russian front.

And now the cook has just come up to say that the maquis are on their way and may get here at Culoz not any day but at any moment of to-day. I wonder. It is now the fourth of July and things certainly are moving.

It's the fourth of July and everybody is on the broad grin. The French black troops with regular French officers are now within eight kilometers of us, they have been parachuted in the region and the Germans scared to death are packing up their bags and moving away and everybody stands around and laughs and with reason. It is a happy day.

To-day I took a long walk and all along there were groups of people telling each other all sorts of things, some had seen Canadians and some had seen English and some had heard on the radio that this department of the Ain was going to be completely emptied of Germans by the fourteenth of July and others had seen the black troops and anyway there was a sound of cannon firing and somebody had heard one of the German soldiers say; the only thing to do to shorten this war is to kill our chiefs, and sometimes when you realise that there have been twenty-four German generals killed or imprisoned in three weeks are they doing it, are they.

There is one thing certain now it is very bad form to mention maquis or mountain boys, you speak respectfully of the French army, in two days the word maquis no longer exists it is with great pride the French army. There are such funny things the new prefect was talking of having he himself been condemned to death by the maquis and the wife of the mayor said yes he will write about it in his memoirs and then she added meditatively condemned to death we are all condemned to death.

It is very pleasant to have a new army with an old name or an old army with a new name, very pleasant.

We were in Belley yesterday and there everybody was excited the night before the maquis had come into the town and walked off with the sous-prefect with the chief of police with a thousand kilos of sugar that one of the cake shops had and lots of other material, and everybody of course was excited and upset, six of us had gone over in a taxi including our mayor, and it was very exciting and then we came home and then that evening the maquis came very near to Culoz and the Germans took out cannon to shoot at them and all to-day they were firing around the mountain and we all stood around talking and everybody said if the maquis come they bring food but if the maquis come and do not succeed then the Germans will take hostages and burn up the farms, oh dear do they want maquis or do they not want maquis, it all is very exciting we now have one hundred and sixty Germans in the town and they are not leaving, we all hoped that they would leave and that would be very comfortable for everybody and they would like to leave but Hitler likes everybody to stay where they are until they are all killed, he likes it like that, so I suppose even these few will stay until they are killed so that now that the railroad is not working any more there is no use in staying but their orders are to stay anyway. A lot get killed when there is a lot and a few get killed when there are a few but the idea is to always stay and get killed. That is the way to create the last battalion which will then be killed and we will all be happy, yes quite happy.

༄

ERNEST HEMINGWAY [1899–1964]

Excerpt from A FAREWELL TO ARMS, *1929, Chapter 28*

What were you going to do if you had a mountain frontier? he asked.

I had not worked that out yet, I said, and we both laughed. "But," I said, "in the old days the Austrians were always whipped in the quadrilateral around Verona. They let them come down onto the plain and whipped them there."

"Yes," said Gino. "But those were Frenchmen and you can work out military problems clearly when you are fighting in somebody else's country."

"Yes," I agreed, "when it is your own country you cannot use it so scientifically."

"The Russians did, to trap Napoleon."

"Yes, but they had plenty of country. If you tried to retreat to trap Napoleon in Italy you would find yourself in Brindisi."

"A terrible place," said Gino. "Have you ever been there?"

"Not to stay."

"I am a patriot," Gino said. "But I cannot love Brindisi or Taranto."

"Do you love the Bainsizza?" I asked.

"The soil is sacred," he said. "But I wish it grew more potatoes. You know when we came here we found fields of potatoes the Austrians had planted."

"Has the food really been short?"

"I myself have never had enough to eat but I am a big eater

and I have not starved. The mess is average. The regiments in the line get pretty good food but those in support don't get so much. Something is wrong somewhere. There should be plenty of food."

"The dogfish are selling it somewhere else."

"Yes, they give the battalions in the front line as much as they can but the ones in back are very short. They have eaten all the Austrians' potatoes and chestnuts from the woods. They ought to feed them better. We are big eaters. I am sure there is plenty of food. It is very bad for the soldiers to be short of food. Have you ever noticed the difference it makes in the way you think?"

"Yes," I said. "It can't win a war but it can lose one."

"We won't talk about losing. There is enough talk about losing. What has been done this summer cannot have been done in vain."

I did not say anything. I was always embarrassed by the words sacred, glorious, and sacrifice and the expression in vain. We had heard them, sometimes standing in the rain almost out of earshot, so that only the shouted words came through, and had read them, on proclamations that were slapped up by billposters over other proclamations, now for a long time, and I had seen nothing sacred, and the things that were glorious had no glory and the sacrifices were like the stockyards at Chicago if nothing was done with the meat except to bury it. There were many words that you could not stand to hear and finally only the names of places had dignity. Certain numbers were the same way and certain dates and these with the names of the places were all you could say and have them mean anything. Abstract words such as glory, honor, courage, or hallow were obscene beside the concrete names of villages, the numbers of roads, the names of rivers, the numbers of regiments and the dates. Gino was a patriot, so he said things that separated us sometimes, but he was also a fine boy and I understood his being a patriot. He was born one. He left with Peduzzi in the car to go back to Gorizia.

It stormed all that day. The wind drove down the rain and everywhere there was standing water and mud. The plaster of the broken houses was gray and wet. Late in the afternoon the rain stopped and from out number two post I saw the bare wet autumn country with clouds over the tops of the hills and the straw screening over the roads wet and dripping. The sun came out once before it went down and shone on the bare woods beyond the ridge. There were many Austrian guns in the woods on that ridge but only a few fired. I watched the sudden round puffs of shrapnel smoke in the sky above a broken farmhouse near where the line was; soft puffs with a yellow white flash in the centre. You saw the flash, then heard the crack, then saw the smoke ball distort and thin in the wind. There were many iron shrapnel balls in the rubble of the houses and on the road beside the broken house where the post was, but they did not shell near the post that afternoon. We loaded two cars and drove down the road that was screened with wet mats and the last of the sun came through in the breaks between the strips of mattings. Before we were out on the clear road behind the hill the sun was down. We went on down the clear road and as it turned a corner into the open and went into the square arched tunnel of matting the rain started again.

The wind rose in the night and at three o'clock in the morning with the rain coming in sheets there was a bombardment and the Croatians came over across the mountain meadows and through patches of woods and into the front line. They fought in the dark in the rain and a counter-attack of scared men from the second line drove them back. There was much shelling and many rockets in the rain and machine-gun and rifle fire all along the line. They did not come again and it was quieter and between the gusts of wind and rain we could hear the sound of a great bombardment far to the north.

❧

WILLIAM FAULKNER [1897–1964]

Excerpt from THE OLD MAN, *1939, Chapter 3*

He did not have to paddle now, he just steered (who had been without food for twenty-four hours now and without any sleep to speak of for fifty) while the skiff sped on across that boiling desolation where he had long since begun to not dare believe he could possibly be where he could not doubt he was, trying with his fragment of splintered plank merely to keep the skiff intact and afloat among the houses and trees and dead animals (the entire towns, stores, residences, parks and farmyards, which leaped and played about him like fish), not trying to reach any destination, just trying to keep the skiff afloat until he did. He wanted so little. He wanted nothing for himself. He just wanted to get rid of the woman, the belly, and he was trying to do that in the right way, not for himself, but for her. He could have put her back into another tree at any time—

"Or you could have jumped out of the boat and let her and it drown," the plump convict said. "Then they could have given you ten years for escaping and then hung you for the murder and charged the boat to your folks."

"Yah," the tall convict said. —But he had not done that. He wanted to do it the right way, find somebody, anybody he could surrender her to, something solid he could set her down on and then jump back into the river, if that would please anyone. That was all he wanted—just to come to something, anything. That didn't seem like a great deal to ask. And he couldn't do it. He told how the skiff fled on—

"Didn't you pass nobody?" the plump convict said. "No steamboat, nothing?"

"I don't know," the tall one said.—while he tried merely to keep it afloat, until the darkness thinned and lifted and revealed—

"Darkness?" the plump convict said. "I thought you said it was already daylight."

"Yah," the tall one said. He was rolling a cigarette, pouring the tobacco carefully from a new sack, into the creased paper. "This was another one. They had several while I was gone."—the skiff to be moving still rapidly up a winding corridor bordered by drowned trees which the convict recognised again to be a river running again in the direction that, until two days ago, had been upstream.

Excerpt from ABSALOM, ABSALOM!, *1936, Chapter 1*

From a little after two o'clock until almost sundown of the long still hot weary dead September afternoon they sat in what Miss Coldfield still called the office because her father had called it that —a dim hot airless room with the blinds all closed and fastened for forty-three summers because when she was a girl someone had believed that light and moving air carried heat and that dark was always cooler, and which (as the sun shone fuller and fuller on that side of the house) became latticed with yellow slashes full of dust motes which Quentin thought of as being flecks of the dead old dried paint itself blown inward from the scaling blinds as wind might have blown them. There was a wistaria vine blooming for the second time that summer on a wooden trellis before the window, into which sparrows came now and then in random gusts, making a dry vivid dusty sound before going away: and opposite Quentin, Miss Coldfield in the eternal black which she had worn for forty-three years now, whether for sister, father, or nothusband none knew, sitting so bolt upright in the straight hard chair that was so tall for her that her legs hung straight and rigid as if she had iron shinbones and ankles, clear of the floor with that air of impotent and static rage like children's feet, and talking in that grim haggard amazed voice until at last listening would renege and hearing-sense self-confound and the long-dead object of her impotent yet indomitable frustration would appear, as though by outraged recapitulation evoked, quiet inattentive and harmless, out of the biding and dreamy and victorious dust.

Her voice would not cease, it would just vanish. There would be the dim coffin-smelling gloom sweet and over-sweet with the twice-bloomed wistaria against the outer wall by the savage quiet September sun impacted distilled and hyperdistilled, into which came now and then the loud cloudy flutter of the sparrows like a flat limber stick whipped by an idle boy, and the rank smell of female old flesh long embattled in virginity while the wan haggard face watched him above the faint triangle of lace at wrists and throat from the too tall chair in which she resembled a crucified child; and the voice not ceasing but vanishing into and then out of the long intervals like a stream, a trickle running from patch to patch of dried sand, and the ghost mused with shadowy docility as if it were the voice which he haunted where a more fortunate one would have had a house. Out of quiet thunderclap he would abrupt (man-horse-demon) upon a scene peaceful and decorous as a schoolprize water color, faint sulphur-reek still in hair clothes and beard, with grouped behind him his band of wild niggers like beasts half tamed to walk upright like men, in attitudes wild and reposed, and manacled among them the French architect with his air grim, haggard, and tatter-ran. Immobile, bearded and hand palm-lifted the horseman sat; behind him the wild blacks and the captive architect huddled quietly, carrying in bloodless paradox the shovels and picks and axes of peaceful conquest. Then in the long unamaze Quentin seemed to watch them overrun suddenly the hundred square miles of tranquil and astonished earth and drag house and formal gardens violently out of the soundless Nothing and clap them down like cards upon a table beneath the up-palm immobile and pontific, creating the Sutpen's Hundred, the *Be Sutpen's Hundred* like the oldentime *Be Light*. Then hearing would reconcile and he would seem to listen to two separate Quentins now—the Quentin Compson preparing for Harvard in the South, the deep South dead since 1865 and peopled with garrulous outraged baffled ghosts, listening, having to listen, to one of the ghosts which had refused to lie still even longer than most had, telling him about old ghost-times; and the Quentin Compson who was still too young to deserve yet to be a ghost, but nevertheless having to be one for all that, since he was born and bred in the deep South the same as she was—the two separate Quentins now talking to one another in the long silence of notpeople, in notlanguage, like this: *It seems that this demon—his name was Sutpen—(Colonel Sutpen)—Colonel Sutpen. Who came out of nowhere and without warning upon the land with a band of strange niggers and built a plantation (Tore violently a plantation, Miss Rosa Coldfield says)—tore violently. And married her sister Ellen and begot a son and a daughter which —(Without gentleness begot, Miss Rosa Coldfield says)—without gentleness. Which should have been the jewels of his pride and the shield and comfort of his old age, only—(Only they destroyed him or something or he destroyed them or something. And died) —and died. Without regret, Miss Rosa Coldfield says—(Save by her) Yes, save by her. (And by Quentin Compson) Yes. And by Quentin Compson.*

"Because you are going away to attend the college at Harvard they tell me," Miss Coldfield said. "So I don't imagine you will ever come back here and settle down as a country lawyer in a little town like Jefferson, since Northern people have already seen to it that there is little left in the South for a young man. So maybe you will enter the literary profession as so many Southern gentlemen and gentlewomen too are doing now and maybe some day you will remember this and write about it. You will be married then I expect and perhaps your wife will want a new gown or a new chair for the house and you can write this and submit it to the magazines. Perhaps you will even remember kindly then the old woman who made you spend a whole afternoon sitting indoors and listening while she talked about people and events you were fortunate enough to escape yourself when you wanted to be out among young friends of your own age."

෴

JOHN DOS PASSOS [1896–   ]

Excerpts from THE BIG MONEY, *1937*

NEWSREEL XLVIII

truly the Steel Corporation stands forth as a corporate colossus both physically and financially

> *Now the folks in Georgia they done gone wild*
> *Over that brand new dancin' style*
> > *Called   Shake   That   Thing*

CARBARNS BLAZE

GYPSY ARRESTED FOR TELLING THE TRUTH

Horsewhipping Hastens Wedding

that strength has long since become almost a truism as steel's expanding career progressed, yet the dimensions thereof need at times to be freshly measured to be caught in proper perspective

DAZED BY MAINE DEMOCRATS CRY FOR MONEY

shake that thing

Woman of Mystery Tries Suicide in Park Lake

shake that thing

OLIVE THOMAS DEAD FROM POISON

LETTER SAID GET OUT OF WALL STREET

BOMB WAGON TRACED TO JERSEY

Shake   That   Thing

Writer of Warnings Arrives

BODY FOUND LASHED TO BICYCLE

FIND BOMB CLOCKWORK

TIN LIZZIE

"*Mr. Ford the automobileer,*" the featurewriter wrote in 1900,

"*Mr. Ford the automobileer began by giving his steed three or four sharp jerks with the lever at the righthand side of the seat; that is, he pulled the lever up and down sharply in order, as he said, to mix air with gasoline and drive the charge into the exploding cylinder. . . . Mr. Ford slipped a small electric switch handle and there followed a puff, puff, puff. . . . The puffing of the machine assumed a higher key. She was flying along about eight miles an hour. The ruts in the road were deep, but the machine certainly went with a dreamlike smoothness. There was none of the bumping common even to a streetcar. . . . By this time the boulevard had been reached, and the automobileer, letting a lever fall a little, let her out. Whiz! She picked up speed with infinite rapidity. As she ran on there was a clattering behind, the new noise of the automobile.*

For twenty years or more,

ever since he'd left his father's farm when he was sixteen to get a job in a Detroit machineshop, Henry Ford had been nuts about machinery. First it was watches, then he designed a steam-tractor, then he built a horseless carriage with an engine adapted from the Otto gasengine he'd read about in *The World of Science*, then a mechanical buggy with a onecylinder fourcycle motor, that would run forward but not back;

at last, in ninetyeight, he felt he was far enough along to risk throwing up his job with the Detroit Edison Company, where he'd worked his way up from night fireman to chief engineer, to put all his time into working on a new gasoline engine,

(in the late eighties he'd met Edison at a meeting of electric-light employees in Atlantic City. He'd gone up to Edison after Edison had delivered an address and asked him if he thought gasoline was practical as a motor fuel. Edison had said yes. If Edison said it, it was true. Edison was the great admiration of Henry Ford's life);

and in driving his mechanical buggy, sitting there at the lever jauntily dressed in a tightbuttoned jacket and a high collar and a derby hat, back and forth over the level illpaved streets of Detroit,

scaring the big brewery horses and the skinny trotting horses and the sleekrumped pacers with the motor's loud explosions,

looking for men scatterbrained enough to invest money in a factory for building automobiles.

He was the eldest son of an Irish immigrant who during the Civil War had married the daughter of a prosperous Pennsylvania Dutch farmer and settled down to farming near Dearborn in Wayne County, Michigan;

like plenty of other Americans, young Henry grew up hating the endless sogging through the mud about the chores, the hauling and pitching manure, the kerosene lamps to clean, the irk and sweat and solitude of the farm.

He was a slender, active youngster, a good skater, clever with his hands; what he liked was to tend the machinery and let the others do the heavy work. His mother had told him not to drink, smoke, gamble or go into debt, and he never did.

When he was in his early twenties his father tried to get him back from Detroit, where he was working as mechanic and repairman for the Drydock Engine Company that built engines for steamboats, by giving him forty acres of land.

Young Henry built himself an uptodate square white dwellinghouse with a false mansard roof and married and settled down on the farm,

but he let the hired men do the farming;

he bought himself a buzzsaw and rented a stationary engine and cut the timber off the woodlots.

He was a thrifty young man who never drank or smoked or gambled or coveted his neighbor's wife, but he couldn't stand living on the farm.

He moved to Detroit, and in the brick barn behind his house tinkered for years in his spare time with a mechanical buggy that would be light enough to run over the clayey wagonroads of Wayne County, Michigan.

By 1900 he had a practicable car to promote.

He was forty years old before the Ford Motor Company was started and production began to move.

Speed was the first thing the early automobile manufacturers went after. Races advertised the makes of cars.

Henry Ford himself hung up several records at the track at Grosse Pointe and on the ice on Lake St. Clair. In his 999 he did the mile in thirtynine and fourfifths seconds.

But it had always been his custom to hire others to do the heavy work. The speed he was busy with was speed in production, the records in efficient output. He hired Barney Oldfield, a stunt bicyclerider from Salt Lake City, to do the racing for him.

Henry Ford had ideas about other things than the designing
of motors, carburetors, magnetos, jigs and fixtures, punches and
dies; he had ideas about sales,
    that the big money was in economical quantity production,
quick turnover, cheap interchangeable easilyreplaced standardized
parts;
    it wasn't until 1909, after years of arguing with his partners,
that Ford put out the first Model T.

    Henry Ford was right.
    That season he sold more than ten thousand tin lizzies, ten
years later he was selling almost a million a year.
    In these years the Taylor Plan was stirring up plantmanagers
and manufacturers all over the country. Efficiency was the word.
The same ingenuity that went into improving the performance
of a machine could go into improving the performance of the
workmen producing the machine.
    In 1913 they established the assemblyline at Ford's. That
season the profits were something like twentyfive million dollars,
but they had trouble in keeping the men on the job, machinists
didn't seem to like it at Ford's.

    Henry Ford had ideas about other things than production.
    He was the largest automobile manufacturer in the world;
he paid high wages; maybe if the steady workers thought they
were getting a cut (a very small cut) in the profits, it would give
trained men an inducement to stick to their jobs,
    wellpaid workers might save enough money to buy a tin
lizzie; the first day Ford's announced that cleancut properlymar-
ried American workers who wanted jobs had a chance to make
five bucks a day (of course it turned out that there were strings
to it; always there were strings to it)

such an enormous crowd waited outside the Highland Park plant

all through the zero January night

that there was a riot when the gates were opened; cops broke heads, jobhunters threw bricks; property, Henry Ford's own property, was destroyed. The company dicks had to turn on the firehose to beat back the crowd.

The American Plan; automotive prosperity seeping down from above; it turned out there were strings to it.

But that five dollars a day

paid to good, clean American workmen

who didn't drink or smoke cigarettes or read or think,

and who didn't commit adultery

and whose wives didn't take in boarders,

made America once more the Yukon of the sweated workers of the world;

made all the tin lizzies and the automotive age, and incidentally,

made Henry Ford the automobileer, the admirer of Edison, the birdlover,

the great American of his time.

But Henry Ford had ideas about other things besides assemblylines and the livinghabits of his employees. He was full of ideas. Instead of going to the city to make his fortune, here was a country boy who'd made his fortune by bringing the city out to the farm. The precepts he'd learned out of McGuffey's Reader, his mother's prejudices and preconceptions, he had preserved clean and unworn as freshprinted bills in the safe in a bank.

He wanted people to know about his ideas, so he bought the *Dearborn Independent* and started a campaign against cigarettesmoking.

When war broke out in Europe, he had ideas about that too. (Suspicion of armymen and soldiering were part of the midwest farm tradition, like thrift, stickativeness, temperance and sharp practice in money matters.) Any intelligent American mechanic could see that if the Europeans hadn't been a lot of ignorant underpaid foreigners who drank, smoked, were loose about women and wasteful in their methods of production, the war could never have happened.

When Rosika Schwimmer broke through the stockade of secretaries and servicemen who surrounded Henry Ford and suggested to him that he could stop the war,

he said sure they'd hire a ship and go over and get the boys out of the trenches by Christmas.

He hired a steamboat, the *Oscar II*, and filled it up with pacifists and socialworkers,

to go over to explain to the princelings of Europe
that what they were doing was vicious and silly.

It wasn't his fault that Poor Richard's commonsense no longer rules the world and that most of the pacifists were nuts,

goofy with headlines.

When William Jennings Bryan went over to Hoboken to see him off, somebody handed William Jennings Bryan a squirrel in a cage; William Jennings Bryan made a speech with the squirrel under his arm. Henry Ford threw American Beauty roses to the crowd. The band played *I Didn't Raise My Boy to Be a Soldier*. Practical jokers let loose more squirrels. An eloping couple was married by a platoon of ministers in the saloon, and Mr. Zero, the flophouse humanitarian, who reached the dock too late to sail,

dove into the North River and swam after the boat.

The *Oscar II* was described as a floating Chautauqua; Henry Ford said it felt like a middlewestern village, but by the time they reached Christiansand in Norway, the reporters had kidded him

so that he had gotten cold feet and gone to bed. The world was too crazy outside of Wayne County, Michigan. Mrs. Ford and the management sent an Episcopal dean after him who brought him home under wraps,
> and the pacifists had to speechify without him.

Two years later Ford's was manufacturing munitions, Eagle boats; Henry Ford was planning oneman tanks, and oneman submarines like the one tried out in the Revolutionary War. He announced to the press that he'd turn over his war profits to the government,
> but there's no record that he ever did.

One thing he brought back from his trip
was the Protocols of the Elders of Zion.
He started a campaign to enlighten the world in the *Dearborn Independent;* the Jews were why the world wasn't like Wayne County, Michigan, in the old horse and buggy days;
the Jews had started the war, Bolshevism, Darwinism, Marxism, Nietzsche, short skirts and lipstick. They were behind Wall Street and the international bankers, and the whiteslave traffic and the movies and the Supreme Court and ragtime and the illegal liquor business.
Henry Ford denounced the Jews and ran for senator and sued the *Chicago Tribune* for libel,
and was the laughingstock of the kept metropolitan press;
but when the metropolitan bankers tried to horn in on his business
he thoroughly outsmarted them.

In 1918 he had borrowed on notes to buy out his minority stockholders for the picayune sum of seventyfive million dollars.

In February, 1920, he needed cash to pay off some of these notes that were coming due. A banker is supposed to have called on him and offered him every facility if the bankers' representative could be made a member of the board of directors. Henry Ford handed the banker his hat,

and went about raising the money in his own way:

he shipped every car and part he had in his plant to his dealers and demanded immediate cash payment. Let the other fellow do the borrowing had always been a cardinal principle. He shut down production and canceled all orders from the supplyfirms. Many dealers were ruined, many supplyfirms failed, but when he reopened his plant,

he owned it absolutely,

the way a man owns an unmortgaged farm with the taxes paid up.

In 1922 there started the Ford boom for President (high wages, waterpower, industry scattered to the small towns) that was skillfully pricked behind the scenes

by another crackerbarrel philosopher,

Calvin Coolidge;

but in 1922 Henry Ford sold one million three hundred and thirtytwo thousand two hundred and nine tin lizzies; he was the richest man in the world.

Good roads had followed the narrow ruts made in the mud by the Model T. The great automotive boom was on. At Ford's production was improving all the time; less waste, more spotters, strawbosses, stoolpigeons (fifteen minutes for lunch, three minutes to go to the toilet, the Taylorized speedup everywhere, reach under, adjust washer, screw down bolt, shove in cotterpin, reachunder adjustwasher, screwdown bolt, reachunderadjustscrewdown-reachunderadjust until every ounce of life was sucked off into production and at night the workmen went home grey shaking husks).

Ford owned every detail of the process from the ore in the hills until the car rolled off the end of the assemblyline under its own power, the plants were rationalized to the last tenthousandth of an inch as measured by the Johansen scale;

in 1926 the production cycle was reduced to eightyone hours from the ore in the mine to the finished salable car proceeding under its own power,

but the Model T was obsolete.

New Era prosperity and the American Plan
(there were strings to it, always there were strings to it)
had killed Tin Lizzie.
Ford's was just one of many automobile plants.

When the stockmarket bubble burst,
Mr. Ford the crackerbarrel philosopher said jubilantly,
"I told you so.
Serves you right for gambling and getting in debt.
The country is sound."
But when the country on cracked shoes, in frayed trousers, belts tightened over hollow bellies,

idle hands cracked and chapped with the cold of that coldest March day of 1932,

started marching from Detroit to Dearborn, asking for work and the American Plan, all they could think of at Ford's was machineguns.

The country was sound, but they mowed the marchers down.

They shot four of them dead.

Henry Ford as an old man
is a passionate antiquarian,
(lives besieged on his father's farm embedded in an estate

of thousands of millionaire acres, protected by an army of servicemen, secretaries, secret agents, dicks under orders of an English
exprizefighter,

always afraid of the feet in broken shoes on the roads, afraid
the gangs will kidnap his grandchildren,

that a crank will shoot him,

that Change and the idle hands out of work will break
through the gates and the high fences;

protected by a private army against

the new America of starved children and hollow bellies and
cracked shoes stamping on souplines,

that has swallowed up the old thrifty farmlands

of Wayne County, Michigan,

as if they had never been).

Henry Ford as an old man
is a passionate antiquarian.

He rebuilt his father's farmhouse and put it back exactly in
the state he remembered it in as a boy. He built a village of museums for buggies, sleighs, coaches, old plows, waterwheels, obsolete models of motorcars. He scoured the country for fiddlers to
play oldfashioned squaredances.

Even old taverns he bought and put back into their original
shape, as well as Thomas Edison's early laboratories.

When he bought the Wayside Inn near Sudbury, Massachusetts, he had the new highway where the newmodel cars roared
and slithered and hissed oilily past (*the new noise of the autmo-
bile*),

moved away from the door,

put back the old bad road,

so that everything might be

the way it used to be,

in the days of horses and buggies.

                              Observe, on page 257, the increasing speed of "Reach under, adjust washer, screw down bolt, shove in cotterpin, reachunder adjustwasher, screwdown bolt, reachunderadjustscrewdownreachunderadjust." Observe that at the highest speed the washer, the bolt and the cotterpin have disappeared.

THE CAMERA EYE (45)

the narrow yellow room teems with talk under the low ceiling and crinkling tendrils of cigarettesmoke twine blue and fade round noses behind ears under the rims of women's hats in arch looks changing arrangements of lips the toss of a bang the wise I-know-it wrinkles round the eyes all scrubbed stroked clipped scraped with the help of lipstick rouge shavingcream razorblades into a certain pattern that implies

    this warmvoiced woman who moves back and forth with a throaty laugh head tossed a little back distributing with teasing looks the parts in the fiveoclock drama

    every man his pigeonhole

    the personality must be kept carefully adjusted over the face

    to facilitate recognition she pins on each of us a badge

    today entails tomorrow

    Thank you but why me? Inhibited? Indeed goodby

    the old brown hat flopped faithful on the chair beside the door successfully snatched

    outside the clinking cocktail voices fade

    even in this elderly brick dwellinghouse made over with green paint orange candles a little tinted calcimine into

    Greenwich Village

    the stairs go up and down

    lead through a hallway ranked with bells names evoking lives tangles unclassified

    into the rainy twoway street where cabs slither slushing foot-

steps plunk slant lights shimmer on the curve of a wet cheek a pair
of freshcolored lips a weatherlined neck a gnarled grimed hand an
old man's bloodshot eye
    street twoway to the corner of the roaring avenue where
in the lilt of the rain and the din the four directions
    (the salty in all of us ocean the protoplasm throbbing through
cells growing dividing sprouting into the billion diverse not yet
labeled not yet named
    always they slip through the fingers
    the changeable the multitudinous lives)
    box dizzingly the compass

☙

SAMUEL BECKETT [1906–   ]

Excerpt from MOLLOY. *French original by Beckett, 1951; English
translation by Beckett and Patrick Bowles, 1955*

I must have fallen asleep, for all of a sudden there was the moon,
a huge moon framed in the window. Two bars divided it in three
segments, of which the middle remained constant, while little by
little the right gained what the left lost. For the moon was moving
from left to right, or the room was moving from right to left, or
both together perhaps, or both were moving from left to right,
but the room not so fast as the moon, or from right to left, but
the moon not so fast as the room. But can one speak of right and
left in such circumstances? That movements of an extreme com-
plexity were taking place seemed certain, and yet what a simple
thing it seemed, that vast yellow light sailing slowly behind my
bars and which little by little the dense wall devoured, and finally
eclipsed. And now its tranquil course was written on the walls, a
radiance scored with shadow, then a brief quivering of leaves, if
they were leaves, then that too went out, leaving me in the dark.

How difficult it is to speak of the moon and not lose one's head, the witless moon.

Excerpts from WATT, *1953*

At ten the steps came, clearer, clearer, fainter, fainter, on the stairs, on the landing, on the stairs again, and through the open door the light, from darkness slowly brightening, to darkness slowly darkening, the steps of Arthur, the light of poor Arthur, little by little mounting to his rest, at his habitual hour.

At eleven the room darkened, the moon having climbed behind a tree. But the tree being small, and the moon's ascension rapid, this transit was brief, and this obscuration.

As by the steps, the light, growing, dying, Watt knew that it was ten, so he knew, when the room darkened, that it was eleven, or thereabouts.

Watt wore a greatcoat, still green here and there. This coat, when last weighed by Watt, weighed between fifteen and sixteen pounds, avoirdupois, or a little more than a stone. Of this Watt was certain, having weighed himself on a machine, first with the coat on, and then with it off, lying on the ground, at his feet. But that was a long time ago, and the coat might have put on weight, since then. Or it might have lost weight. This coat was of such length, that Watt's trousers, which he wore very baggy, in order to conceal the shapes of his legs, were hidden by it from view. This coat was of a very respectable age, as such coats go, having been bought at secondhand, for a small sum, from a meritorious widow, by Watt's father, when Watt's father was a young man, and motoring in its infancy, that is to say some seventy years before. This coat had not, since then, at any time been washed, except imperfectly by the rain, and the snow, and the sleet, and of course occasional fleeting immersion in canal water, nor dry-cleaned, nor turned, nor brushed, and it was no doubt to these precautions that its preservation, as a unit, was due. The material of this coat, though liberally scored and contunded, especially in the rear, was so thick, and so strong, that it remained exempt from perforation, in the strict meaning of the word, nor was its thread elsewhere exposed, than at the seat, and elbows. This coat continued to button, up the front, with nine buttons, various now in shape, and colour, but without exception of such exceptional size as to remain, once buttoned, buttoned. Aloft in the flowerhole brooded the remains of a factitious murrey chrysanthemum. Patches of velvet clung to the collar. The skirts were not divided.

Watt wore, on his head, a block hat, of a pepper colour. This excellent hat had belonged to his grandfather, who had picked it up, on a racecourse, from off the ground, where it lay, and carried it home. Then mustard, now it was pepper, in colour.

It was to be observed that the colours, on the one hand of this coat, on the other of this hat, drew closer and closer, the one to the other, with every passing lustre. Yet how different had been their beginnings! The one green! The other yellow! So it is with time, that lightens what is dark, that darkens what is light.

It was to be expected that, once met, they would not stay, no, but continue, each as it must, to age, until the hat was green, the coat yellow, and then through the last circles paling, deepening, swooning cease, the hat to be a hat, the coat to be a coat. For so it is with time.

Watt wore, on his feet, a boot, brown in colour, and a shoe, happily of a brownish colour also. This boot Watt had bought, for eight pence, from a one-legged man who, having lost his leg, and a fortiori his foot, in an accident, was happy to realize, on his discharge from hospital, for such a sum, his unique remaining marketable asset. He little suspected that he owed this good fortune to Watt's having found, some days before, on the sea-shore, the shoe, stiff with brine, but otherwise shipshape.

This shoe and this boot were so close in colour, the one to the other, and so veiled, as to their uppers, in the first place by the trousers, and in the second by the greatcoat, that they might almost have been taken, not for a shoe on the one hand, and on the other for a boot, but for a true pair, of boots, or of shoes, had not the boot been blunt, and the shoe sharp, at the toe.

In this boot, a twelve, and in this shoe, a ten, Watt, whose size was eleven, suffered, if not agony, at least pain, with his feet, of which each would willingly have changed places with the other, if only for a moment.

By wearing, on the foot that was too small, not one sock of his pair of socks, but both, and on the foot that was too large, not the other, but none, Watt strove in vain to correct this asymmetry. But logic was on his side, and he remained faithful, when involved in a journey of any length, to this distribution of his socks, in preference to the other three.

Of Watt's coat and waistcoat, of his shirt his vest and his drawers, much might be written, of great interest and significance. The drawers, in particular, were remarkable, from more than one point of view. But they were hidden, coat and waistcoat, shirt and underclothes, all hidden, from the eye.

Watt wore no tie, nor any collar. Had he had a collar, he would no doubt have found a tie, to go with it. And had he had a tie, he might perhaps have procured a collar, to carry it. But having neither tie, nor collar, he had neither collar, nor tie.

❧

VLADIMIR NABOKOV [1901–   ]

Excerpt from "Mademoiselle O," 1951, in NABOKOV'S DOZEN, *1958*

A kerosene lamp is steered into the gloaming. Gently it floats and comes down; the hand of memory, now in a footman's white cotton glove, places it in the centre of a round table. The flame is nicely adjusted, and a rosy, silk-flounced lamp shade crowns the light. Revealed: a warm, bright room in a snow-muffled house— soon to be termed *le château*—built by my great-grandfather, who, being afraid of fires, had the staircase made of iron, so that when the house did get burnt to the ground, sometime after the Soviet Revolution, those fretted steps remained standing there, all alone but still leading up.

Some more about that room, please. The oval mirror. Hanging on taut cords, its pure brow inclined, it strives to retain the falling furniture and a slope of bright floor that keep slipping from its embrace. The chandelier pendants. These emit a delicate tinkling whenever anything is moved in an upstairs room. Coloured pencils. That tiny heap of emerald pencil dust on the oilcloth where a penknife has just done its recurrent duty. We are sitting at the table, my brother and I and Miss Robinson, who now and then looks at her watch: roads must be dreadful with all that snow; and anyway many professional hardships lie in wait for the vague French person who will replace her.

Now the coloured pencils in more detail. The green one, by a mere whirl of the wrist, could be made to produce a ruffled tree, or the chimney smoke of a house where spinach was cooking. The blue one drew a simple line across the page—and the horizon of all seas was there. A nondescript blunt one kept getting into one's way. The brown one was always broken, and so was the red, but sometimes, just after it had snapped, one could still make it serve by holding it so that the loose tip was propped, none too securely, by a jutting splinter. The little purple fellow, a special favourite of mine, had now worn down so short as to become scarcely manageable. The white one alone, that lanky albino among pencils, kept its original length, or at least did so until I discovered that, far from being a fraud leaving no mark on the page, it was the ideal tool since I could imagine whatever I wished while I scrawled.

❦

THORSTEIN VEBLEN [1857–1929]

Excerpts from THE THEORY OF THE LEISURE CLASS, *1899*

From Chapter 3, "Conspicuous Leisure"

Abstention from labour is not only a honorific or meritorious act, but it presently comes to be a requisite of decency. The insistence on property as the basis of reputability is very naïve and very imperious during the early stages of the accumulation of wealth. Abstention from labour is the conventional evidence of wealth and is therefore the conventional mark of social standing; and this insistence on the meritoriousness of wealth leads to a more strenuous insistence on leisure. *Nota notæ est nota rei ipsius.* [A sign of a sign is a sign of the thing itself.] According to well-established laws of human nature, prescription presently seizes upon this conventional evidence of wealth and fixes it in men's habits of thought as something that is in itself substantially meritorious and ennobling; while productive labour at the same time and by a like process becomes in a double sense intrinsically unworthy. Prescription ends by making labour not only disreputable in the eyes of the community, but morally impossible to the noble, freeborn man, and incompatible with a worthy life.

This tabu on labour has a further consequence in the industrial differentiation of classes. As the population increases in density and the predatory group grows into a settled industrial community, the constituted authorities and the customs governing ownership gain in scope and consistency. It then presently becomes impracticable to accumulate wealth by simple seizure, and, in logical consistency, acquisition by industry is equally impossible for high-minded and impecunious men. The alternative open to them is beggary or privation. Wherever the canon of conspicuous leisure has a chance undisturbed to work out its tendency, there will therefore emerge a secondary, and in a sense spurious, leisure class—abjectly poor and living a precarious life of want and discomfort, but morally unable to stoop to gainful pursuits. The decayed gentleman and the lady who has seen better days are by no means unfamiliar phenomena even now. This pervading sense of the indignity of the slightest manual labour is familiar to all civilised peoples, as well as to peoples of a less advanced pecuniary culture. In persons of delicate sensibility, who have long been habituated to gentle manners, the sense of the shamefulness of manual labour may become so strong that, at a critical juncture, it will even set aside the instinct of self-preservation. So, for instance, we are told of certain Polynesian chiefs, who, under the stress of good form, preferred to starve rather than carry their food to their mouths with their own hands. It is true, this conduct may have been due, at least in part, to an excessive sanctity or tabu attaching to the chief's person. The tabu would have been communicated by the contact of his hands, and so would have made anything touched by him unfit for human food. But the tabu is itself a derivative of the unworthiness or moral incompatibility of labour; so that even when construed in this sense the conduct of the Polynesian chiefs is truer to the canon of honorific leisure than would at first appear. A better illustration, or at least a more unmistakable one, is afforded by a certain king of France, who is said to have lost his life through an excess of moral stamina in the observance of good form. In the absence of the functionary whose office it was to shift his master's seat, the king sat uncomplaining before the fire and suffered his royal person to be toasted beyond recovery. But in so doing he saved his Most Christian Majesty from menial contamination.

Summum crede nefas animam præferre pudori,
Et propter vitam vivendi perdere causas.
[*Believe it the worst of sins to purchase life with dishonor,*
And in order to live to lose all reason for living.]

From Chapter 10, "Modern Survivals of Prowess"

Apart from warlike activity proper, the institution of the duel is also an expression of the same superior readiness for combat; and the duel is a leisure-class institution. The duel is in substance a more or less deliberate resort to a fight as a final settlement of a difference of opinion. In civilised communities it prevails as a normal phenomenon only where there is an hereditary leisure class, and almost exclusively among that class. The exceptions are (1) military and naval officers—who are ordinarily members of the leisure class, and who are at the same time specially trained to predatory habits of mind—and (2) the lower-class delinquents— who are by inheritance, or training, or both, of a similarly predatory disposition and habit. It is only the high-bred gentleman and the rowdy that normally resort to blows as the universal solvent of differences of opinion. The plain man will ordinarily fight only when excessive momentary irritation or alcoholic exaltation act to inhibit the more complex habits of response to the stimuli that make for provocation. He is then thrown back upon the simpler, less differentiated forms of the instinct of self-assertion; that is to say, he reverts temporarily and without reflection to an archaic habit of mind.

From Chapter 11, "The Belief in Luck"

While the belief in luck is the basis of the gambling habit, it is not the only element that enters into the habit of betting. Betting on the issue of contests of strength and skill proceeds on a further motive, without which the belief in luck would scarcely come in as a prominent feature of sporting life. This further motive is the desire of the anticipated winner, or the partisan of the anticipated winning side, to heighten his side's ascendency at the cost of the loser. Not only does the stronger side score a more signal victory, and the losing side suffer a more painful and humiliating defeat, in proportion as the pecuniary gain and loss in the wager is large; although this alone is a consideration of material weight. But the wager is commonly laid also with a view, not avowed in words nor even recognised in set terms *in petto*, to enhancing the chances of success for the contestant on which it is laid. It is felt that substance and solicitude expended to this end can not go for naught in the issue. There is here a special manifestation of the instinct of workmanship, backed by an even more manifest sense that the animistic congruity of things must decide for a victorious outcome for the side in whose behalf the propensity inherent in events has been propitiated and fortified by so much of conative and kinetic urging.

Exercises

Don't let anything run to more than two pages.

1. You are in a large section of a course that you are taking only because it is required. You are present only because the professor calls the roll. He is delivering a dull lecture in a loud voice. It has to be loud because a giant vacuum cleaner is removing the leaves from the lawn just outside the classroom. The student to your right keeps passing you notes. The student to your left, a distractingly attractive specimen of the opposite sex, keeps whispering to you words that you don't quite catch. A fly keeps settling on your forehead. And you are trying to read an important chapter in a textbook on another subject, because you will be quizzed on it during the next period. Give us two pages of your stream of consciousness, in the manner of *Ulysses*.

2. Describe the way you live now, or the way you lived at some time in the past, in the manner of Gertrude Stein's "The Winner Loses."

3. Describe your relations with a friend, in the manner of Gertrude Stein's account of her relations with Hemingway.

4. Discuss the work of a justly famous person, in the manner of Gertrude Stein's "Picasso." By "justly famous" I mean famous for the quality of his work. That eliminates all TV stars, especially the good ones; all dictators and would-be dictators; all singers who sing with their hips, and all painters who paint by kicking the paint bucket. Write about somebody who does with rare skill something that is worth doing.

5. Write a piece of indirect discourse, with interruptions, in the manner of Faulkner's "The Old Man."

6. Do a "Camera Eye" piece on a student party. The basic idea is to suggest the nature of the party by means of images presented without comment. Either kind of party will do—evening or political.

7. Many people believe that the sum of all wisdom is to say nothing that anybody might possibly disagree with, and to do nothing that anybody might possibly disapprove of. Discuss this view, in the style of Thorstein Veblen.

APPENDICES

*Every feeling experienced by us will
assume an aesthetic character, provided
that it has been* suggested, *and not* caused.

HENRI BERGSON
Time and Free Will

⌒⋆⌒ THE FIRST of these appendices shows how the foremost avant-garde writer of the twentieth century, whose boldest techniques have not even begun to be assimilated by other writers, uses in his boldest experiment a traditional rhythmic pattern; the second discusses the physiological sources of the rhythms of poetry and prose; the third defines the uses of symmetry and asymmetry, regularity and irregularity, rhythm and random, in another art.

"The Prankquean," an episode from the first chapter of *Finnegans Wake*, is in terms of structure a paradigm of the whole novel. It has the traditional four-part pattern of such fairy tales as "Jack the Giant-Killer," "Goldilocks and the Three Bears," and "The Three Billy-Goats Gruff": three similar actions and a coda that concludes them. By following the numbers that I have written under the motifs, you can easily see the design: the first motif occurs at 21.5, 21.33 and 22.21: and remember that in all such fairy tales the third time is the charm.

André Spire (1868–   ),[1] a social poet inspired by Whitman and Tolstoy, thought of writing as a manifestation of the writer's vital force; "The Ear and the Mouth" expresses this view. An interesting piece to compare with it, which I have not included here because it is available in any decent library, is Oliver Wendell Holmes's "The Physiology of Versification," the ninth paper in *Pages from an Old Volume of Life*.

[1] As I add this footnote, in May 1967, that remarkable man is still living.

Sartre's essay on Alexander Calder's mobiles, though it says nothing directly about the art of writing, expresses a point of view that many of the most interesting contemporary novelists share. For better and for worse, there is a school of writers now who believe that nothing matters but form, structure, organization, design, internal validity: style; and that all other values come from style or are implicit in it. I do not agree. Some of the best-executed novels of our own time seem to me empty of thought and feeling, and therefore, notwithstanding their wonderfully ingenious construction and brilliant finish, hardly worth reading more than once. On the other hand, much of the contemporary literature of "thought" and "feeling" is not worth reading even once, because the form that constitutes its "thought" and "feeling" is at best commonplace and more often inept. It is as if, by way of theater, we had to choose between a troupe of wonderfully skillful acrobats and a troupe of earnest ham actors performing a wooden play about a hair-tearing young man torn between Idealizzum and Ambishun, written by a playwright whose only equipment was a big strong heart and a small weak brain. Most of our most skillful writers, for various invalid reasons, have chosen to ignore the great problems of our time or of any time; and most writers who are concerned with such problems don't write well. Those of us who choose the acrobats—as I do—wish there were something more interesting to choose.

There is of course no necessary conflict between moral sensitivity and literary sensitivity; in fact, as I intimated in the Introduction, we may very well question the moral sensitivity of a writer whose vague or inaccurate or clumsy language obviously blunts his perceptions. But Zola wrote well. Proust wrote well. Joyce wrote well. Kafka wrote well. Italo Svevo wrote well. Hermann Broch wrote well. Samuel Beckett writes well. Günter Grass writes well. And they all have or had good hearts as well as good heads. It is my hope that this book will help college students with good hearts to develop a sense of form and some skill in handling it. Their decency will become clearer and be more effective as they grow more articulate.

APPENDIX ONE

JAMES JOYCE

THE PRANKQUEAN: A FAIRY TALE

[The numbers in the margins indicate pages and lines in the text of *Finnegans Wake:* 21.5 means page 21, line 5. The numbers under the lines are intended to help us locate verbal motifs.]

It was of a night, late, lang time agone, in an auldstane eld,   21.5
1 1 1 1 1 1 1 1 1 1 1 1 1 1 1 1 1 1
when Adam was delvin and his madameen spinning watersilts,
when mulk mountynotty man was everybully and the first leal
ribberrobber that ever had her ainway everybuddy to his love-
saking eyes and everybilly lived alove with everybiddy else, and
2 2 2
Jarl van Hoother had his burnt head high up in his lamphouse,   21.1
2 2 2 2 2 2 2 2 2 2 2 2 2 2 2 2 2 2 2 2 2 2 2 2 2 2 2 2 2 2
laying cold hands on himself. And his two little jiminies, cousins
2 2 2 2 2 2 2 2 2 2 2 2 2 2 3 3 3 3 3 3 3 3 3 3 3 3 3 3 3 3 3 3
of ourn, Tristopher and Hilary, were kickaheeling their dummy
3 3 3 3 3 3 3 3 3 3 3 3 3 3 3 3 3 3 3 3 3 3 3 3 3 3 3 3 3 3 3 3
on the oil cloth flure of his homerigh, castle and earthenhouse.
3 3 3 3 3 3 3 3 3 3 3 3 3 3 3 3 3 3 3 3 3 3 3 3 3 3 3 3 3 3 3 3
And, be dermot, who come to the keep of his inn only the neice-
4 4 4 4 4 4 4 4 4 4 4 4 4 4 4 4 4 4 4 4 4 4 4 4 4 4 4 4 4 4 4 4 4 4 4 4
of-his-in-law, the prankquean. And the prankquean pulled a rosy   21.1
4 4 4 4 4 4 4 4 4 4 4 4 4 4 5 5 5 5 5 5 5 5 5 5 5 5 5 5 5 5 5
one and made her wit foreninst the dour. And she lit up and fire-
5 5 5 5 5 5 5 5 5 5 5 5 5 5 5 5 5 5 5 5 5 5 5 5 5 5 5 5

land was ablaze. And spoke she to the dour in her petty perusi-
5 5 5 5 5 5 5 5 6 6 6 6 6 6 6 6 6 6 6 6 6 6 6 6 6 6 6 6 6 6 6 6

enne: Mark the Wans, why do I am alook alike a poss of porter-
6 6 6 6 6 6 6 6 6 6 6 6 6 6 6 6 6 6 6 6 6 6 6 6 6 6 6 6 6 6

pease? And that was how the skirtmisshes began. But the dour
6 6 6   7 7 7 7 7 7 7 7 7 7 7 7 7 7 7 7 7 7 7 7 7   8 8 8 8 8 8 8

21.20 handworded her grace in dootch nossow: Shut! So her grace
8 8 8 8 8 8 8 8 8 8 8 8 8 8 8 8 8 8 8 8 8 8 8 9 9 9 9 9 9

o'malice kidsnapped up the jiminy Tristopher and into the shan-
9 9 9 9 9 9 9 9 9 9 9 9 9 9 9 9 9 9 9 9 9 9 9 9 9 9 9 9 9 9

dy westerness she rain, rain, rain. And Jarl van Hoother war-
9 9 9 9 9 9 9 9 9 9 9 9 9 9 9 9   10 10 10 10 10 10 10 10 10 10

lessed after her with soft dovesgall: Stop deef stop come back to
10 10 10 10 10 10 10 10 10 10 10 10 10 10 10 10 10 10 10 10 10 10 10

my earin stop. But she swaradid to him: Unlikelihud. And there
10 10 10 10 10 10 10 10 10 10 10 10 10 10 10 10 10 10 10   11 11 11 11

21.25 was a brannewail that same sabboath night of falling angles some-
11 11 11 11 11 11 11 11 11 11 11 11 11 11 11 11 11 11 11 11 11 11 11

where in Erio. And the prankquean went for her forty years'
11 11 11 11 11   12 12 12 12 12 12 12 12 12 12 12 12 12 12 12 12 12 12

walk in Tourlemonde and she washed the blessings of the love-
12 12 12 12 12 12 12 12 12 12 12 12 12 12 12 12 12 12 12 12 12

spots off the jiminy with soap sulliver suddles and she had her
12 12 12 12 12 12 12 12 12 12 12 12 12 12 12 12 12 12 12 12 12

four owlers masters for to tauch him his tickles and she convor-
12 12 12 12 12 12 12 12 12 12 12 12 12 12 12 12 12 12 12 12 12

21.30 ted him to the onesure allgood and he became a luderman. So then
12 12 12 12 12 12 12 12 12 12 12 12 12 12 12 12 12 12 12 12 4 4 4 4

she started to rain and to rain and, be redtom, she was back again
4 4 4 4 4 4 4 4 4 4 4 4 4 4 4 4 4 4 4 4 4 4 4 4 4 4 4 4

at Jarl van Hoother's in a brace of samers and the jiminy with
4 4 4 4 4 4 4 4 4 4 4 4 4 4 4 4 4 4 4 4 4 4 4 4 4 4 4 4

her in her pinafrond, lace at night, at another time. And where
4 4 4 4 4 4 4 4 4 1 1 1 1 1 1 1 1 1 1 1 1 1 4 4 4 4 4 4

did she come but to the bar of his bristolry. And Jarl von Hoo-
4 4 4 4 4 4 4 4 4 4 4 4 4 4 4 4 4 4 4 4 2 2 2 2 2 2 2 2 2

ther had his baretholobruised heels drowned in his cellarmalt,   21.35
2 2 2 2 2 2 2 2 2 2 2 2 2 2 2 2 2 2 2 2 2 2 2 2 2 2 2 2 2 2

shaking warm hands with himself and the jiminy Hilary and
2 2 2 2 2 2 2 2 2 2 2 2 2 2 2 2 3 3 3 3 3 3 3 3 3 3 3 3 3

the dummy in their first infancy were below on the tearsheet,   22.1
3 3 3 3 3 3 3 3 3 3 3 3 3 3 3 3 3 3 3 3 3 3 3 3 3 3 3 3 3 3

wringing and coughing, like brodhar and histher. And the prank-
3 3 3 3 3 3 3 3 3 3 3 3 3 3 3 3 3 3 3 3 3 3 3 3 5 5 5 5 5 5 5

quean nipped a paly one and lit up again and redcocks flew flack-
5 5 5 5 5 5 5 5 5 5 5 5 5 5 5 5 5 5 5 5 5 5 5 5 5 5 5 5 5 5

ering from the hillcombs. And she made her witter before the
5 5 5 5 5 5 5 5 5 5 5 5 5 5 5 5 5 5 5 5 5 5 5 5 5 5 5 5 5 5

wicked, saying: Mark the Twy, who do I am alook alike two poss   22.5
5 5 5 5 6 6 6 6 6 6 6 6 6 6 6 6 6 6 6 6 6 6 6 6 6 6 6 6 6 6

of porterpease? And: Shut! says the wicked, handwording her
6 6 6 6 6 6 6 8 8 8 8 8 8 8 8 8 8 8 8 8 8 8 8 8 8 8 8 8 8 8

madesty. So her madesty a forethought set down a jiminy and
8 8 8 8 9 9 9 9 9 9 9 9 9 9 9 9 9 9 9 9 9 9 9 9 9 9 9 9 9 9

took up a jiminy and all the lilipath ways to Woeman's land she
9 9 9 9 9 9 9 9 9 9 9 9 9 9 9 9 9 9 9 9 9 9 9 9 9 9 9 9 9 9

rain, rain, rain. And Jarl von Hoother bleethered atter her with
9 9 9 9 9 9 9 10 10 10 10 10 10 10 10 10 10 10 10 10 10 10 10 10

a loud finegale: Stop domb stop come back with my earring stop.   22.10
10 10 10 10 10 10 10 10 10 10 10 10 10 10 10 10 10 10 10 10 10

But the prankquean swaradid: Am liking it. And there was a wild
10 10 10 10 10 10 10 10 10 10 10 10 10 10 11 11 11 11 11 11 11 11

old grannewwail that laurency night of starshootings somewhere
11 11 11 11 11 11 11 11 11 11 11 11 11 11 11 11 11 11 11 11 11 11

in Erio. And the prankquean went for her forty years' walk in
11 11 11 12 12 12 12 12 12 12 12 12 12 12 12 12 12 12 12 12 12

Turnlemeem and she punched the curses of cromcruwell with
12 12 12 12 12 12 12 12 12 12 12 12 12 12 12 12 12 12 12 12

the nail of a top into the jiminy and she had her four larksical   22.15
12 12 12 12 12 12 12 12 12 12 12 12 12 12 12 12 12 12 12 12 12

monitrix to touch him his tears and she provorted him to the
12 12 12 12 12 12 12 12 12 12 12 12 12 12 12 12 12 12 12 12 12

onecertain allsecure and he became a tristian. So then she started
12 12 12 12 12 12 12 12 12 12 12 12 12 12 15 4 4 4 4 4 4 4 4
raining, raining, and in a pair of changers, be dom ter, she was
4 4 4 4 4 4 4 4 4 4 4 4 4 4 4 4 4 4 4 4 4 4 4 4 4 4 4 4 4
back again at Jarl von Hoother's and the Larryhill with her under
4 4 4 4 4 4 4 4 4 4 4 4 4 4 4 4 4 4 4 4 4 4 4 4 4 4 4 4 4

22.20 her abromette. And why would she halt at all if not by the ward
4 4 4 4 4 4 4 4 4 4 4 4 4 4 4 4 4 4 4 4 4 4 4 4 4 4 4 4 4
of his mansionhome of another nice lace for the third charm?
4 4 4 4 4 4 4 4 4 4 1 1 1 1 1 1 1 1 1 1 1 1 1 1 1 1 1 1 1
And Jarl von Hoother had his hurricane hips up to his pantry-
2 2 2 2 2 2 2 2 2 2 2 2 2 2 2 2 2 2 2 2 2 2 2 2 2 2 2 2
box, ruminating in his holdfour stomachs (Dare! O dare!), and
2 2 2 2 2 2 2 2 2 2 2 2 2 2 2 2 2 2 2 2 2 2 2 2 2 2 3 3
the jiminy Toughertrees and the dummy were belove on the
3 3 3 3 3 3 3 3 3 3 3 3 3 3 3 3 3 3 3 3 3 3 3 3 3 3 3 3

22.25 watercloth, kissing and spitting, and roguing and poghuing, like
3 3 3 3 3 3 3 3 3 3 3 3 3 3 3 3 3 3 3 3 3 3 3 3 3 3 3 3
knavepaltry and naivebride and in their second infancy. And the
3 3 3 3 3 3 3 3 3 3 3 3 3 3 3 3 3 3 3 3 3 3 3 3 5 5 5 5
prankquean picked a blank and lit out and the valleys lay twink-
5 5 5 5 5 5 5 5 5 5 5 5 5 5 5 5 5 5 5 5 5 5 5 5 5 5 5 5
ling. And she made her wittest in front of the arkway of trihump,
5 5 5 5 5 5 5 5 5 5 5 5 5 5 5 5 5 5 5 5 5 5 5 5 5 5 5 5
asking: Mark the Tris, why do I am alook alike three poss of por-
6 6 6 6 6 6 6 6 6 6 6 6 6 6 6 6 6 6 6 6 6 6 6 6 6 6 6 6

22.30 ter pease? But that was how the skirtmishes endupped. For like
6 6 6 6 7 7 7 7 7 7 7 7 7 7 7 7 7 7 7 7 7 7 7 7 7
the campbells acoming with a fork lance of lightning, Jarl von
Hoother Boanerges himself, the old terror of the dames, came
hip hop handihap out through the pikeopened arkway of his
three shuttoned castles, in his broadginger hat and his civic chol-

22.35 lar and his allabuff hemmed and his bullbraggin soxangloves
and his ladbrook breeks and his cattegut bandolair and his fur-

23.1 framed panuncular cumbottes like a rudd yellan gruebleen or-

angeman in his violet indigonation, to the whole length of the
strongth of his bowman's bill. And he clopped his rude hand to
his eacy hitch and he ordurd and his thick spch spck for her to
8 8 8 8 8 8 8 8 8 8 8 8 8 8 8 8
shut up shop, dappy. And the duppy shot the shutter clup (Per-　23.5
8 8 8 8 8 8 8 8 8 8 8 8 8 8 8 8 8 8 8 8 8 8 8 8 8 8
kodhuskurunbarggruauyagokgorlayorgromgrammitghundhurth-
rumathunaradidillifaititillibumullunukkunun!) And they all drank
free. For one man in his armour was a fat match always for any
girls under shurts. And that was the first peace of illiterative
7 7 7 7 7 7 7
porthery in all the flamend floody flatuous world. How kirssy the　23.10
7 7 7 7 7 7 7
tiler made a sweet unclose to the Narwhealian captol. Saw fore
7 7 7 7 7 7 7 7 7 7 7 7 7 7 7 7 7 7 7 7 7 7 7 7 7 7 7 7 7 7 7
shalt thou sea. Betoun ye and be. The prankquean was to hold
7 7 7 7 7 7 7
her dummyship and the jiminies was to keep the peacewave
and van Hoother was to git the wind up. Thus the hearsomeness
of the burger felicitates the whole of the polis.

The prankquean's riddle
occurs from time to time throughout *Finnegans Wake:* unmistakably at 21.18, 22.5, 22.29, 223.23, 224.14, 260.5, 301.F1, 311.22,
317.22, 324.12, 365.34, 372.4, 417.7, 493.29 and 623.14, and possibly
at 38.5, 466.30 and 511.19.

APPENDIX TWO

ANDRÉ SPIRE

PLAISIR POÉTIQUE ET PLAISIR MUSCULAIRE, *1949, Chapter 2, "The*
*Ear and the Mouth"**

The poet is not merely a dreamer, who needs only solitude and his

* Notes to this section appear on pp. 296–312.

dream. He wants to give a certain substantiality to his dream; he wants to keep some trace of the happiness. But such communion is not achieved in a state of ecstasy or by the laying on of hands in silence.

It requires a medium: words.

These words, on their graphic side, are composed of visual elements called letters; on their oral side they are composed of sound elements, which linguists, in order to distinguish them from the other sounds given by nature and used or studied in other human activities, artistic and scientific, have designated by the name of *phonemes*.

The phonemes are divided into vowels and consonants—a difference of function rather than of nature, since in certain cases the same phonemes may be used sometimes as vowels, sometimes as consonants.[1] Consonants and vowels are parts of "a natural series of which only the ends are clearly separate."[2]

But in no languages are phonemes used in isolation. The articulatory movements that create them are combined in phrases, which themselves are divided into words and syllables.

Experience has shown that the feeling of the separation of words is less natural than the feeling of the separation of syllables.[3] In speech, there are "syllables and even groups of syllables which one does not know whether to utter as independent words or to attach to neighboring words. The division is sharper in some languages than in others."[4] Every normal person feels the syllable as the elementary division of language; and the history of languages supports this feeling. The first alphabets were not of phonemes but of syllables. To pass from the notion of the syllable to that of the letter, it is necessary to have developed a capacity for long and delicate analysis—to have arrived at a state in which the faculties of observation are singularly refined, but in which language evolves from expressiveness toward signification, from the *concrete value* to the *algebraic value* of words.

These words, whose duration in sound and extent in space are rather poorly defined, these words whose sense depends on the text that envelops them, form phrases whose total or partial unity is more easily recognizable.

Let us listen, for example, to an orator. If we are too far away to understand him, we perceive "groups of sounds, varying in length and separated by silences." Let us come closer. The "groups of sounds perceived by the ear awake in our mind groups of related representations, each of which constitutes, grammatically speaking, a phrase."[5]

The phrase, which is not a collection of word-images but everywhere a specific phenomenon simpler than the word,[6] the phrase which alone expresses a thought, is a linguistic unity which recovers a primordial linguistic act, beyond which the linguist has no means of penetrating.[7] It is the fundamental element of language.[8]

The phrase may be very short—one or two words: Yes. No. Certainly! For example. My God! It may extend to the balanced dimensions of a Ciceronian period, or wind like a serpent through the subordinate clauses of Marcel Proust. In the province of the phrase are "systems, linked or opposed, . . . of varying degrees of differentiation. There are simple systems, clearly differentiated, which can be comprehended immediately because they suggest the fewest alternative choices: interjections, exclamations, stereotyped expressions such as the formulas of politeness, or those 'refrains' which adorn certain rabble-rousing speeches or which are traditional in certain ethnic groups—the *Allah alone is great* of the Mohammedans."[9]

But even a ready-made expression may be a quite complicated system. Below this level are simpler elements, "little blocks, solid and compact,"[10] each forming a whole which is psychologically, semantically, rhythmically indissoluble.[11] These are elementary phrases, propositions composed in general of a subject, a verb and a complement, or groups smaller still, composed of a word (substantive, adjective or verb) preceded by a particle such as an article or a preposition or some other word which has not, either by nature or by position, any independent existence, but which is in effect a part of the word that follows it.[12]

Nevertheless—save in exceptional cases of oral improvisation which are basically mnemonic, or when writing in a surrealistic trance to the dictation of a muse hidden in the recesses of the unconscious—though the poet while composing feels a kind of expectancy, desire, attraction, hope, toward these little solid, compact groups, the happily poised assembly of which will in the future constitute his verse—nevertheless, while he is in the process of arranging it, of giving it form, he must work with even simpler elements of the phrase.[13] The elements he combines, juxtaposes, tries to work into patterns, are syllables or combinations of syllables, words themselves.

Thus, his creative activity—instinctively, no doubt, and concretely, yet analytically too—is concerned with the same elements of his poem which will engage the activity of the grammarian and the linguist when they study the completed poem.

Let us then use the classifications of these devoted experts to guide us through the hazardous labyrinths of language. Aided also by the confidences of poets, of which there is no lack, let us try to understand what are, *for a poet in the act of composing*, the elements of the grand linguistic unities he assembles: those "nothings" which are "the substratum, the necessity, . . . the form, the color and the odor . . . the vehicle" of thought: words.[14]

At the call of the eager mind,[15] there awakes a world of possibilities sleeping in the depth of our being. Some, *images* more or less precise, more or less isolated or associated with memories or anticipations visual, auditory, gustatory, kinesthetic,[16] are *concrete* representations:[17] a certain face, a certain flavor of a certain fruit, a certain color, a certain odor of a certain flower, a certain gesture of certain hands, or a certain complex ensemble of objects, of movements, of attitudes, of affective states, of sounds, of tastes, of odors. Others, which transcend the facts on which they are based,[18] are *abstract* and general notions, rudimentary judgments,[19] instruments of social thought incorporated in language, of reflective thought, of science, of knowledge: *concepts.* Here, things, states, acts are no longer considered in terms of their particular and unique attributes, but are departicularized, in a sense disincarnated, and characterized only by what they have in common.[20]

Escaping farther and farther from the things it represents, the concept, less and less an image and more and more a notion, is no longer "a simple fragment of the things of common sense." It is not "a copy, but a shadow, an appearance . . . in which resemblance to things has been replaced by a set of logical conditions."[21] In some cases[22] the concept tends to be nothing more than a phantom, a mere label with no sensible content, a sort of algebraic sign[23] freed from any relationship to the actual, such as "the words September, October, November, December, which in our calendar designate respectively the ninth, tenth, eleventh and twelfth months; or the proper names Blanche, Melanie, Sophie . . . conferred with no thought of their etymology."[24]

Also phantoms are the *grammatical tools:* articles, pronouns, prepositions, conjunctions, auxiliary verbs and their substitutes, which—while the living elements of language (nouns, adjectives, verbs, certain adverbs)[25] represent objects, feelings, actions, ideas, qualities—can express nothing but relations, grammatical categories.[26] Some are words which formerly had representative content: for example, *chez,* which meant *casa* (house), and other prepositions which are only participles or adjectives separated from the rest of the formulas of which they are part: *during* (the night), *notwithstanding* (the proscription), *despite* (the rain), *except* (Sundays), *sauf* (erreur), *plein* (la rue). Some are words that were formerly concrete and full of meaning, the shells of old autonomous words, emptied of their own sense and used now simply as exponents, as symbols."[27]

But these images, which are the *sensible, emotional, intellectual* content of the word and which the poet seeks, are not all there is to the word. The psychic unity anterior to utterance is "at once a representation elaborated by thought looking toward expression in language and an ensemble of phonetic possibilities ready to be realized."[28] *The word is a complex of sense and sound*, single and double at the same time, and there is no need to demonstrate that it has no real effect save as a totality. But for purposes of study we may legitimately isolate its various psychological and linguistic elements.

On the side of sound, the word, for the poet in the act of composing, is also a voluntary or spontaneous resurrection of past sensations: a representation, an image. These verbal images which the poet calls up, touches, draws to himself, puts aside, draws to himself again, until they give him, by their contact and their coincidence with the meaning of the word, the sense of beauty or at least of success, are themselves nothing but the "playing back" of sensations: sensations experienced by the poet, when at school he learned or recited or heard poems, or when as a child serving his apprenticeship to language he associated (while acquiring lifelong automatisms) certain mental operations with certain movements or certain sound-phenomena.[29]

These images,[30] in their contours no less imprecise and unstable than those that float in the fugitive content of words, electric accumulators continually charging and discharging, not only involve one or several of our senses, but also echo in our general sensibility (muscular, visceral, glandular).

Consider first the auditory images. They are extremely complex. Our ear perceives air vibrations in a certain range of frequencies only. For us, frequencies below 15 or 20 cycles or above

15,000 or 20,000 cycles per second are silent. On the other hand, the ear is not the only part with which we perceive relatively slow vibrations, such as the low notes of the cello, of the piano, and perhaps of certain bass or contralto voices. They can also be perceived as resonances through the responsive vibrations of the sound-boxes or tubes of instruments held in the hand, or of our diaphragm, our thoracic cage, or various other vibrating parts of our body. As for sharper sounds, perceived as purely auditory sensations, they are not without their physiological action, as has been shown by experiments with the harmonics of the highest audible fundamental sounds. In all cases the bombarding of the body, the skin, the flesh, the resonators of the hollow parts, by the millions of slow or rapid movements in the atmosphere and the vibrating walls and partitions of the room, explain well enough—much better than pleasure of a purely musical order—that state of exaltation, of ecstasy, of being lifted out of oneself, of being crushed, of bewilderment even, in which some particularly sensitive persons are found at the end of a concert.[31]

Moreover, our ear is not merely a simple acoustic receiver in which air vibrations of a certain frequency become audible. Just as our eye is at once an organ for receiving vibrations of visible frequency, and a contractile and mobile organ which, lending itself to all sorts of movements of accommodation, of direction, of secretion, is a motor of vision, and hence an organ of muscular sensations and muscular images, so our ear—composed, in addition to the auditory nerve, of motor nerves, of muscles, of cartilages, of membranes, of large and small bones,[32] of canals, of liquids whose movements or modifications play a role in our hearing of certain sounds, in our accommodation to intensity and distance, in our appreciation of the direction of sounds, in orientation and balance[33]—acts as a motor organ of hearing.[34] Its functioning gives rise to auditory sensations accompanied by muscular movements provoking various feelings of effort, of tenseness, of discomfort, of sadness even,[35] occasioned by vibrations of certain frequencies, or by the too rapid, too slow, too irregular or too intense succession of noises or sounds.[36]

Many associations also contribute to the production of our voice: associations between the parts and functions of our ear and those of our laryngo-buccal system—that is to say, of all its organs: diaphragm, lungs, bronchi, tracheae, larynx, pharynx, nasal fossae, and resonant cavities from the base of the diaphragm to the attachment of the lips. There are associations which have their origin in common or neighboring organs, in cerebral or nervous connections, in muscular intricacies well known to anatomists, to psycho-physiologists and to phoneticians. As a result, sensations or certain images can arise not only from localized reflexes in a part of the ear or in one of the organs of the vocal apparatus, but also from irradiations in the totality of these organs or in one and another at the same time.

There are analogous associations between these various organs and functions and those of our neck, our head, our face, which are the seat of facial mimicry;[37] and similarly with the secretory systems of the ear, the salivary and lachrymal glands, the motor organs of the eye, the tactile organs of the skin and the tongue,[38] the sense of smell, and the whole motor system of the arms, the hands, the legs—our whole body.[38a]

That is why an *auditory excitation*, an unexpected or a sudden noise, can provoke separate or concomitant motor reactions, accompanied by more or less vague consciousness of them—movements or cessations of movement of all sorts, attitudes of various parts of our face and our body, mute gestures of our upper and lower extremities, phonetic gestures such as words or cries.

But these peripheral animal excitations are not the only ones that originate movements or the images of movements.

The functioning of the cerebral-organic mechanism embraces not only direct actions but actions at a distance, and so many derivations, equivalences, substitutions, levelings out—in short, "such a diffusion of emotional excitation that perhaps not a single cell of the organism is untouched by emotion."[39]

That is why not only external stimuli but any physical or intellectual effort, any emotion or sentiment—hope, desire, fear, moral anguish—can provoke such reactions: the more or less obvious reactions of our muscles, gestures silent or vocal, and in addition circulatory, respiratory, visceral, glandular reactions.[40] These reactions, which give us internal sensations of local or general contraction, of pain, of oppression, of shortness of breath, indirectly modify our attitudes and gestures, our facial expression, the movements of our throat and the nuances of our voice.[41]

This setting in lively motion of all the interrelated elements of our being by the slightest reception or representation,[42] by the innumerable events of our affective life, is accomplished in part by auditory operations. They play an important, an indispensable part—but only a part. They originate movements in the same way that the small explosion of a percussion cap liberates formidable forces, potential but inert, in a bomb. If, in its modest receiving operation, the ear experiences some sign, some pleasure or pain of an auditory nature, that experience is very little by comparison with all the sensations, precise or diffused, which vibrations of sound can evoke in our external tactile sensibility—in our scalp, the skin of our face, the skin over the various tissues of our members and the partitions of our body[43]—and in our internal sensibility: kinesthetic reactions that accompany our conscious listening, to say nothing of the coenesthetic phenomena which cannot be dissociated from them.[44]

It is a profound sensibility, for the sensations or images which impinge on it engage even those elements which are farthest removed from the surface of our body; they engage our internal organs in relations with the external world, which prepare our communications with it: our diaphragm, seat of respiration and voice; our lungs, our tracheae, our larynx, the various laryngo-buccal organs by which we breathe in the air of life and breathe it out charged with sounds that transmit to other human beings, together with the nuances of our emotions, the very heat of our body.

But among the mass of *natural associations*, of *spontaneous movements* and biochemical functions which evince the unity of our being[45] as it responds by complexes of reactions to the innumerable solicitations of the universe, social life can make choices. It can regard the manifestation of some reactions as less useful, of others as inconvenient, disadvantageous or dangerous, of yet others as indispensable to its ends. Little by little, some are atrophied, dissimulated or dissolved.[46] Others grow stronger spontaneously or are artificially strengthened.

This is evident from the diversity of forms taken by the language with which at different times and places men have tried to communicate with each other or to respond to the movements and actions of the beings, visible and invisible, with which they feel themselves surrounded.

There is mimic language, consisting of gestures, attitudes, passionate emissions of voice, cries, chants, variously modulated or articulated according to the structure of the vocal organs, which modern psychology calls "vocal patterns of emotion."[47] In this language auditory associations lose all or part of their importance, since it is the *mute language* of silent populations, whose expressive bodies, by means of manual gesticulations, facial movements, and attitudes of the whole, have become "all face." This language is still used, as either a principal or an auxiliary means of communication, by the Bushmen and by the Indians of North and South America. It still serves as the common inter-tribal language.[48] It is so rich "that Indians of two different tribes, not one of whom knows a single word of the other's language, can spend half a day talking and gossiping, telling all sorts of stories by movements of their fingers, heads and feet."[49] But this language, in which the hand sketches and evokes in space the forms, the characteristic gestures and the reciprocal actions of beings and objects, in which the face and the body reproduce the movements and emotional attitudes by which they habitually respond to the movements and actions of the external world, this language in which the "gestural name" is not only a sign but "the essence of the thing, its essential action," imitated concretely,[50] could be an instrument of only intermittent expression and communication. Plastic, mute, it supposes visible movements. It requires the collaboration of an idle body and unoccupied hands, and of the light of day or at least of a campfire.

Humanity generally has preferred the language of sounds, produced by the collaboration of senses and organs that permit it to converse in the dark: *the ear*, that sense of the night, as Alain calls it—the ear, that organ of "sensations infinitely numerous and subtle;"[51] and *the mouth*, with "muscles even more supple and adaptable than those of the hand"[52]—all the laryngo-buccal apparatus, "susceptible of great variety and great delicacy of movement, in a small space and with very little effort."[53]

In the elaboration of this sound-automatism, the association of auditory sensations with auricular and laryngo-buccal movements has been strengthened to the detriment of other associations that function in manual or total mimicry. Gesture loses its importance. It is no longer the whole of language, the principal instrument of communication. But gesture does not *die*. It subsists, an internal accompaniment to the language of sounds, always ready to manifest itself when the content of a word is of such a nature that the word alone cannot express all its affective nuances. Moreover, it communicates its basic value to spoken language, which is merely an extension of the language of gestures,[54] a language of gestures less ample—often hardly visible—by all the parts of our body that transform the movements of our respiratory apparatus into sounds. But there are always gestures, the laryngobuccal reduction and transposition of bodily mimicry. They are the natural expression of man, whose elementary movements are always of unequal duration and force, but who, being "a two-sided animal,"[55] whose principal organs—arms, legs, eyes, ears—come in pairs, has a tendency to physical balance, to the rhythmic regularization of his unequal movements.

The rhythmic character of language, whose motor and auditory associations can be strengthened by the deliberate creation of powerful mnemonic automatisms, lends itself to the faithful and almost indefinite preservation of poems. Poems if you will—or rather chronicles, didactic and historical collections—solidified in rhythm, recited by their authors or confided to the organic memory of the mouths and throats of trained rhapsodes, who spoke or rather chanted their ascending and descending verses, sustained at once by "adjuvant melodies at fixed intervals"[56] and by rhythmic movements of their arms and bodies, analogous to those of our accordionists and jazz singers.

During this period of *oral style*,[57] when writing was used only for memoranda or for the purpose of fixing in definitive form a text liable to corruption in the course of time,[58] the poet did not compose as a writer. He improvised collections of clichés, "he strung together and juxtaposed traditional formulas in unexpected and often inspired patterns,"[59] by trying their rhythms, playing with them—tasting them, as it were—in his mouth and throat.

This was the manner of composition of the Hebrew prophets, the Ionian poets, the singers, rhapsodes, bards, minstrels, troubadours, the Venetian gondoliers; it is still the manner of composition among primitive peoples and in Eastern Europe, where the majority of the population is illiterate.[60]

In some individuals there manifests itself or develops what modern psycho-physiologists of language call the verbo-motor temperament. In individuals of this type there is not, between the thought and the spoken word, *any auditory interval*. The verbo-motor thinks and remembers with his laryngo-buccal apparatus. For him, the word, whether isolated or assimilated to a group, is not something written or seen, hardly even something understood, but rather something felt as a laryngo-buccal movement, actual or potential.

In others the verbo-motor temperament, less clearly defined, is complicated by auditory images; this appears to be the case with oracles, prophets and inspired people generally—those who, at certain privileged moments of their lives or in certain states induced by ascetic or ritual methods, by repetitions of gestures, of sounds, of rhythms, by gyrating dances, by some "mechanism of enthusiasm" which constrains the spirit and forces inspiration to come,[61] feel being born within them "quasi-spontaneous and often compulsive improvisations, forming rhythms in the mouth and more or less distinctly sounding in the ears."[62]

But with the development of writing, the industrial production of paper, the invention of printing, the diffusion of books and journals, humanity entered the period of *written style*, in which "many civilized people communicate with their peers even more than by conversation."[63]

In this modern phase of language, the visual and auditory association with the simplest movements of the eye, the hand, the ear, have been developed to the detriment of the associations that involved the most ample movements of the body and its members; there is a lessening even of the more limited movements, which often have powerful effects, of the respiratory and laryngo-buccal apparatus. Here the word offers hardly any resistance to the hand that glides over the page, to the eye which by minuscule and almost insensible movements follows the lines from left to right or right to left or down the page from top to bottom. Their efforts and fatigue have hardly any connection[64] with anything but the quality of the light, the pen, the paper, not with the realities evoked by the content of the words. When it is written and read, the word is no longer the thing itself or the emotion suggested by the thing.[65] An abstract concept, it is no longer anything but a substitute for the thing, chosen not for its expressive value but because it is easier to manipulate and communicate. It is merely a label, a sign emptied of content, algebraized.[66]

The prevalence of associations between graphic motor images and visual and tactile sensations over associations between phonetic images and auditory sensations[67] has given birth to a new style, the *manual style*, which in expressive value is much inferior to manual or bodily mimicry. It has also given birth to a graphic-visual temperament, in which all thought and all emotion take the form of movements of the hand and tend to issue in writing. The graphic-visual composes only with strokes in space, with fly-tracks and crossings-out. Just as a stenographer or typist comes to think with the tips of her fingers, the graphic-visual comes to think with "manual concepts"—not with phrases, words or syllables but with letters formed or scrawled by the penholder which is his hand. For him, words have no value except as written signs; they are deprived of almost all their auditory value, as they were for de Musset's character who "couldn't clearly understand anything not written in Spencerian script."[68] This visual type often occurs, either in the pure state or combined with the graphic type, among schoolmasters and professors, journalists as a rule, men of letters, and people who write rhymes for the eye.[69] These visuals and graphics, from long habituation to writing and reading rather than reciting and listening, have undergone such an attenuation of their auditory consciousness that they believe there is a correspondence between written letters and the actual sounds of spoken language. Even worse, they believe in the reality of the sounds conventionally represented by letters and conserved in orthography, those simple mute souvenirs of sounds uttered long ago.[70] It is probable, however, that this type of sensibility will tend to evolve toward types less impoverished, in proportion as the development of the typewriter, the phonograph and the radio tends to convert all wielders of pens—be they industrialists, merchants or writers —into people who dictate; the daily newspaper into the news broadcast, and reading into recitation.

But even in our period of written style there are few writers whose temperament is exclusively of the graphic-visual type. Even among writers preoccupied with graphic problems, such as Mallarmé and Péguy,[71] for whom the typographic appearance of the works they composed or printed assumed an almost morbid importance, auditory and phonetic images and sensations were not totally supplanted by graphic and visual associations. Equally rare are writers of the exclusively auditory type, to whom words come as images more or less strong, more or less clearly defined, localized in the ears—or even as auditory hallucinations analogous to those we experience in certain psychopathic states or in hypnagogic dreams,[72] such as voices heard in the waking state in certain cases of intellectual or affective tension. Romain Rolland has created, in his *Jean-Christophe*, a type of the "perfect auditory."[73] But if Romain Rolland as a musician resembled his character, as a writer, as a poet, especially in his *Colas Breugnon*, he is infinitely more complex.

With Mohammed, with Goethe, auditory hallucinations were accompanied by actual or intended movements of articulation.[74] Even in the cases of Lamartine and de Musset, those inspired men who "wrote to the dictation of the Muse," the words are something quite other than pure sounds.

In fact, except among those in whom graphism has finally paralysed all muscles but those of the eye and the hand, vision, audition, respiration, gestures and bodily attitudes all participate, in various degrees according to the disposition of the day and the hour, in the poet's battle with the external form of words.[75] Every poet belongs more or less to the verbo-auditory type, in whom the ear, the mouth, all the organs of sound collaborate. And since poetic tension is strong enough to efface the impress of social conventions, to overcome all the constraints and prudences of mundane living that have weakened the spontaneous reactions of natural language, gesture reappears and laryngo-buccal gesticulation is intensified. The poet of today rediscovers the original nature of the composer in the oral style, thinking rhythmically, dancing his thought with his body, with all the movements of his throat and his articulating mouth.

"*We are . . . at the sources of the creation of style.* At these depths, the style is the *whole* man . . . dancing and balancing, in harmony with the living and logical laws of the human complex of flesh and spirit."[76]

Retracing in some sort the evolution of his maternal tongue from the beginning, the poet becomes once more a maker of gestures, a mime, a verbo-motor.[77]

"See him walking up and down, rubbing his hands; he beats time, he growls something between his teeth. And little by little, under that rhythmic impulsion, between the two roles of imagination and desire, the flood of words and ideas begins to gush out."[78]

But even when it stops gushing, when the poet sits down, stretches out in an armchair or lies on a sofa, when having played with words for a long time he commits them to writing, he is still talking. It is an *internal speech*, not simply mental: he *articulates* his words, sounds them, albeit so softly that an observer can neither hear a sound nor see anything more than a slight moving of the lips or the throat. This is a representation in motion. And if the poet is not always clearly conscious of it, the resistance which certain words offer to his choice indicates that he has a dim awareness of these reduced movements, that he feels them.[79] Here all is soliloquy, monologue: interior monologue,[80] which takes place in the depths of the being, at the junction of the biological and the mental, where all images vanish and only movement remains, where man no longer sees or hears, but utters himself, babbles out his poem.

And this poem: those who will hear it recited or declaimed, and those who will read it in their silent rooms, will themselves pronounce it.

For *to read is to pronounce*. Look at the priest on the bus, the nun in the train, who in reading the breviary move their lips.[81]

To hear is also to pronounce, as in the case of the automobilist who catches himself humming the song of his engine, or the listener who finishes under his breath—and sometimes aloud—the phrase we are uttering. "Often what we call hearing comprises a beginning of silent articulation, of weak, half-completed movements of the vocal apparatus," says Ribot;[82] it is "talking to oneself," says Bergson.[83]

In the act of *listening*, which supposes a more attentive direction of the mind, the whole mechanism of interior monologue functions, but more actively. A person who listens to us, says Michel Bréal,[84] "speaks inwardly at the same time as we. . . . His thought follows, accompanies or precedes our own," as does that of the reader, who "is virtually an auditor."[85]

And just as a musician who reads a part in a symphony and the person who hears it both recreate it, play it within themselves as if they held the conductor's baton;[86] just as the spectator, an "involuntary actor,"[87] participates with his whole being in the performance of a tragedy, as at the music-hall he follows with his muscles the movements of an acrobat,[88] so the reader and the hearer of a poem reproduce the movements of the mouth in which it was formed; they have in their mouths, with all their motor and affective values, the very voice of the poet.

The book, with the sounds it brings to their eyes and ears, is only a conductor between two moving mouths.

Notes

1. J. Vendryès, *Le langage. Introduction linguistique à l'histoire*. Paris, La Renaissance du Livre, 1921, p. 25.

2. Abbé Rousselot, *Principes de phonétique expérimentale*. Paris, Didier, 1924, p. 634.

3. Vendryès, *Le langage*, p. 64.

4. *Ibid.*, p. 25.

5. *Ibid.*, p. 77.

6. K. Goldstein, "L'analyse de l'aphasie et l'étude de l'essence du langage," *Psychologie du langage*, Paris, Alcan, 1933, pp. 467–468.

7. Vendryès, "Sur les tâches de la linguistique statique," *Psychologie du langage*, p. 81.

8. That fundamental element of language, the phrase, which is neither phoneme nor syllable, is the verbal image, "that image with two faces, which on one side looks into the depths of thought and on the other is reflected in the mechanism of sound-production." Vendryès, *Le langage*, pp. xii, 79, 81 ff. Cf. also I. Meyerson, "Les images," in Georges Dumas, *Nouveau traité de psychologie*. Paris, Alcan, 1933, Tome II, p. 557, and H. Delacroix, "La pensée et les images," in Dumas, *Nouveau traité de psychologie*, II, 101: "The order and the structure of the phrase are governed by the synthetic unity of a complex thought."

9. A. Ombredanne, "Le langage," in Dumas, *Nouveau traité*, III, 433.

10. E. Boucly, "Le style oral dans les milieux palestiniens," *Revue juive de Genève*, mai 1934, p. 332.

11. These "solid blocks" are also called phonetic words or accentual groups. Cf. M. Grammont, *Traité de phonétique*, Paris, Delagrave, 1933, pp. 143, 363; and F. Lefèvre, "Une heure avec Pierre Janet," *Nouvelles littéraires*, 17 mars 1928, p. 79.

12. Cf. G. Lote, "Le silence et la ponctuation dans l'alexandrin français," *Revue de phonétique*, Paris, 1911, Tome I, fasc. III, p. 264. The

words which have not by nature any independent existence are the grammatical tools discussed later in this chapter.

13. André Ombredanne has shown that what he calls "reflective improvisation," that is, every work of verbal creation, written or not, "requires an uncompromising distrust of verbal automatism, a constant effort to break away from clichés, constant experimentation with new constructions and use of new types of phrases," a distrust that tends to destroy clichés of all kinds, semantic, grammatical and rhythmic. "Le langage," p. 372.

14. Remy de Gourmont, quoted by G. Lote in "La poétique du symbolisme," *Revue des cours et conférences*, 30 juillet 1934.

15. In the period anterior to the effort of expression, thought, when it is very active, must remain free of all images. But, as unconscious act of the mind, it requires, in order to become fully conscious, images and words. A. Binet, cited and summarized by L. Barat, "Les images," revised by I. Meyerson, in Dumas, *Traité de psychologie*, Paris, Alcan, 1923–1924, Tome I, pp. 510–511; cf. Meyerson in Dumas, *Nouveau traité de psychologie*, p. 573.

16. Meyerson, *ibid.*, p. 598 ff.; cf. infra., note 44.

17. These images, "a complex fact tied up . . . with the functioning of thought," can be defined as "sensible, concrete subjects of consciousness, having some correspondence with the world of things—objects, situations, reality—and reminding us of them in some manner, . . . [but] existing outside actual perception, outside any actual stimulation of the sense organs, or at least having no correspondence with any actual stimulation; appearing spontaneously after an effort of evocation or of search." Meyerson, *ibid.*, p. 542.

18. Delacroix, "Les opérations intellectuelles," in Dumas, *Nouveau traité*, V, 111.

19. "The isolated concept is nothing. Every concept is a rudimentary judgment. . . . Without the beginnings of judgment, it is not a concept that I have in mind, but only a concrete representation; what distinguishes the concept of man from the image of a man is the presence of

judgments about the man, which are potential in the concept and which are more or less precisely formulated." Delacroix, *ibid.*, p. 116.

20. Meyerson, "Les images," pp. 557, 576; Delacroix, "Les opérations intellectuelles," pp. 103, 110, and passim. In the elaboration of the concept by means of the most complete abstraction, we go "from substitution to substitution, and end by letting into consciousness only brief and rapid allusions superimposed on each other, each of which is a translucent screen that further obscures the image of things, in such a way that the concrete objects become so blurred, so different from each other and at the same time so analogous to each other, that they take on the appearance of total inequation and we seem to be observing a pure work of pure function." A. Spaier, *Le pensée concrète*, Paris, Alcan, 1927, p. 131.

21. Meyerson, "Les images," p. 584.

22. Meyerson, "Images-éclairs," *Journal de psychologie*, 1926, pp. 575–576.

23. I say sign, not symbol. For according to Saussure's distinction, cited by Meyerson, "Les images," p. 579, the sign is arbitrary and unmotivated but the symbol is not altogether arbitrary: "It is not empty; there is something of a natural connection between it and what it symbolizes. The symbol of justice, the balance, could not be replaced by just anything, a car for example."

24. G. Revault d'Allonnes, "L'attention," in Dumas, *Traité*, I, 861, note 1.

25. Vendryès, *Le langage*, p. 158. Here is a more detailed list of tool-words, from C. Bruneau and M. Heulluy, *Grammaire française*, Paris, Delagrave, 1937, pp. 28, 49, 184 ff., 389 ff.: *Tool-words that clarify or replace the noun:* articles, possessive, demonstrative and indefinite particles, personal and relative pronouns, numbers; *tool-verbs:* the auxiliaries and their substitutes; *invariable tool-words:* certain adverbs and adverbial locutions; prepositions and prepositional locutions, conjunctions and conjunctive locutions. Though they have no meaning of their own and often no accent, in some cases they can have a certain expressive value—a rhythmic value.

26. *Ibid.*, pp. 106 ff. p. 86.

27. *Ibid.*, p. 196.

28. *Ibid.*, p. 78.

29. "Words are not listed in the mind as in the columns of a book. . . . We don't know from just what level of our intellectual activity to pull them in order to fit them into phrases and slip them, fully equipped, into our phonetic organs." *Ibid.*, p. 220. Certain experiments in directed evocation have shown that the desired word "appeared after a sort of continued pushing, or, on the contrary, quite suddenly. One experiences a feeling of relief. The word may be uttered aloud immediately, or be preceded by a verbal image or by a beginning of unconscious articulation. It is often said as if by compulsion, automatically; it may be accompanied by affective states." Meyerson, "Les images," p. 562.

30. These images are classed according to the nature of the sensations (auditory, visual, tactile, etc.) to which they correspond. *Ibid.*, pp. 598–600.

31. Exil, "La machine parlante électrique," *Radio-Magazine.* 2 nov. 1930; P. Bonnier, *La voix. Sa culture physiologique. Théorie nouvelle de la phonation*, 4ème éd., Paris, Alcan, 1913, pp. 81, 82, 146, 241; L. Bourguès et A. Dénéréaz, *La musique et la vie intérieure*, Paris, Alcan, 1921, pp. 5–6: "Every sensation of sound is accompanied by a tactile sensation. . . . The epithets designating the quality of sound are all taken from the tactile vocabulary." Cf. also J. d'Udine, *L'art et le geste*, Paris, Alcan, 1910, p. 90, for whom each of our senses is synesthetically related to the four others, in such a way that "gesture and attitude become the constant intermediaries of all our emotions, and the sense of touch [which for d'Udine includes the muscular sense] functions every time life or a work of art interests one or several of our senses, even when they most seem to be affected in isolation." Cf. also H. Bergson, *Essai sur les données immédiates de la conscience*, 19ème éd., Paris, Alcan, 1920, p. 32; A. Spire, "Un musicien: Conte," *Réfuges*, Paris, La Belle Page, 1926; G. Dumas, *Traité*, pp. 199, 309. On the motor, circulatory and respiratory conditions of auditory attention, cf. Revault d'Allonnes, "L'attention," p. 881. On the physical effects of music—accelera-

tion of circulation, dynamogeny, ecstasy, trembling, spasms, convulsions, tears—and on the vibrations of concert halls, cf. H. Berlioz, *À travers chants. Études musicales, adorations, boutades et critiques*, Paris, Calmann Lévy, 1898, pp. 94 ff.

32. A. Malherbe, R. Vilenski et N. Herman, *Recherches sur les restes d'audition chez les sourds-muets. Étude de la perception osseuse, son utilisation pédagogique*, Paris, Masson, 1935; cf. H. Pieron, "L'attention," in Dumas, *Nouveau traité*, IV, 49–55.

33. P. Jacques et H. Grimaud, "État actuel de la psychologie de l'audition," *Annales des maladies de l'oreille, du larynx, du nez et du pharynx*, 1930, XLIX, 126, 130 ff., 140 ff., 152 ff.; Ombredanne, "Le langage," pp. 7 ff.

34. M. Jousse, "Études de psychologie linguistique. Le style oral rhythmique et mnémotechnique chez les verbomoteurs," *Archives de philosophie*, 1925, II, Ch. IV, 56.

35. "The acute vowels penetrate our ear like a sharp point and sometimes create in us a feeling close to sadness." Grammont, *Traité de phonétique*, p. 404; cf. also Berlioz, *À travers chants*, p. 226.

36. Jacques et Grimmaud, pp. 126, 152.

37. Cf. the description of the facial nerves and the muscles of the face, in Dumas, *Nouveau traité*, III, 121 and 125, particularly figures 62 and 63.

38. Cf. V. Egger, *La parole intérieure. Essai de psychologie déscriptive*, Paris, Germer-Baillière et Cie., 1881, pp. 76, 101. Cf. also D. Lagache, *Les hallucinations verbales et la parole*, Paris, Alcan, 1934, p. 16: "Various sensory and sensitive impressions accompany the exercise of speaking: auditory impressions produced by the sound of the voice; in the mucous membranes, the sensations produced by the passage of exhaled air and the sensations of double contact produced by the movements of the tongue and the lips; the vibratory sensations of the air passages—sensations whose exact location depends on the pitch of the voice; the sensations produced by the muscular activity of the diaphragm, the larynx, the epiglottis, the tongue and the lips; in short, the exterocep-

tive, interoceptive and proprioceptive impressions. This sensitive-sensory complex helps us to distinguish the words we speak from those we only hear; external sounds are revealed to us only by hearing—strongly reinforced, if they are sufficiently intense, by the perception of vibrations, and, if they are loud, sudden and surprising, by the shutting of the eyes (the ocleo-palpebral reflex). The spoken word, on the other hand, has a sensible intimacy which seems to be the surest guarantee of its belonging to us alone and of its specifically personal character."

38a. For Dumas, *Nouveau traité*, III, 307–308, certain mimic movements of our mouth originate in olfactory and gustatory contacts. For the working together of the muscles of the tongue, the jaw, the mouth, with the other muscles of the body, a collaboration which can be consciously developed by education, cf. Revault d'Allonnes, "L'attention," pp. 876 ff., and Pieron, "L'attention," pp. 12 ff., 49 ff.; cf. G. Hytier, *Le plaisir poétique. Étude de psychologie*, Paris, Les Presses Universitaires, 1923, p. 86. Finally, Dumas, *Nouveau traité*, pp. 20 ff., gives examples of the motor reactions of the eye on the sudden approach of an object or a flash of light (blinking), or the appearance of a photo-motor reflex of dilation resulting not only from a decrease in light but simply from the idea of darkness, and examples of muscular reflexes, both ocular and general, of auditory origin: sudden closing of the eyes, and jumping up with arrest of breathing, Goldstein, "L'analyse de l'aphasie," pp. 452, 492, points out, in certain cases of aphasia, modifications of facial expression (absence, fixity, confusion, alarm), and "serious disturbances of optic or tactile recognition."

39. Dumas, *Nouveau traité*, III, 205; cf. also 17, note 3.

40. Dumas, "Le choc émotionel. (Réactions glandulaires et musculaires)," *Nouveau traité*, II, 348.

41. On the association of auditory associations and images with the various muscular phenomena of vocal and corporal mimicry, and with muscular, viseral and glandular sensibility, in the phenomena of physical and intellectual effort, in attention, cf. Revault d'Allonnes, "L'attention," pp. 876–878.

42. Jousse, "Études de psychologie linguistique," p. 23.

43. P. Bourdon, "Les sensations," in Dumas, *Nouveau traité*, III, 90 ff.

44. By *kinesthesia* is meant the ensemble of sensations and perceptions arising from the muscles and the joints: sensations of movement, of effort and of muscular resistance. By *coenesthesia* is meant the ensemble of sensations and perceptions arising from the internal organs, the viscera, the glands, etc. Under this head come the sensations of hunger, of thirst, of nausea, etc. The coenesthetic sensibility also gives us vague general impressions of malaise, of well-being, of euphoria, often promoted by the absorption of certain substances or the odor of certain perfumes, or by the repetition of certain movements or sounds. Cf. Bourdon, "Les sensations," pp. 112 ff., 121 ff.

45. Jousse, "Etudes de psychologie linguistique," pp. 31-32; Goldstein, "L'analyse de l'aphasie," p. 435; Cf. also C. Blondel, "Les volitions," in Dumas, *Nouveau traité*, VI, fasc. 3, 365: "*Every state of consciousness,* left to itself and not contradicted by antagonistic states, *tends to externalize itself in movements,* if only in movements of *verbal articulation,* and the connection of the states of consciousness with their corresponding movements is as evident as it is inexplicable.... Experience confirms that certain psychic states are followed by certain physiological manifestations of a motor order." There are often very vague states of consciousness which are revealed only by the memory of these motor manifestations. A personal example: When I was 13 years old, we spent the summer in the country near Nancy. Grandparents, parents, uncle, aunt, cousins. One morning I get up at daybreak. A luminous sky. Coolness before the great heat that will come after sunrise. I climb from branch to branch in a big fir tree. I sing, then I climb until I reach the top. And there I sing again, I sing!—until my grandfather, the earliest riser of the family, opens the blinds and shuts me up. Why this sudden need to climb and sing? An excess of strength? The onset of puberty? More oxygen than usual in the air of that beautiful morning? All that remains is the memory of an intense joy. Also that I was something different, a more vital being than those people in bed; that I would perhaps wake them, and that it would shock them to see that I had become a squirrel, a bird.

46. Dumas, "L'excitation et le mouvement," in *Nouveau traité*, II, 27-28.

47. Revault d'Allonnes, "L'attention," pp. 898 ff. Did this mimic language appear before the others? It is not necessary to take sides on such questions of priority. In any case, this is not the historical point of view apparently taken by d'Udine (that pioneer whose name and work are too unjustly forgotten, but not his ideas or his felicitous expressions) in *L'art et le geste*, p. 86, when, by way of pointing out that gesture is the mediator among various orders of sensations, and between the creative artist and the public, he writes: we can "substitute for Hans von Bülow's celebrated phrase *In the beginning was rhythm* a formula at once more precise and more general: *In the beginning was gesture*."

48. Wherever there are human groups with different languages, who do not know any language but their own, there is gestural language.

49. L. Lévy-Bruhl, *Les fonctions mentales dans les sociétés inférieures*, 2ème ed., Paris, Alcan, 1912, pp. 177–178. I neglect the other forms of manual language. For the spontaneous or systematized language of deaf-mutes, see Jousse, "Études de psychologie linguistique," Chapters IV, V.

50. Lefèvre, "Une heure avec Pierre Janet," p. 70. For Jousse, "Etudes de psychologie linguistique," pp. 43 ff., the eminently expressive quality of gestural language comes from the fact that the subject "*reviews in his gestures the phases of action in the order in which he saw them occur*." These different phases are expressed in a continuous gesture, a *propositional gesture*, corresponding in the language of sounds to the simple proposition of speech or to the more complex proposition of written language. Without adopting Jousse's expression "propositional gesture," Ombredanne, "Le langage," pp. 364-366, agrees with him in affirming that gestural language comes closer to reality, conveys it more exactly than oral language, and still more exactly than written language: "If significative gesture properly socalled has a universality, a transparency which is not found in oral language, it is because there the sign is closer to the thing signified. . . . The hand portrays not things

but movements, the movement of the subject, the movement of the object, the movement by which the subject acts on the object. Such a language develops as a game in which the significative gesture constantly participates in the action it is imitating, a language without the economies and refinements of abstraction, but a language faithfully representative, in which the name is truly 'the essence of the thing,' since it reproduces, in the movement of their generation and of their succession, attitudes and behavior. Here, semantic effort is reduced to the minimum. The nominal abstraction and the grammaticism proper to our modern tongues do not exist. By so much are diminished the detours we never cease making between the order of the action recalled or imagined and the proper order of the tongue employed." On the expressiveness of hand movements, see Stefan Zweig's admirable novel, *Twenty-Four Hours in the Life of a Woman*. On all that bodily gesticulation can express, see Balzac, *Traité de la vie élégante, suivi de la théorie de la démarche*; and the extraordinary pantomime played by the feet of the dancer Francesca in Heine's *The Baths of Lucca*.

51, 52, 53. Jousse, "Études de psychologie linguistique," p. 37.

54. A. Spire, *Plaisir poétique et plaisir musculaire*, New York, S. F. Vanni, 1949, pp. 115 ff.

55. Jousse, "Études de psychologie linguistique," pp. 36 ff., and his course at l'École des Hautes Études (Sorbonne), passim.; cf. also Spire, *Plaisir poétique*, p. 114.

56. Lefèvre, "Une heure avec Pierre Janet," p. 90.

57. The oral style is, according to Jousse, still alive in the Basque country, where shepherds improvise in free rhythms "made exclusively for improvisation"; among the Achantis, where severe and sometimes cruel methods are used in developing the memories of the recitateurs, who, once admitted into the caste, are punished with death for the slightest error, "be it in the text or in the recitation"; among the natives of Madagascar, in whose *hain-tenys* Jean Paulhan has pointed out a parallelism similar to that of the prophets of Israel; among the guslars, nomadic recitateurs of Yugoslavia. There were analogous methods of rhythmic and mnemonic swaying among the Biblical prophets and the

rabbis of Israel, for purposes of memorization and improvisation. Cf. Jousse, "Études de psychologie linguistique," passim., and especially Ch. XI, pp. 108 ff.; Ch. XXI, pp. 113 ff.; Ch. XIII, pp. 119 ff.; Ch. XV, pp. 169, 180, 189. As for the development of the Greek rhapsodes from the primitive period, it has been shown by V. Bérard, *Introduction à l'Odyssée*, Paris, Les Belles Lettres, 1924-1925, pp. 81 ff., 129 ff., and passim., and *La résurrection d'Homère*, 7ème éd., Paris, Grasset, 1930, p. 49. To the oral style belongs also the Finnish folk epic *The Kalevala*, of which the French translator, J. L. Perret, says, p. 15: "The popular Finnish songs, which were customarily accompanied by the music of the kantele [a three-stringed zither], were performed by two singers seated face to face on a bench. With folded hands, they rocked back and forth. The first bard would sing a verse alone, and his companion, who joined him in the last foot of the verse, would say the following octosyllable alone, which the first singer would terminate in unison with him and go on alone to the third verse. This cooperative singing often lasted all day." On the rhythmic gesticulation that accompanied the swaying and the recitation of improvisers in the oral style, cf. Spire, *Plaisir poétique*, pp. 117 ff.

58. The Bible, the Targumim, the Iliad and the Odyssey were recited for long periods of time before being put into writing.

59. Jousse, *Les rabbis d'Israel. Les récitatifs rhythmiques parallèles. I—Genre de la maxime*, Paris, Spes, 1929, p. xxv.

60. Cf. above, note 57, and Jousse, "Etudes de psychologie linguistique," Ch. VIII, especially pp. 60 ff. Cf. Spire, *Plaisir poétique*, pp. 118 ff. On the improvisations of the Venetian gondoliers, see Georges Sand, "La dernière Aldini," *Oeuvres de Georges Sand*, Paris, Félix Bonnaire, 1838, XIX, 17 ff., and *Lettres d'un voyageur*, Paris, Michel Lévy, 1857, pp. 53–56.

61. "Religion, inspiration: whence come these divine things? Could there be artificial means to lift us up to them? Means to constrain the spirit, to force inspiration to come! A mechanism of enthusiasm! Think of Mozart: when the musical idea wouldn't come to him, he said his rosary. This repetition of the apostrophes of love set in motion the heart of genius. As the mystic has certain procedures for entering into

his most exalted states, does not the artist have some for finding his creative animation? To read a great poet releases in us a certain power which a minute before was sleeping. All this would lead us to the knowledge of certain rhythms more capable than others of speeding the birth of ecstasy. All this would make us return to the origin of the literary processes of cadence, rhyme, alliteration. We would understand the various strophes, the bell-stroke of *Nevermore*, all the primitivism of poetry, of the orator's art." M. Barrès, "Konia, Ville des Danseurs," in *Enquête aux pays du Levant*, Paris, Plon, 1923, II, 156. Cf. *ibid.*, p. 228, p. 156, note 17. Cf. also A. Schaeffner, *Origine des instruments de musique*, Paris, Payot, 1936, pp. 133–134.

62. Jousse, "Études de psychologie linguistique," p. 228.

63. Vendryès, *Le langage*, p. 399.

64. Connections which are manifested by movements so slight that the writing subject is, so to speak, never conscious of them, and whose significance can be revealed only by the methods of graphology or psychoanalysis.

65. Vendryès, *Le langage*, pp. 214–215.

66. Cf. above, p. 5.

67. Grammont, *Traité de phonétique*, pp. 24–25.

68. Vendryès, *Le langage*, p. 400.

69. It exists also among bankers. One told me at the beginning of 1938, "I can't read books any more. I am so used to reading the columns of the stock market reports that I can only read from top to bottom, not from left to right." It is possible that for the Chinese, who read from top to bottom, the apprenticeship to European books requires an adaptation of eye movements which does not come without a great deal of fatigue or at least discomfort.

70. This graphic-visual type exists also among musicians. "Debussy could more justly have complained that in music people attached more importance to *notes* than to *sounds*, if he himself had never been a slave to notes, to their spontaneous associations—guides for the eye and the hand of the musician, or, in Pascal's words, *false windows for*

symmetry, where the correctness of the written characters takes precedence over the accuracy of the utterance. It is a symmetry merely of notes which requires that an interval of a third or a fourth be followed by another and yet another; that the *imitations* answer from octave to octave; in short, that the eye see and inscribe before the ear has really heard or understood." Schaeffner, "Évolution harmonique et fixité tonale dans la musique contemporaine," *Journal de psychologie normale et pathologique*, 1926, XXIII, 228.

71. For Mallarmé, cf. "La catastrophe d'Igitur," in P. Claudel, *Positions et propositions*, Paris, Nouvelle Revue Française, 1928–1934, pp. 195 ff., and P. Valéry, "Le coup de Dés," in *Variéte*, Paris, Nouvelle Revue Française, 1924–1936, II, 193 ff. For Péguy, cf. below, note 77.

72. L. Barat, "Le langage," revised by P. Chaslin, in Dumas *Traité*, I, 749.

73. C. Sénéchal, *Les grands courants de la littérature française contemporaine*, Paris, E. Malfère, 1934, p. 40; in the purely auditory type, it seems, we must include the father of pure *poetry*, the Abbé Henri Bremond. Cf. Jousse, "Henri Bremond et la psychologie de la lecture," *Revue des cours et conférences*, 1933, pp. 22 ff. Georges Sand seems to have experienced music not only by hearing but also by tactile and muscular sensations. "What you tell me about Franz," she writes to Marie d'Agoult on July 10, 1836, "gives me a sick, furious longing to hear him. As you know, I get under the piano when he plays. I have very strong feelings, and I never find any instrument powerful enough." *Corréspondance de Georges Sand*, Paris, Calmann Lévy, 1882, II, 4. Cf. Spire, "Un musicien: Conte," and above, note 31. As for Lamennais, he was an absolute verbo-motor. "Lamennais went every morning to walk out his thoughts in Liszt's room at La Chenaie." T. Marix-Spire, "Du piano à l'action sociale. Franz Liszt et Georges Sand militants socialistes d'après des documents inédits," in *Renaissance*, New York, l'École Libre des Hautes Études, 1945, p. 201. The psychology of mathematicians shows the interplay of several kinds of temperament. "The attention of the pure analyst is directed to nothing but combinations of letters and numbers; the sensory or muscular side is reduced to the minimum. It is thus very abstract. . . . But under what form do

mathematicians represent to themselves symbols and notions, when they have no symbols or words before their eyes? Some are visuals, others are motors or verbo-auditories; in short, they are like other people. Thus, most mathematical prodigies have been visuals, but Inaudi was a motor and verbo-auditory, and Poincaré was entirely without visual images; he used motor images of the eye and the limbs, and spoken words." P. Chaslin, in Dumas, *Traité*, I, 688–691.

74. On Mohammed's undertaking to repeat word for word the chants in *sadj'*, which he believed to be inspired by the angel Gabriel or by Allah himself, cf. Jousse, "Études de psychologie linguistique," p. 228. On Goethe, cf. Romain Rolland, "Goethe musicien," *Europe*, 15 juillet 1930: "Goethe composed many of his poems walking and singing like Beethoven, and it is not for nothing that a number of them bear the title *Wanderer*. A typical passage of the *Wanderjahre of Wilhelm Meister* reveals the musical character of the creative process: 'It often seems that a hidden genius whispers to me something so rhythmical that as I walk my steps keep time to its measure; and at the same time I seem to perceive faint sounds accompanying certain songs, which are pleasantly manifested in one way or another.' " If one takes account of the fact that for Goethe music was only a stimulus, a help in composing poetry (P. Landormy, "Goethe musicien," *Les Nouvelles Littéraires*, 9 avril 1932), it appears that for him singing meant pronouncing words accompanied by music. We find in him the union of auditory phenomena with dynamic laryngo-buccal and corporal phenomena. There was the same union in Apollinaire: cf. Spire, *Plaisir poétique*, Appendix III, pp. 474–475. It seems that Gérard de Nerval and Guillaume Apollinaire had the delusion that their poetic creation was accompanied by a sort of musical creation: the *Cydalises* came, "in spite of myself, in the form of song; I found words and melody at the same time; I was obliged to write the melody down, and it conformed closely to the words." "I am convinced that every poet could easily make music of his verses if he had some knowledge of notation." G. de Nerval, *Poésies*, Édition de Jean Perrier, Paris, Éditions d'art d'Edouard Pelletan, 1924, pp. 15, 55.

75. A personal example will show the various kinds of images a verbal

pattern can evoke. It concerns not poetic creation but internal recitation. I have memorized, in no particular order, several poems of Ronsard. At night, before falling asleep, I repeat them. The text of these poems, which I have recited so many times, never awakens in me any visual sensation. It gives me only sensations of movement, together with sensations of a rising and falling in my ears. But when I amused myself by trying to recite them in the order of the collection in which they were printed, I failed until I made an effort to *see* them in that order. Then I succeeded. Whenever I recite, without regard to the order of impression, one or several of these poems, they give me no visual sensation at all. When I wish to recite them in order, I vaguely see their position (they are nearly all sonnets) at the top, in the middle, or at the bottom of the page. But it seems to me that if I had from the beginning studied these poems in the order of impression I would remember them in that order without the aid of visual sensations, simply by linking the last verse of each poem to the first verse of the next, as I do with the verses of any rather long poem, for example the song *Plus estroit que la vigne à l'ormeau se marie*, which has 52 lines.

76. Jousse, summarized by Lefèvre, "Une heure avec Pierre Janet," p. 39.

77. We are all verbo-motors: the more one studies the question the more one is convinced of the predominance of this type, says Pierre Janet, cited by Jousse, "Études de psychologie linguistique," p. 58. Cf. also R. de Souza, "Marcel Jousse: le style oral rhythmique," etc., *Mercure de France*, 1er nov. 1929, 15 janv., 1er avril, 15 août 1930; 15 févr. 1931, p. 711. Claudel seems to belong to the verbo-motor type, and so, with an admixture of visual and graphic elements, does Péguy, whose balanced rhythms Lefèvre has compared to those of the recitateurs of the age of oral style, in *Marcel Jousse: une nouvelle psychologie de langage*, Paris, Librairie de France, 1926, pp. 87–88. The typographical manias of Péguy are well known. A graphologist, to whom I showed the strongly designed handwriting of one of his notes, cried, "That is the hand of a typographer!" Cf. also R. Dreyfus, "Péguy typographe," in *De Monsieur Thiers à Marcel Proust*, Paris, Plon,

1939. As for Valéry, the alliterative example given by Lefèvre in *Marcel Jousse*, p. 86, does not convince me that there is not in him a preponderance of graphic and visual elements.

78. Claudel, *Positions et propositions*, I, 95. The verbo-motor poet today is like the improvising bard. For example: "Now a desire seizes me, in my mind a thought is born: I want to sing, I want to shape my words: words rush together in my mouth, words escape, fly from my tongue, rush out between my teeth." *The Kalevala*, Book I. Cf. above, note 57. The same need for muscular activity in creation is seen in Barbey d'Aurévilly and in Kierkegaard: "The mother of my friend LeClercq, who lived directly across the street from the Hotel Granval, sometimes saw Barbey d'Aurévilly gesticulating before his mirror for hours on end: he lived, he acted out his *Diaboliques*." Quoted by Ch.–H. Hirsch in *Cahiers Aurévilliens*, décembre 1937. Soeren Kierkegaard "worked a large part of the night. Georg Brandes says he could be seen from the street, pacing with long strides through the brightly lit rooms of his vast apartments. In each room he had a writing table and paper, so as to be able to write down, in the course of his interminable promenade, the phrases he had just composed." D. de Rougemont, "Soeren Kierkegaard," in *Jean-Jacques*, févr. 1938.

79. "Verbal language, which is only a reduction of the language of gestures, can show every possible gradation, from speech clearly perceptible by an outside observer to speech so reduced that it is limited to a mere idea of motion perceptible only by the speaking subject." Lefèvre, "Une heure avec André Spire, poète et essayiste," *Les Nouvelles Littéraires*, 31 janv. 1933. According to Ribot, "A man who meditates gets into position. More, an organ works: his larynx; we hardly think without speaking, or at least preparing with closed lips the enunciation of our thought. Even the most abstract thought has a corporal base, namely a muscular substratum furnished by language, however slight." Revault d'Allonnes, "L'attention," p. 885. Cf. also Revault d'Allonnes, *Les inclinations. Leur rôle dans la psychologie des sentiments*, Paris, Alcan, 1907, p. 18, and Bergson, *Essai sur les données immédiates de la conscience*, p. 47; "When we think, it is seldom that we do not talk to ourselves; we sketch, we prepare, if we do not actu-

ally carry them out, the movements of articulation by which our thought is expressed." There are analogous remarks in Jousse, "Études de psychologie linguistique," pp. 25–26, 57–58, and Vendryès, *Le langage*, p. 78; also in Barat, "Le langage," pp. 752 ff., where the author discusses the thesis of Victor Egger on *internal speech*. He states that it is true, as Egger believes, that in certain individuals there is a predominance of muscular images and motor patterns of articulation and phonation, but that it is extremely rare for anyone to "use visual verbal images of writing or printing." Poetic composition being only a thought, a meditation which is externalized, all the foregoing is applicable to it.

80. E. Dujardin, *Le monologue intérieur*, Paris, Messein, 1931.

81. Ombredanne, "Le langage," p. 376. Cf. also Barat and Chaslin, "Le langage," p. 762: "It is in silent reading and in writing that internal speech is most easily observed. Watch a man writing a letter. It is seldom that his lips don't move or that he doesn't whisper words. Dramatists, when they make a man who is writing a letter speak it out, merely intensify, by making audible, a phenomenon of potential phonation." This "latent endophasic" phenomenon, as Jousse calls it, was particularly lively in Arthur Fontaine, president of the International Labor Office, whose assistant I was in the Ministry of Labor. When he was revising a letter I had prepared for him, he moved not only his lips but his jaws. He chewed his words.

82. Quoted by M. Bréal, *Essai de sémantique*, 2ème éd., Paris, Hachette, 1899, p. 157.

83. Bergson, *Essai sur les données immédiates de la conscience*, p. 33.

84. *Essai de sémantique*, p. 157.

85. P. Lasserre, "Musique et mouvement dans la prose," *Nouvelles littéraires*, 20 oct. 1928.

86. J. Combarteu, *La musique, ses lois, son évolution*, Paris, Flammarion, 1907, p. 246, and L. Landry, *La sensibilité musicale. Ses éléments. Sa formation*, Nouv. éd., Paris, Alcan, 1930, p. 126.

87. Landry, *ibid.*, p. 112.

88. This is true of the spectator of any physical exercise or game of movement. Cf. the very interesting article of A. Arnoux, "Le sport au cinéma," *Nouvelles littéraires,* 28 avril 1928: "It is impossible for me to watch a well-performed exercise without imitating it internally, without accompanying it, by some secret innervation, to the end— without, in a word, joining in the exercise, not only with my eyes but with my viscera and my muscles." Cf. also J. Prévost, *Plaisirs et sports, Essais sur le corps humain,* Paris, Nouvelle Revue Française, 1925.

APPENDIX THREE

JEAN-PAUL SARTRE

"*Calder's Mobiles,*" *from* SITUATIONS, III, *1949*

If it is true that sculpture must carve motion in the immobile, it is wrong to relate Calder's art to that of the sculptor. He doesn't suggest motion, he collects it; he doesn't want to fix it forever in bronze or gold, those glorious and stupid materials committed by nature to immobility. With cheap and flimsy materials, with little bones or pieces of tin or zinc, he mounts curious arrangements of rods and plates, of quoits, leaves, petals. They are resonators, traps, they hang at the end of a wire like a spider at the end of her thread, or they rest on a pedestal, torpid, inert, apparently asleep; a light breeze passes, is caught by them, stirs them into life; they turn it and give it a fleeting form: a *Mobile* is born.

A Mobile: a little local celebration, an object defined by its motion and nonexistent apart from it, a flower that fades as soon as it stops, a pure play of motion as there are pure plays of light. Sometimes Calder amuses himself by imitating an unfamiliar form: he has made me a present of a bird of paradise with iron wings; if a little warm air escaping through the window passes it, that is enough: the bird smooths itself out, clinking; it stands up, leaps, balances its tufted head, rolls and reels, and suddenly, as if obeying an invisible sign, sinks down, sprawling. But most of the time he doesn't imitate anything, and I know no art less deceitful than his. Sculpture suggests motion, painting suggests depth or light. Calder doesn't suggest anything: he catches real living movements and works with them. His mobiles suggest nothing, refer to nothing but themselves: they are, that is all; they are absolutes. In them "the Devil's share" is perhaps larger than in any other creation of man. They have too many possibilities, and too complex, for any mind —even their creator's—to be able to foresee all their combinations. For each of them, Calder establishes a general destiny of movement, to which he then abandons it; the time of day, the sun, the temperature, the wind will determine each particular dance. Thus the object lives forever midway between the servitude of the statue and the independence of natural events; each of its evolutions is the inspiration of the moment; we discern in each the theme composed by its author, on which, however, it elaborates a thousand personal variations; it is a little hot-jazz improvisation, unique and ephemeral as the sky, as the morning; if you miss it, you have lost it forever. Valéry used to say of the sea that it is always rebeginning. An object by Calder is like the sea and weaves the same enchantment: always rebeginning, always new. To glance at it in passing is not enough; we must live in commerce with it and be fascinated by it. Then the imagination delights in the interchanges of those pure forms, at once free and ordered.[1]

These movements that have no purpose but to please, to enchant our eyes, nevertheless have a profound and as it were metaphysical import. For mobility must come from somewhere to the mobiles. Formerly Calder fed them with an electric motor; now he abandons them to nature's means, in a garden, near an open window, he lets them tremble to the wind like Aeolian harps; they feed on air, they breathe, they take their life from the living waves of the atmosphere. In addition, their mobility is of a quite par-

[1] Cf. Philippe Sollers on the waves of the sea: "always the same though infinitely various."—J.M.M.

ticular kind. Although they are human productions, they never have the precision or efficiency of Vaucanson's automata.[2] But the charm of the automaton lies precisely in the fact that it fans itself or plays a guitar like a human being and that the movements of its hands nevertheless have the blind and inescapable rigor of the merely mechanical. Calder's mobile, on the contrary, undulates, hesitates, seems to err and correct itself. I have seen in his studio a gong and a hammer suspended high in the air; at the slightest breath the hammer pursued the gong, which turned freely; it got in position to strike, threw itself at the gong and missed, like a clumsy hand—and then, just when we least expected it, swung around and struck it right in the center, with a frightful noise. And yet, these movements are too artfully arranged to be compared to those of a ball on an uneven floor, whose course depends entirely on the accidents of the terrain. They have a life of their own. One day while I was talking with Calder in his studio, a mobile which had been quite still was seized with a violent agitation and moved straight at me. I stepped back, and thought I had moved out of its range. But suddenly, when the agitation had passed and it seemed to have died, its long, majestic tail, which had not stirred, began to move indolently and as if regretfully, turned in the air, and passed under my nose. These hesitations, these reconsiderations, these gropings, these awkwardnesses, these sudden decisions, and especially this marvellous, swanlike nobility, made Calder's mobiles strange beings, midway between matter and life. Now their displacements seem to be purposeful, now they seem to have lost the idea on the way and to dawdle, balancing idly. My bird flies, floats, swims like a swan, like a petrel, it is one, a solitary bird, and then suddenly, all at once, it disintegrates, it is nothing but bits of metal stirred by meaningless little quivers. These mobiles, which are

2 "Vaucanson (Jacques de), French machinist, born at Grenoble (1709–1782). His automata, the *Flute Player* and especially the *Duck*, were famous."—*Petit Larousse*—J.M.M.

neither quite alive nor altogether mechanical, which change at every moment but always return to their original position, are like aquatic plants pulled by the current,[3] like the petals of the sensitive plant, like the legs of a decerebrated frog, like algae lifted by a swirl of water. In a word, though Calder has no wish to imitate— for he wishes only to create scales and chords of unknown movements—they are at the same time lyric inventions, combinations that are technical and almost mathematical, and visible symbols of Nature, of that great vague Nature that squanders pollen and suddenly produces flights of a thousand butterflies, and of which we never know whether it is the mere blind concatenation of causes and effects or the timid, ceaselessly retarded, deranged and interrupted development of an Idea.

[3] Cf. Proust's description, in *Swann's Way*, of the water lily which the current carried ceaselessly back and forth across the Vivonne.—J.M.M.

OSTSCRIPT

Kafka's *The Trial* is the story of Joseph K., an extraordinarily ordinary man, who although he had done nothing wrong was arrested, and although he was never tried or imprisoned was knifed to death by the executioners. His dying words were, "Like a dog!"

Joseph K. died like a dog because he had lived like a dog. He was guilty of not having done anything wrong. He was guilty of not resisting arrest. He was guilty of acknowledging the jurisdiction of the court. He was guilty of going to the court when summoned and leaving when dismissed. He was guilty of passively submitting to the executioners. He was guilty of innocence.

Before the first set of exercises in this book, I advised you "to suppress for the time being your deepest moral and emotional preoccupations," and, "at the beginning, to avoid subjects on which your emotion may distract you from the choice and marshaling of words." For the time being. At the beginning. Not permanently. In all dictatorships, both of the right and of the left, writers live and die like good obedient innocent dogs. One thinks of the Fascist Marinetti and the Communist Sholokhov. But they are not innocent. Kafka profoundly realized that such innocence is disingenuous and immoral.

The problem for a writer is not to refrain from protesting against the injustices he is aware of, but to learn how to protest effectively. There is a temptation, in writing with anger, to forget style and resort to <u>underscorings</u>, *italics*, exclamation points and CAPITAL LETTERS!!!!!!!! Such pitifully easy tricks are no substitute for command of language. We must develop such command. We must command our anger in order to express it. Where there is no style, there is in effect no anger.